the Breath of Abundant Life!

Robert Leslie Holmes

with foreword by Dr. Lloyd John Ogilvie

AMBASSADOR-EMERALD INTERNATIONAL
GREENVILLE, SOUTH CAROLINA • BELFAST, NORTHERN IRELAND

ISBN 1-889893-47-1

Published by:
Ambassador-Emerald International
1 Chick Springs Road, Suite 203
Greenville, SC 29609 USA

and

Ambassador Productions
16 Hillview Avenue
Belfast, Northern Ireland
BT5 6JR

Cover design © 1999 Grand Design
Cover and internal design by Matt Donovan
Cover photos © 1999 Photodisc
Copyediting by Becky J. Smith

www.emeraldhouse.com

To my mentors
Dr. Samuel W. Heslip and Dr. Arthur M. Schneider Jr.
for their positive influence on my life and ministry
and, as always,
to
Barbara
a woman full of the Spirit and of wisdom,
this book is dedicated with love and thanksgiving.

Contents

Foreword

You are about to begin an exciting adventure. Reading this book will introduce you to life as God meant it to be lived. You'll receive the love of God in greater depth. You'll be able to relish the grace of Christ as Savior and Lord, and you will be given the secret of living the abundant life through the indwelling power of the Holy Spirit.

With biblical clarity and authority, one of America's finest pastors and scholar preachers invites us to join him in discovering the often untapped supernatural gifts and resources of the Holy Spirit. Robert Leslie Holmes is a competent biblical theologian, empathetic counselor, and impelling communicator in both the spoken and, as you will witness, the written word. He writes as he speaks—with conviction, warmth, and insight. His gift of illustrating each biblical truth with stories of historical and contemporary people makes this book an enjoyable, inspiring experience. Holmes knows people and understands how to reach their deepest hurts and hopes. You'll often exclaim, "How does he know how I feel?" It's because he has discovered the importance of listening to people. And, as you will see, he first listens to God in his prayers and study of the Scriptures.

Dr. Holmes opens the rich treasure of the Bible on the theme of the Holy Spirit and examines the most important verses, holding up the jewels of truth so they can flash their magnificent insights for us today.

Many Christians settle for two-thirds of God. For them, God is way up there—aloof and apart from their daily lives. Christ is out there—between them and the Father. The Holy Spirit is often some kind of vague force or impersonal power they hear about but do not know intimately. They overlook the clear biblical assertion that "no man can say that Jesus is the Lord, but by the Holy Ghost" (I Cor. 12:3) and that Christ engenders the gift of faith and enables us to appropriate the abundant life.

Too often, Christians make their commitment to Christ and press on with their own strength. Later, they realize they are attempting the impossible.

Their lives become a cycle of brave attempts and sad failures. They feel defeated, impotent, and frustrated. When a big crisis hits, they suddenly realize that they don't have what it takes and cry out for help.

Often this is the sublime moment when Christians open themselves to learn about the Holy Spirit for the first time, even though He has been at work in them before and after their conversion. It's an immense sense of relief for them to realize that they no longer need to run their own lives through sheer willpower. The inner wells of their lives can be replenished with artesian joy, peace, and wisdom.

My good friend Robert Leslie Holmes has been reflecting on the power of the Holy Spirit for the past thirty years. His book explores the transforming work of the Spirit in a believer's life. Here is a realistic approach to finding the guidance of the Holy Spirit in everyday circumstances.

I wholeheartedly recommend the Breath of Abundant Life because it shares the secret of finding God's practical power available to all His people. Through the use of Bible-based examples, Dr. Holmes provides a means by which we can reexamine our own lives in the Spirit.

Read this book to discover the Holy Spirit as your companion, counselor, and courage. And then rejoice because *The Breath of Abundant Life* will give you spiritual stamina for a dynamic life.

Dr. Lloyd John Ogilvie
United States Senate Chaplain
Washington, D.C.

Preface

Nobody has a monopoly on the Holy Spirit and nobody has the last word either!" In many ways, those words spoken to a young immigrant from Ulster over thirty years ago were the inspiration for this book. My uncle Sam Heslip who spoke them, was advising me to "prove all things; hold fast that which is good" (I Thess. 5:21). It was his gentle warning not to naively accept everything I was hearing from some well-intentioned friends at that time but to test them in the light of the Scriptures. It is wise for us to carefully check out what we are told and reject everything that is not founded in what the Bible says.

This book does not pretend to be the last word on the Holy Spirit either, but everything it says about the Spirit of God, the Breath of Abundant Life, is firmly grounded in God's Word. I've never quite fully recovered from Uncle Sam's admonition, and the life and work of the Spirit in the Scriptures has been an ongoing pursuit of mine. I've learned a lot I didn't know back then, and, more than that, I've become more and more convinced that I have much more to learn. So consider this book to be, at best, an exploration of the work of the Spirit in the Bible along with solid application examples that will help you live today. This much I know for certain: there is a plan for each of us who trust Christ and that plan is accomplished only when we open our lives to embrace Christ's Holy Spirit. That is why this book had to be written.

You will quickly discern that like my previous books this is no one-man effort. The influence of many people flows through the keyboard that sends these words to you. Their names sometimes appear in the chapters. Others are silent heroes. I am indebted to them all. Some deserve special mention. Especially helpful was Dr. Arthur Schneider, my dear friend and mentor of over thirty years. "A man full of faith and of the Holy Ghost" (Acts 6:5), his encouragement has been a continual well of blessing and I owe him a debt far greater than I can pay. His life is an illustration of what it means to live in the Spirit.

Don and Pauline Gielow and Darryl and Bernice Compton from our San Mateo church family encouraged me to focus on writing as a means of getting out Christ's message.

Paul and Jean Moore, wonderful friends from our Pascagoula church family, generously allowed me to stay in their home in Destin, Florida, where in quietness and peace I could complete much of this work inspired by the splendid white sands and emerald green waters of the Gulf of Mexico. For this and much more, Barbara and I are deeply grateful for all Paul and Jean are and mean to us.

Tomm Knutson, my publisher at Ambassador-Emerald, International, was superb with his encouragement and patience. Thanks, Tomm!

A special word of thanks is due to our present church family at First Presbyterian Church of Pittsburgh. Their encouragement and affirmation is a true blessing from God. Betty Chapman, my assistant, has been especially helpful and deserves special credit.

And, of course, Barbara has as ever been one of the Lord's greatest blessings in my life. A constant channel of inspiration, she has sacrificed her own plans more than once to assist me in this project. Every word you will read, she has read before you. In many cases, she made suggestions that were better by far than my own ideas and they are incorporated in these pages. She deserves special credit.

There are illustrations, parables, legends, and personal accounts in these pages that all have one purpose and that is to help you, the reader, to see Jesus Christ more clearly. Where it has been possible, I have traced down the source of each one and sought permission to use it. If I've retold something you told me either by word of mouth or in your writings and you have not been credited, please know that the omission was unintentional. If you let me know, I'll make sure you receive proper credit in future editions of this work.

This book is but one man's reflections on the Holy Spirit and how He guides and motivates our lives daily for the glory of Jesus if we give Him control. It is not about the man. He is merely a message boy for the King of Kings. It is about the Holy Spirit, and if it is about the Spirit, it is about Jesus, for the Spirit's job, and mine, is to draw attention to Him whom to know is life abundant and eternal. Speaking about the Spirit as a dove, Charles Spurgeon is reported to have said, "I looked to Christ and the Dove flew in. I looked at the Dove and it disappeared." My prayer is that by reading these pages about the Dove, you will see Christ more clearly than ever before. If that happens, my purpose has been served and I am amply rewarded.

Soli Deo Gloria!
Robert Leslie Holmes
Spring 1999

1

The eternal love triangle

Shema', Yisrael, Yehovah Elohenu, Yehovah 'echad!" This declaration, which translates into English as "Hear, O Israel: The Lord our God is one Lord!" (Deut. 6:4), is the bedrock of Jewish theology. It distinguishes the religion of Israel from the religions of the polytheistic nations all around them. Unlike the surrounding nations, Israel has but one God. On the surface, it even seems to separate Israel's understanding of God from the Christian understanding of God. Why, after all, would anyone with even a simple understanding of logic believe there could be any direct connection between people who understand God to be one and people who believe in a triune Deity?

An evangelical Presbyterian minister friend in Dublin writes about the inauguration of the Republic of Ireland's new president. In connection with the installation ceremony, a service of worship was to be organized. This service was originally intended to incorporate representatives of various religious groups active in that country. The platform would include, among others, a Jewish rabbi and a Moslem imam. Each would participate with prayers and readings from his religion. My friend found himself in a difficult place. As a Christian, he saw that this widely broadcast service provided an opportunity to speak a word for the gospel of Christ. If he did not participate, that opportunity might be lost. No one would be there to speak a word that would point to Christ. At the same time, he felt his presence among that group chosen more for political correctness than religious commitment might give the appearance of endorsing religions that deny who Christ is. After studying the Scriptures and giving time to prayer, the minister wrote a polite letter declining the invitation. In his letter he explained that unless the service was exclusively Trinitarian: that is, that it would honor God as Father, Son, and Holy Spirit, he could not participate for reasons of conscience. As it happened, the Jewish and Moslem religious leaders also declined to attend because of internal strife among members of their own groups. The result was that only Christian ministers participated. My friend was able, after all, to give testimony to the saving power of Christ who is part of the Trinity.

Every major branch of the Christian faith teaches the doctrine of the Trinity: that is, that there are three Persons in the Godhead. They are God the Father, God the Son, and God the Holy Spirit. In short, we believe that One plus One plus One equals One.

ONE PLUS ONE PLUS ONE EQUALS ONE

It sounds confusing, does it not? Even Augustine, the father of reformed theology, struggled with the mystery of the Trinity. One story about his life tells how his intellectual tension found relief one day as he walked along the side of the ocean pondering the mystery. There the former brilliant pagan philosopher, who by grace was drawn to Christ and became a great Christian scholar, noticed a young boy playing with a seashell. The lad scooped a load of sand in the seashell, leaving a pock mark in the pristine beach. He carried it down to the water's edge where he poured out the sand and filled his shell with seawater. Returning to the hole he had just made in the sand, he poured out the water. Augustine watched as the child made that trip repeatedly before commencing a conversation with him. "What are you trying to do, my little friend?" Augustine asked. The little fellow replied, "I'm pouring the whole ocean into this hole, sir, because I want to control it all." Suddenly, a light went on inside Augustine's head and he realized, "That's what I have been trying to do. Standing on the edge of the ocean of God's infinity, I have been attempting to make it understandable to my finite mind."

For nearly two thousand years finite minds have attempted to understand and explain the doctrine of the Trinity. Through hymns and sermons and in books and essays on theology we have sung, written, and spoken of this faith mystery. Yet we still struggle to describe the essence of this foundational Christian doctrine.

This book is written not to try to explain the Trinity so much as to help Christians find the power the Trinity makes available to us through the Holy Spirit. It is important, however, that we first consider the roots of the member of the Godhead who is the principle focus of this volume. Therefore, we begin by considering the Trinity as a whole.

The fact of the Trinity is the focus of many of our great Christian hymns. None is any better known than Reginald Heber's famous attempt to capture the essence of the Godhead:

> Holy, holy, holy! Lord God Almighty!
> Early in the morning our song shall rise to thee;
> Holy, holy, holy! Merciful and mighty!
> God in three Persons, blessed Trinity!
>
> Holy, holy, holy! All the saints adore thee,
> Casting down their golden crowns around the glassy sea;
> Cherubim and seraphim falling down before thee,
> Which wert and art, and evermore shalt be.
>
> Holy, holy, holy! Though the darkness hide thee,
> Though the eye of sinful man thy glory may not see,
> Only thou art holy; there is none beside thee
> Perfect in power, in love, and purity.
>
> Holy, holy, holy! Lord God Almighty!
> All thy works shall praise Thy name, in earth, and sky, and sea:
> Holy, holy, holy! Merciful and mighty!
> God in three Persons, blessed Trinity!

"God in three Persons, blessed Trinity!" The essence of Augustine's problem, and of the problem we all have, is well stated in Heber's third stanza when he writes that "the eye of sinful man thy glory may not see." It is impossible for us, because we are sinners, to fully comprehend the greatness and glory of God. Augustine was right! We stand on the edge of infinity and try with limited, finite minds to comprehend what can be received only by faith.

This truth has never stopped us from trying to understand and describe the Trinity by crude allusion, however. Mighty servants of Christ, such as Patrick, who in the fifth century blazed a trail for Christ in pagan Ireland, tried to make it easier for us. Patrick is said to have plucked a shamrock leaf from the green glens of County Antrim one day. "Look," he explained to his congregation, "you can see the idea of the Trinity every-where in nature, even in this simple leaf. Notice its three branches, all are separate, yet all are equal and all become one in the stem."

Others allude to H_2O, suggesting that in its frozen form it is ice, whilst in its liquid form it is water, and in its heated gaseous form it is steam. Capture some steam in a bottle. Allow it to cool and you have water. Freeze it below 32 degrees Fahrenheit and it becomes ice. Now, reverse the process: apply heat to the ice and it becomes water. Boil the water and it becomes steam again. Did the essential substance change? No, it is always the same substance, yet it is revealed in three distinct forms. Such formulas as these might help to shed a little light on our understanding of the Bible's eternal love Triangle, but they still leave us grasping for more answers.

THE SUBSTANTIAL DIFFERENCE SUBSTANCE CAN MAKE

When you stop and think about it, sometimes the Trinitarian formula sounds remarkably like some complicated theological theory developed by a group of heady theologians. In one sense, that is what it is, except that the group of theologians who gave us the most succinct definition of the Trinity hardly qualifies for the term *modern*.

Over sixteen centuries ago, in 325 A.D., a council of Christian leaders gathered in a hamlet near the Black Sea called Nicea. Teachers and preachers throughout the Christian world gathered to deal with a growing heresy about Jesus. In the course of their discussions, they made some his-torically valuable contributions to our understanding of God. Not only did they define the person and work of Christ, they defined the essence of Christian faith and the Trinity. Their Scripturally based definitions are unsurpassed even today.

In a sense they did more than they planned to do. Together those great leaders of the Christian church produced a powerful Bible-based statement that has served Christ's church well for the past sixteen hundred years. The Nicene Creed, which they produced, helps clarify the individual and collective roles of each of the persons in the Trinity. In our congregation, as in many others around the world, we still recite the Nicene Creed as an occasional part of our worship services:

> We believe in one God, the Father Almighty,
> Maker of heaven and earth, of all things visible and invisible.
> And in one Lord Jesus Christ, the only-begotten Son of God,
> begotten of His Father before all worlds,
> God of God, Light of Light, very God of very God,
> begotten not made, being of one substance with the Father;
> by whom all things were made;
> who for us and for our salvation came down from heaven,
> and was incarnate by the Holy Spirit of the virgin Mary,
> and was made man;
> and was crucified also for us under Pontius Pilate;
> He suffered and was buried;
> and the third day He rose again according to the Scriptures,
> and ascended into heaven, and is seated at the right hand of the
> Father;
> and he shall come again, with glory, to judge both the living and the
> dead;
> whose kingdom shall have no end.
> And we believe in the Holy Spirit, the Lord and giver of life,
> who proceeds from the Father and the Son;
> who with the Father and the Son together is worshiped and glorified;
> who spoke by the prophets;
> and we believe in one holy catholic and apostolic church;
> we acknowledge one baptism for the remission of sins;
> and we look for the resurrection of the dead,
> and the life of the world to come. Amen.

In distinct terms, the Nicene authors wrote a creed that described God as one who reveals Himself in three ways: Father, Son, and Holy Spirit. What is more, they described this God who is at the same time three and one as having three distinct roles: the Father is God, the Maker of heaven and earth. The Lord Jesus Christ is God and came down for our salvation from heaven. The Holy Spirit is God who spoke by the prophets.

All three are God. Does this mean Christians have three Gods? No. In a splendid word picture, the Christian scholars at Nicea illustrated a God who is one and three all at the same time. Three principle parties, each with a divergent view of Christ, made up that Nicene Council.

CREATURE OR CREATOR?

The primary reason for the calling of the council at Nicea was a heretical new teaching advocated by one of those three theological parties called the Arians. They took their name from their leader Arius, an elder from Alexandria in Egypt. Arius and his followers taught that Jesus Christ was the greatest creature God ever made but that He was nothing more than that. The disciples of Arius denied Christ's pre-existent deity. They did teach that Christ was a very good man and a gifted teacher. Yet He was not God. Arius and his followers argued their position using a Greek word, *heterousion.* This word is composed of two Greek words, *heteros,* meaning "essentially different" and *ousia,* which means "substance." Christ, they asserted, did not exist before He was born in Bethlehem. This view, still with us, comprises the fundamental eternal difference between biblical Christianity and two of the larger cults of our day, the Mormons and the Jehovah's Witnesses.

CHILDREN OF THE LESSER CHRIST

The philosophical next-door neighbors to the Arians at Nicea were the Semi-arians or Subordinationists. As their name suggests, they were a compromise party who tried to walk a middle ground between Arianism and orthodox Christianity. They described Christ with another Greek term, *homoiosousion. Homoio* means "one who is similar," while *ousia* speaks of "style, character, or substance to another."

"Here is what happened," the proponents of this theory suggested, "somewhere back in eternity God caused Christ to proceed from Himself. Jesus, whilst God, is not God to the degree that the Father is God. Nevertheless, Jesus and the Father are so similar that it is virtually impossible to distinguish between the two. Christ existed before He was born in Bethlehem, but He did not always exist."

The Semi-arians asserted that Jesus, although God, was not eternal. They portrayed a Jesus who was a kind of God Jr., who was subordinate to the Father, therefore, not equal.

Do we see this view today also? Absolutely. It is the subtle underlying belief of every person who makes an attempt to buy Christ off with compromised commitment. It is the essence of the theology for those people whose understanding of the Son of God stops with "Gentle Jesus meek and mild." There are still those about us who are satisfied to leave Jesus in a Bethlehem manger and not give Him credit for all He is and did when He walked among us. Not for them the Christ of glory, who rose again and "is seated at the right hand of the Father; and he shall come again, with glory, to judge both the living and the dead; whose kingdom shall have no end."

VERY GOD

In addition to the Arians and Semi-arians, a third group was present at Nicea. These were the Orthodox believers. Their view of Christ, founded solely on the teachings of the Scriptures, prevailed at the Council of Nicea. It is the standard for orthodox Christianity today. This view, expressed in yet another Greek word, *homoousion,* which means "exactly and at the same time identical or all one."

One of the delights of post World War II childhood in Northern Ireland was opening the daily bottle of milk left on the doorstep by the milkman in the wee hours each morning. Since the cream always rises to the top, whoever opened the milk first poured the layer of cream out of the bottle onto his breakfast porridge. Whoever came second missed that treat.

Perhaps the first sacrifice of life in America was giving up that delicious cream. American milk goes through a process called *homogenization,* which mixes the milk and cream together. This process supposedly makes the milk better for us, or so we are told. I've never been quite convinced that it is not all part of some great conspiracy secretly conceived in the minds of someone like my two sisters, who liked to sleep later than me and, as a result, seldom got the cream. Because of homogenization, all milk, whether at the top or bottom of the container, looks and tastes exactly alike. Cream and milk are so thoroughly mixed that it is impossible to tell where one begins and the other ends. That first part of the word *homogenization* is from the same Greek root, *homos,* for "identical." As cream and milk are one through the process of homogenization, so also the Father and Son are one.

In the words of the Nicene Creed, Jesus Christ is "the only-begotten Son of God, begotten of His Father before all worlds, God of God, Light of Light, very God of very God, begotten not made, being of one substance with the Father."

GOD THE HOLY SPIRIT

The same, said the Council of Nicea, is true for the Holy Spirit: "And we believe in the Holy Spirit, the Lord and giver of life, who proceeds from the Father and the Son; who with the Father and the Son together is worshiped and glorified; who spoke by the prophets." This is the essence of the message behind this book. This God of the Bible reveals Himself to us in three distinct personalities, each of whom plays a distinct role in history and in your life. One of those personalities is the Holy Spirit. He is God in every way, and you need to know Him.

THE BIBLE AND THE TRINITY

"The grace of the Lord Jesus Christ, and the love of God, and the communion of the Holy Ghost be with you all. Amen" (II Cor. 13:14). How can God be one and three all at the same time? A pastor asked a Sunday school student, "What is the Trinity?" The boy's weak voice was muffled by a noisy window air conditioner in the room. "I'm sorry. I can't understand you," the pastor rejoined after the student had responded. Now the bright young student replied, "I know, sir, it's supposed to be a mystery."

That lad was right. None of us can fully understand the Trinity. No one will ever have the final word on all there is to know about the God of the Bible. This book is not the last word on God's Holy Spirit. I trust that reading this book will, however, help you understand the Holy Spirit better than you do now and that understanding Him better you will love Christ more and serve Him better.

THE ONE WHO HAS IT ALL TOGETHER

The Hebrew *Sh'ma,* with which this chapter opens, contributes to our understanding of who God is: "Shema',Yisrael,Yehovah Elohenu,Yehovah 'echad!" "Hear, O Israel: The Lord our God is one Lord!" The word *'echad,* translated *one,* is used over eight hundred times in the Hebrew Scriptures. It refers to a single unit that is composed of more than one part. This is God's idea of solidarity.

God's model of solidarity is seen first in the Genesis Creation account. There, two elements, morning and evening, are made into one day: "God called the light Day, and the darkness He called Night. And the evening and the morning were the first day" (Gen. 1:5).

In the next chapter we read, "A man shall leave his father and his mother, and [be joined] to his wife, and they shall be one flesh" (Gen. 2:24). Marriage between a man and a woman makes two people *'echad,* "one." In marriage, God joins the man and woman together. God's ideal is that they complement each other as a team unit.

Later in Genesis, just before Babel, *'echad* speaks of the unified language of all the people: "The people is one, and they have all one language" (Gen. 11:6). There were many people, but there was only one language.

David uses *'echad* in a negative sense: "They have all turned aside, They have together become corrupt" (Ps. 14:3). He sees many people caught up in a common sin. All have gone off in a similar wrong direction. In Isaiah 53:6 we get a different picture of sin's impact on many people: "We have turned every one to his own way." The difference is that David notes the uniformity, *'echad,* of his people's sinful behavior, whereas Isaiah's concern is that each one does his or her own thing. For this reason, Isaiah uses a word other than *'echad.*

In Numbers 13:23 *'echad* describes a huge cluster of grapes carried out of Canaan to demonstrate the fertility of the land there: "They came unto the brook of Eshcol, and cut down from thence a branch with one cluster of grapes." It was many grapes but only one cluster. It reminds us again of Saint Patrick's shamrock illustration.

9

In the New Testament, Jesus demonstrates the unity of the Godhead in His choice of words for the Great Commission: "Go ye therefore, and [make disciples of] all nations, baptizing them in the name of the Father, and of the Son, and of the Holy Ghost" (Matt. 28:19). The "name" is singular, but the personalities are three. Jesus understood Himself to be one with His Father and the Holy Spirit.

Is this so hard to understand? Think of it in purely human terms using this illustration: Barbara, my wife, is her parents' daughter. She is also our children's mother. Now, when Barbara is alone with me, does that mean she ceases for the time being to be the mother of our children? When she is with her mother and I am elsewhere, does it mean she is temporarily not my wife? Are there times when she is forced to reject two roles in order to fulfill one? Of course not, for these three roles are not mutually exclusive. There may, of course, be times when one role is more apparent than the others, but that does not mean the others are temporarily abandoned. Although distinct, all three roles are fulfilled in one very special person. Her parents, her husband, and her children each think of her differently. For each of us she meets different needs. Members of our family may expect her to play different roles depending on who we are but she is still only one person. She never ceases to be Barbara.

In another sense, each of us is a kind of trinity. We are at the same time body, mind, and spirit.

THE ETERNAL LOVE TRIANGLE

What is true of Barbara and of you and me is even more true about the Triune God. The Father did not cease to exist when the Son came to earth to live as a human being for thirty-three years. Nor did the Son somehow dissipate when He gave His Holy Spirit to the church. All continue to exist. All are equal and all are God. Each manifests a different role in our lives out of gracious love for us. This is the great eternal love triangle of the Bible and of the ages.

The Father loves us with a love so great He made a world for us to enjoy. At Eden's Gate, when sin broke our relationship with Him, He immediately devised a plan for our salvation. That love is unlike any love the world ever knew before. It is so great a whole new Greek word, *agapao,* was coined to describe it. "Behold, what manner of love the Father has bestowed on us, that we should be called the sons of God" (I John 3:1). This is love with no limits!

The Son's love for us made Him willing to endure the pain of Calvary's cross as the atoning sacrifice for our sin. "God so loved the world that he gave his only begotten Son, that whosoever believeth in him should not perish, but have everlasting life" (John 3:16).

This great love of the Father and the Son would have been in vain and would have never been personalized in our hearts without the patient, infinite love of the Holy Spirit: "The love of God is shed abroad in our hearts by the Holy Ghost which is given unto us" (Rom. 5:5).

The Holy Spirit, whose life and unique ministry is the subject of each chapter ahead, is not like some vague force or influence. He is not like the imaginary force of a *Star Wars* movie. He is as real as you are except that He does not have a body like yours or mine. As we shall see, he was present at creation and is present in the world today. He loves, guides and directs us. He has a job. His job is to help us trust in Jesus for eternal life in heaven. When we do, He comes and lives within us and helps us to grow more like Christ every day.

As I look back over my life, I can see that this great Holy Spirit love nudged me in boyhood to observe the faithful testimony of my sainted grandmother. As a young man and new immigrant to the United States, it was Holy Spirit love that gave life to my uncle Sam Heslip's words that convicted me of my sin. It was Holy Spirit love that convinced me I was forgiven by Christ who died for me on Calvary's cross. It was Holy Spirit love that persuaded me God loved me despite my sin and that further delay in surrendering my life to the Savior would be utterly foolish. In the years since I was drawn to make that commitment, it has been the love of the Spirit of God that has kept me and nurtured me in my faith. He has made me aware of God's love through good times and bad. This is the love of abundant life; hence, the title and theme of this book, *The Breath of Abundant Life.*

Yet, as we shall see, this is only part of what the Holy Spirit does for us. In Moscow's Red Square, tourists gather to see the tomb of Lenin. He is

11

dead. He speaks no longer to his followers. Similarly, when Mohammed died, he left no promises for his devotees. For as long as he lived, Buddha was a light for all his students. As he neared the end of his life, however, he told them somewhat abruptly to make their own light. Each of these men left their followers as orphans. Jesus Christ is different. He made a specific promise that set Him apart from every other great historical or religious leader: "I will not leave you comfortless: I will come to you" (John 14:18). He even told us how this would come to pass: "I will pray the Father, and he shall give you another Comforter, that he may abide with you forever; the Spirit of truth; whom the world cannot receive, because it seeth him not, neither knoweth him: but ye know him; for he dwelleth with you, and shall be in you." (John 14:16-17).

Line up all the great leaders who have ever lived and see that Christ did far more than any of them. He left us the promise of a living Spirit to comfort, guide, inspire, lead and help us: "These things I said not unto you at the beginning, because I was with you. But now I go away to him who sent Me ...I tell you the truth; it is expedient for you that I go away: for if I go not away, will not come unto you; but if I depart, I will send him unto you" (John 16:4-7).

This promised Spirit is the Breath of Abundant Life. One of the great catastrophes of our time is that more inconsistent theology has been taught about the Holy Spirit than in all the previous generations of the Christian faith combined. The Third Person of the Trinity has been misrepresented, slighted, ignored, and abused. What a tragedy this is!

No Christian teaching needs more reemphasis today than the doctrine of the Holy Spirit. He can and will come into your life and bring renewal in your walk with Christ. He will be a positive and intensely practical force in your relationships with other people, in your marriage, with your family, on your job, or in your business. That is a primary thrust throughout the chapters of this book. Wherever you need help, there the Holy Spirit will be present looking out for you.

Without this Breath of Abundant Life it is impossible to experience the life-changing power Christ promises. Who is this Holy Spirit and what can He do in your life? In the pages ahead, you will learn the answers to these and many other questions. You will see what the Bible has to say about what it really means to live new life in the Holy Spirit as a practical and wonderful life-transforming experience. Read on and grow in the knowledge and love of the Son of the living God who sent His Spirit into the world for you.

2

The breath of abundant life!

As part of their basic flight training, U.S. Air Force student pilots are paired off in an altitude simulation chamber. With oxygen masks on, they are taken to a simulated height of thirty thousand feet. One of the two students takes his oxygen mask off. At that point, he or she is asked to write answers to simple questions on a sheet of paper. After a few minutes, the partner who has continued to wear his oxygen mask forces the oxygen mask back onto the uncovered mouth and nose of the person writing. After a few gulps of air, the one writing is amazed at what he has just written. Earlier, he was sure his answers made perfectly logical sense. In reality, while his first answers make sense, his later answers are nonsense. He was on the verge of losing total consciousness and he did not even know it. That is how important breath is.

GOD'S BREATH

The Bible speaks only three times about God's breathing. One is in Paul's letter to Timothy, the young preacher. There he writes, "All scripture is given by inspiration of God, and is profitable for doctrine, for reproof, for correction, for instruction in righteousness: that the man of God may be perfect, throughly furnished unto all good works" (II Tim. 3:16-17).

Since the Garden of Eden, one of Satan's principle areas of attack has been the credibility of what God says. There is probably no more damaging attack for people than to say that they are not to be believed that they do not tell the truth, that they exaggerate or overstate reality. Undermine the credibility of someone's speech and you strike a death blow to his reputation for honesty. This is a common practice in the court system of our country. Lawyers try hard to erode the integrity of a person by calling into question his basic truthfulness. Important cases are sometimes won and lost by whether the lawyers succeed. In Eden that was Satan's strategy. He attempted to rattle Eve's confidence in God's Word: "The serpent said unto the woman, Ye shall not surely die" (Gen. 3:4). A look at the full record demonstrates that he was aided and abetted by Eve's own tendency to overstate the facts. She stretched God's earlier statement "Of every tree of the garden thou mayest freely eat: but of the tree of the knowledge of good and evil, thou shalt not eat of it: for in the day that thou eatest thereof thou shalt surely die" (Gen. 2:16-17) into, "God hath said, Ye shall not eat of it, neither shall ye touch it, lest ye die" (Gen. 3:3). By saying that God had said that she and Adam were not to even touch the tree, Eve demonstrated her own vulnerability at this point. The crafty Satan, having now uncovered her weakness, knew how to attack.

A few days ago, my attention was attracted by a business magazine interview of a friend of mine who is president of a major shipbuilding operation on the Mississippi Gulf Coast. Jerry St. Pe spoke about some of the latest weapons in the arsenal of the United States Navy. Included among them is a missile capable of being programmed to travel from hundreds of miles away out in the ocean. It speeds over land and water until it weaves its way through a chosen neighborhood and travels down the middle of a preselected street right through the front door of a prepicked house. Like a letter mailed from overseas, the missile arrives at the front door of an address "written" on it by computer technology.

Satan's strategy is not like that as a rule. He is seldom one for a frontal attack. He is rarely, if ever, a front door visitor. He is far too cunning for that. He is more likely to show up unannounced through some unexpected entrance. That was what he did in Eden. With a subtle, indignant-sounding exclamation of disbelief, the Devil cunningly seduced Eve into believing that God did not really mean what she had heard Him say. "The serpent said unto the woman, Ye shall not surely die" (Gen. 3:4). That expression of mock unbelief and pretended concern for Eve was designed to attack God's credibility.

I've sometimes wondered if even Satan knew how successful his ingenious ploy would be. It accomplished his goal in an unbelievable way. In one fell swoop it brought about the spiritual downfall of the entire human race. "By one man sin entered into the world, and death by sin; and so death passed upon all men, for that all have sinned" (Rom. 5:12). An old Hungarian proverb says, "Adam ate the apple and we've all had the toothache ever since."

It's the truth! Satan's first attempt at disrupting human peace worked so well it is no wonder he made it a permanent part of his armory. It was not that he attacked with strong weapons that would have alienated Adam and Eve immediately. Rather, approaching Eve with a soft-sell approach, he set out to undermine the integrity of God's Word. His mock concern was laced with the poison of cynicism. Sincere people are still being seduced into believing that God's Word has a credibility problem. Nobody knows how many potentially great preachers, teachers, missionaries, and other good servants of Christ have fallen for Satan's wily ways. The credibility of the Bible continues to be a major issue in our time.

It was a problem in the first-century church too. Paul recognized this in the life and ministry of Timothy, his son in the faith. Timothy, a young pastor of the congregation at Ephesus, found his ministry floundering for authority. Paul wrote to assure him that his authority was based on what God had said. Cutting to the chase, the apostle pointed out the ultimate source of the Scriptures. "All scripture is given by inspiration of God," said he. To make his point, he coined a strong new Greek word, *theopneustos,* translated "by inspiration of God." Paul's word may have been new, but its message was clear. It was a compound of two other words, *theos,* meaning, "divine" or "God," and *pneustos,* from *pneuma* (from which we derive our English word *pneumatic*), meaning "breathed." "God breathed all Scripture," Paul declared to his young preacher friend. For Paul that made the Bible reliable beyond any question. It ought to do the same for us.

The other two references to God's breath are the principle starting place for the subject of this chapter. The first is from the Creation account in Genesis 2:7, "The Lord God ... breathed into his nostrils the breath of life; and man became a living soul." The second comes at the point of the first encounter between the risen Christ and His disciples in the upper room: Jesus "breathed on them, and saith unto them, 'Receive ye the Holy Ghost'" (John 20:22).

The first of these I call the breath of eternal life. The second is the one from which this book borrows its title. I call it the Breath of Abundant Life. When Jesus Christ told His disciples, "I am come that they might have life, and that they might have it more abundantly" (John 10:10), this is what He meant.

THE BREATH OF ETERNAL LIFE

Last week a man from our congregation had open-heart surgery. As is usually the case with surgery like his, it was necessary that for a time, David's heart be stopped. His breathing was stopped too. During the time his heart and breathing were stopped, his life was sustained by a heart-lung machine. The breath from that machine kept him alive while surgeons performed their delicate work. After the surgeon had performed his intricate operation, the machine was disconnected. David breathed unassisted once more. Afterwards, the chief surgeon reported his success to David's wife and children. "As soon as we disconnected him from the heart-lung machine, he started breathing on his own again and that is what we were hoping for," he said. The resumption of natural breathing was a major indicator that his surgery had gone according to plan.

Last week, our local newspaper carried a report about a child who was rescued from the bottom of a community swimming pool. When the lifeguard rescued the little boy, the child had already stopped breathing. The well-trained lifeguard knew what to do. Laying the child's tiny limp body flat on the ground, she performed CPR. For a while, she breathed for him. The breath of her lungs was passed from her mouth to his mouth and into his lungs. When he resumed breathing without her help, the rescue was deemed successful.

As wonderful as these two events are, the resumed breathing of an open-heart surgery patient and a child near death, the "breath of life" God breathed into Adam is even more wonderful. That holy breath on Adam set Adam apart from every other created thing. It kindled the beginning of a bond between the Creator and His special creature that nothing else in all creation would ever equal. It ignited a unique spiritual link between God and man that gives each a heart for the other. We were made for eter-

nal fellowship with Him. We are spiritual beings. There is an inherent long-
ing deep within us for a relationship that goes further than any other relationship we can ever experience. We try in every way we can imagine to
satisfy it. This is Blaise Pascal's "God-shaped vacuum" that creates a fundamental dissatisfaction at the center of our existence until it is filled. It is
Augustine's recognition that God made us for Himself in such a way that
we have restless hearts until we rest our heart in God. It is David's recognition that "as the hart panteth after the water brooks, So panteth my soul
after thee, O God" (Ps. 42:1). In short, we can neither deny nor get away
from this breath of life.

ROMANCE THAT NEVER RUNS OUT

William Jennings Bryan, the great American orator and defender of
the faith, was at one point in his midlife having his portrait painted. The
artist, in helping to make Bryan "picture-perfect" inquired of him, "Sir, why
do you wear your hair over your ears like that?" William Jennings Bryan
replied, "Actually, there is a romance connected with it. When I first pursued Mrs. Bryan, she declined my every invitation. Later a close confidant
of hers whispered to me that it was not that she did not like me but that
there was something about the way my ears stick out that turned her off. I
decided then and there to remedy the situation. So as to remove that
obstacle to our relationship, I grew my hair long enough to cover my
offending parts."

"That was a long time ago and fashions have changed, sir," the artist
responded. "Would you consider cutting your hair now?" "Absolutely not,"
said the statesman-orator, "I'm still pursuing my romance with Mrs. Bryan."

True romance never runs out. An advertisement in the Personals section of a local newspaper was headlined "Husband for Sale." The text
below read, "Age 52, in good health. Out of sorts most of the time. No
longer verbalizes 'I love you.' Is only rarely touching or tender. Asking price
2 cents. NOTE: Price negotiable!"

According to the wife who placed that message in the newspaper, her
husband is not worth even two cents. We chuckle at such an advertisement;
then we hope for all the world that it really is just a joke. William Jennings

Bryan was aware that when romance leaves a marriage, holy wedlock becomes holy deadlock. Something bad has happened to that relationship.

The same is true in our relationship with our Maker. It can deteriorate to the place where it is virtually worthless. We need constant reminders that fashions come and go, times and circumstances change, but our romance with God through Christ must not be allowed to fluctuate. We were made for intimacy with Him, and it is always in our best interests to deal with any part of our life that offends Him. In the sacrifice of His Son, God made it possible for us to cover our offending parts. No relationship on earth will ever substitute for this relationship He makes possible. None will ever take its place. Indeed, no relationship on earth will ever be truly right without our intimate connection with God first being in place.

How can I say this with such certainty? First, because the Bible says it is so. Our relationship with God is at the same time the foundation and the model for our relationship with one another. Second, I can testify to this point because of a wonderful personal experience. Barbara and I were not committed to Christ when we married. Baptized as children, we were brought up in church but we somehow missed understanding the reality of God's redeeming grace through Christ. We were married, in the church and had a good and loving relationship from the beginning. When we married we were committed to each other for life. We were still not Christians, however. It was sometime after our second wedding anniversary that we each, at separate times, came to faith in Christ. When Christ entered our lives individually and when He entered our life together, we found a level of closeness and love for one another that we had no idea existed before. This romance of ours, after over thirty-three years of marriage, is stronger than ever, and we agree that it is because God is at the center of it.

That is not to say that making a commitment to Christ is a Pollyanna recipe for a good marriage nor that all marital problems somehow float away just because a couple commit their way to Christ. It does mean that when Christ is at the center of a marriage, the issues and concerns that are a normal part of married life are seen from a different perspective. When Christ is at the center there is a renewed sense of commitment to working through difficulties in a way that is positive and constructive for both the husband and the wife. The family that prays together really does stay together. The Christian principles that make for better marriages are true for other relationships as well.

THE BREATH OF ABUNDANT LIFE

The third time God breathed is recorded in John's Gospel: Jesus "breathed on them, and said to them, 'Receive the Holy Spirit.'" When the resurrected Jesus breathed on the disciples in the upper room, something exciting beyond their wildest dreams had just happened. The cross had just been conquered. Death had been destroyed. Its sting had been blunted. The Lord of Calvary had just come through bolted doors. That, too, was a miracle. Human flesh had never walked through a closed door before. The very notion of it still puzzles our minds. What Christ found there was a room filled with a spirit of apprehension. A group of men who only a few days before had boldly pledged to support their leader now gathered in fear. Believing their Master was dead, they waited with certainty that their enemies would soon ferret them out and send them to the death they had seen Him die.

What they did not, could not, know was that something exciting had just happened and that something exciting was about to happen! Having been raised from the dead, the Lord of Calvary's cross came to usher them to the next chapter in mankind's life with God. They were about to embark on life at a higher level.

God's first breath had made man alive in a way that was different from every other created thing by giving him life for all eternity. God's second breath, the Holy Spirit, would bring men power to be God's principle representatives on earth. "Jesus said to them again, Peace be unto you: as my Father hath sent me, even so send I you" (John 20:21). Moments before, they felt defeated, lost, powerless, and more scared than they had ever been. Now they would go forward appointed and empowered in Christ's authority with a message of life the like of which the world had never heard before. This new era would be officially commissioned at Pentecost. That was the moment God had chosen to break this exciting news to the world. In the meantime, this was a pre-Pentecost leadership training session.

Until this moment the Holy Spirit, as part of the Trinity, generally occupied a somewhat subdued position in the background. He had never been the member of the Trinity to get the Scripture headlines. He was always there. He had helped shape creation: "The Spirit of God moved upon the face of the waters" (Gen. 1:2). He was there. He was vitally involved. It was just that in the grander scheme of what was happening, the Holy Spirit was not singled out for a headline role. Many Christians read through the first chapter of the Bible and overlook His presence completely.

He led the Exodus of the children of Israel from Egypt. God revealed to Moses that special gifts were given to Bezalel, Oholiab, and all the craftsmen in order that they might accomplish their special tasks: "I have filled him with the spirit of God, in wisdom, and in understanding, and in knowledge, and in all manner of workmanship, to devise cunning works, to work in gold, and in silver, and in brass, and in cutting of stones, to set them, and in carving of timber, to work in all manner of workmanship" (Exod. 31:3-5).

Throughout the psalms he is there renewing hearts and transforming lives. The penitent David begged that God not mete the most severe punishment the fallen psalmist-king could imagine: "Cast me not away from thy presence; and take not thy holy spirit from me" (Ps. 51:11).

The Holy Spirit was present repeatedly in the prophets. Isaiah mentions the Spirit's ministry more than any of the other prophets: "The spirit of the Lord God is upon me; because the Lord hath anointed me to preach good tidings unto the meek; he hath sent me to bind up the broken-hearted, to proclaim liberty to the captives, and the opening of the prison to them that are bound. To proclaim the acceptable year of the Lord, and the day of vengeance of our God; to comfort all that mourn; To appoint unto them that mourn in Zion, to give unto them beauty for ashes, the oil of joy for mourning, the garment of praise for the spirit of heaviness; that they might be called trees of righteousness, the planting of the Lord, that he might be glorified" (61:1-3).

Jesus made Isaiah's words His synagogue text at the beginning of his earthly ministry. He stopped midway through Isaiah's second verse and validated this prophecy: "This day is this scripture fulfilled in your ears" (Luke

4:21). Not only did He validate Isaiah's ministry, Christ also pointed out that the same power behind Isaiah's ministry would empower His own ministry.

Before that day when Christ recited these words in the synagogue, however, Luke records another incident in which the Spirit played a quiet though vital role: "The angel answered and said unto her, The Holy Ghost shall come upon thee, and the power of the Highest shall overshadow thee: therefore also that holy thing which shall be born of thee shall be called the Son of God" (Luke 1:35).

Matthew records the Spirit's presence at Christ's baptism: "Jesus, when he was baptized, went up straightway out of the water: and, lo, the heavens were opened unto him, and he saw the Spirit of God descending like a dove, and lighting upon him" (Matt. 3:16). He was there at all the vital minutes. It is just that He never trumpeted His presence. He was always in the background. It is the way of the Holy Spirit to keep out of the limelight.

QUIET BUT VITAL

Not long after the fiftieth anniversary of D-Day, I was seated on an airplane next to a veteran on his way home from the anniversary celebrations. We were flying from London to Atlanta. During that eight-hour journey across the Atlantic, he told me about some of his experiences from the recent past. He spoke movingly of his felt need to go back for his buddies who did not survive. When General Eisenhower ordered the C-47 aircraft into the night skies over Normandy on June 6, 1944, great doubt remained about who would prevail. Even before it was under way, the Normandy invasion was identified by many experts as the final great decisive battle of World War II. As part of the famous United States 82nd Airborne, the old veteran sitting beside me spoke of parachuting behind enemy lines during the first hours of D-Day. Those brave young men who would change the course of human history were transported high across the English Channel from England to France on C-47 troop carriers. Their mission was stated in simple words: Stop Hitler's onslaught of tyranny in Europe and save democracy. Only the words were simple. The mission these men were commanded to perform was anything but a simple one. It was necessary that the operation be carried out under cover of darkness and a moonless night was chosen. Realizing the inherent risks of getting separated from one another in strange enemy territory under those conditions, I asked what, if any, provision was made in case they might become detached from one another. He reached into his pant's pocket and pulled out a small metal clicker he had treasured for fifty years. That and his hat were the only personal effects he carried to remind him of his contribution to peace. With all the enthusiasm of a child on Christmas morning, he demonstrated how the clicker worked. As the paratroopers groped their way in the darkness, they were to listen carefully for the sounds of others. When they heard a sound signaling the presence of someone nearby, they were to click the clicker one time. After ten seconds of silence, a buddy hearing that first click would respond with two clicks from his own clicker. Another minute of intentional silence passed, and the series of clicks were repeated; one click followed by ten seconds of silence then two clicks. It was an ingenious idea that doubtless shored up the hope and confidence of many a scared soldier. The sound was so quiet it was barely audible. To the untrained or unexpecting ear, it was nothing more than a meaningless background noise in the night. For a paratrooper separated from his buddies, however, it was music to the ears, a vital evidence that he had a friend nearby. Quiet but vital!

World Changers

We too have a friend nearby who works with us to change the world. His name is the Holy Spirit. He is always there in our times of darkness, coming alongside us. He shines His light from somewhere back of us so that we can see Jesus and know Him to be real. The Spirit whispers into the ear of our heart in such a way as to give Christ's words life and make them intensely personal to us. His Greek name, *paraclete,* means "someone nearby to help." We may not always be conscious of His presence, but He is there nevertheless and He is on our side. Indeed, He is more than just a friend; He is a whole army for "the Lord of hosts is with us; the God of Jacob is our refuge" (Ps. 46:7). When trouble comes and you are afraid a whole army waits nearby, your "click" is a simple prayer thanking God for His never failing nearness. Just because He keeps Himself out of sight does not mean He has gone away. It is simply that He directs all the glory toward Jesus, for it is, after all, the Father's design to glorify the Son.

Quiet but vital! These three words in sequence describe the Holy Spirit's ministry throughout the Old Testament. He was always there, always seemingly in the background, and always in a supporting role, just as He was with Isaiah. It was no different when He came to Mary whom God had chosen to bear His Son.

When Jesus breathed on the disciples and said, "Receive ye the Holy Ghost," He was signaling that from now on the ministry of the Spirit would be different. While He would never be a headline grabber, from this time forward God's people would be more aware of their dependence on God the Holy Spirit. He would come with power upon all God's people to support and encourage their ministry in the name of Christ.

MORE THAN A PRESENCE

Having said all this, there remains yet one signal point to be made. It is that when Christ breathed on the disciples in the upper room, He gave them more than some inanimate presence, for the Holy Spirit of God is, first and foremost, a person.

A young Christian executive spoke about a business conference he had attended. There a motivational speaker concluded his speech by comparing God's power at work in us to the "force" in the *Star Wars* movies. "As you leave today, may the Force be with you," he said, perhaps oblivious to the vast theological difference between what he said and what Christ said. It was probably intended as nothing more than a well meaning "good luck" wish. It is possible to think of the Holy Spirit as nothing more than a mere force. If we do that, however, we miss the true essence of what Jesus gave the disciples in the upper room. We also miss the true significance of Pentecost. The Holy Spirit is first and foremost a person. He always was and always will be.

The authors of the Nicene Creed helped clarify this with their statement, "We believe in the Holy Spirit, the Lord and giver of life." This was entirely in line with Christ's own teaching: "I will pray the Father, and he shall give you another Comforter, that he may abide with you for ever; even the Spirit of truth; whom the world cannot receive, because it seeth him not, neither knoweth him: but ye know him; for he dwelleth with you, and shall be in you" (John 14:16-17). When you read that promise, make special note of the personal pronouns in these phrases: "He may abide with you for ever"; "It seeth him not neither knoweth him: but ye know him for he dwelleth with you, and shall be in you." The Master's choice of the personal pronouns *he* and *him* signify that Christ regards the Holy Spirit as a person and not merely a force or object. Christ promised more than some inanimate force. He gives us a person who is inseparably connected to the Father and the Son. The Holy Spirit is a person. More than that, He is a divine person; God in us. This was what made the difference in the upper room. This is what made Pentecost a signal moment in the life of the early church. This will make the difference in your life.

STILL SCARED!

The author of a Christian magazine article about the future of the church asked me, "What, in your opinion, will be the church's principle mission in the new millennium?" I thought about that question for only a moment before the answer seemed clear. "The principle mission of the church in the new millennium," I replied, "is the same as the church's principle mission for the last two thousand years." It is really very simple: God wants us to tell His story in our lives and invite others to share this journey of faith with us.

THE UNCHANGING CHALLENGE

Tell the story and invite. Ask any advertising professional and you will hear that the best way to get the word out is by word of mouth. "Go ye therefore, and teach all nations, baptizing them in the name of the Father, and of the Son, and of the Holy Ghost: teaching them to observe all things whatsoever I have commanded you: and, lo, I am with you alway, even unto the end of the world" (Matt. 28:19-20). "Ye shall receive power, after that the Holy Ghost is come upon you: and ye shall be witnesses unto me both in Jerusalem, and in all Judaea, and in Samaria, and unto the uttermost part of the earth" (Acts 1:8).

A group of laborers was assigned the meaningless task of digging holes four feet deep in the ground and filling them in again. The work was frustrating, trivial, absurd. When lunchtime arrived, they drew straws with the idea that whoever picked the smallest straw was delegated to approach the foreman and tell him the news. "We quit!" the short-straw-drawer announced to the boss. "We're tired of just digging holes and filling them in again." "Okay," replied the boss, "but this is the only way we'll ever find the broken sewer pipe." The spokesman, fumbling with his short straw, walked back to his workmates. He told them what the foreman had said about finding the broken pipe. In just a minute the spokesman was back talking to the boss. "Okay boss," he said, "tell us where you want us to dig the next hole."

Intelligent people agree that life is more meaningful when it has a sense of purpose. The diggers sense of purpose was found in learning that they were doing something more than merely digging holes in the ground and filling them in again. Ours comes in realizing that Christ came to earth to do two things: First, to create His church, a community of Christian believers He entrusted with the gift of eternal life; and second, to commission them to take His message of abundant life to the world outside. That's the mandate Christ gave His church just before He left it to return to heaven. That was the challenge of the first century and it shall be the challenge of the twenty-first century, and in every century thereafter should the Lord choose to tarry. It is the unchanging mission of every Christian. That's the reason God saved us. It is our first mission as a Christian. It is the reason He gave us His Spirit.

Yet the single greatest tragedy of the church in our times is that we have not taken Christ's promise of the Holy Spirit in us and the Great Commission seriously. Like those upper room disciples, we are, it seems, still afraid to tell His story.

What are we afraid of? As a pastor, I have heard these fears expressed by modern disciples in a variety of forms.

FEAR OF REJECTION

"I am afraid my invitation to receive Christ or join His church will be rejected." The amazing thing about that statement is that the last person who said it to me is a successful real estate salesperson. Each year he books business in the millions of dollars. I asked in response to that answer, "When you ask a prospect to buy a house, do you fear he or she might decline?" "No," he replied, "because I know that while a certain percentage will decline, asking for a commitment is part and parcel of my success in real estate."

He is, I am sure, right about that. One does not succeed for long in sales without asking for the commitment that signals a deal is done. The same is true in all our lives. We invite a friend to join us for dinner at a favorite restaurant. We invite someone home to watch the Super Bowl. We ask the girl of our dreams to marry us. Inviting other people to make decisions is a natural part of life in the real world. Do people ever decline our invitations? Of course, they do. That, too, is part of life in the real world.

The invitation to receive Christ or to come to church is not much different. Some will gladly accept our invitation. Others may reject it. The law of averages would suggest, however, that more are likely to accept than reject. There are people in each of our lives who are waiting for our invitation. God sent them to us because He expects us to issue the invitation that will transform their lives forever, and He sent us to them because He knows they are ready to say yes.

FEAR OF OFFENDING

"I'm afraid of offending someone who is already a Christian." This too is a poor excuse for not obeying the commission to go and tell the story of Jesus. If someone is a Christian, he has an obligation to fulfill the same duty. He will understand and appreciate your responsibility to tell and invite. The fact remains, however, that approximately 70 percent of the people in your town have never made a commitment to Christ and His church. How do I know? Statistics tell us that approximately 30 percent of the people in the United States openly profess faith in Christ and participate regularly in His church. In other parts of the world, the number is often not that high. If you live outside the United States, your opportunities to tell the best news the world will ever hear may be even greater and more compelling. Go and tell and invite!

AFRAID OF CHANGE

One church member of long standing responded to my invitation to go and tell Christ's story with an especially candid response. "I'm afraid," he said, "that the people I would invite might come here and change things." This, I suspect, is a far more prevalent reason that we do not invite new people to church than many of us would like to admit.

The fact is, however, that no matter how hard we try it is impossible to maintain the status quo. Change is a fact of life. We can no more avoid it than we can stop the tide from changing or, for that matter, than the Pharisees could have stopped Pentecost. Christ has saved us and entrusted us with the cure for the ills of humanity. Into our hands He has placed the only sure way to stop pornography, broken homes, the rising rate of illegitimate births, child abuse, addiction problems, teen suicides, poverty, and the other evils of our time. Despite that, we choose to keep it to ourselves. Shame on us! Would we do that with a cure for cancer or Alzheimer's disease? Of course not! We would trumpet our discovery by every means available and nothing at our disposal would ever take the place of a simple word of mouth testimony between friends. Do not be afraid!

"God hath not given us the spirit of fear; but of power, and of love, and of a sound mind" (II Tim. 1:7). Whatever our fear, the One who gives us the Breath of Abundant Life says, "Fear not, little flock; for it is your Father's good pleasure to give you the kingdom" (Luke 12:32). The world is ours to claim for Christ in the power of the Holy Spirit.

Jesus Christ has given us His Spirit to do better things and to do things better. This Third Person in the Godhead has come among us. Let fear be gone. Loosen the bars of your doors and exclaim, "Welcome Holy Spirit!" Go forth and tell Christ's story and invite people in. It is within our power to make a better world.

3

This spirit is not spooky

In his classic *A Tale of Two Cities,* Charles Dickens presents a model illustration of practical friendship. Set during the French Revolution, it is the story of two friends, Charles Darnay and Sydney Carton. Darnay, the young Frenchman, has been thrown in a dungeon to await his appointment with the guillotine. Carton, a wasted English lawyer, has lived a life of wanton reprobation. Carton slips into the dungeon late one afternoon and exchanges clothes with the young prisoner. Darnay, now wearing Carton's garb, is able to escape as night falls. The next morning, Sydney Carton, the lawyer whose life had heretofore been wasted, makes his way up the steps that lead to the guillotine. As he reaches the spot where he shall breathe his last and die in the place of someone else, he raises his voice in final triumph and declares, "I see the lives for which I lay down my life, peaceful, useful, prosperous and happy, in that England which I shall see no more—it is a far, far better thing that I do, than I have ever done; it is a far, far better rest that I go to than I have ever known."

Dickens's expressed intention was to provide the pseudo-sophisticated literary world of his day with a practical allegory of Christ's atonement for us. He wanted his contemporaries to know that the death of Jesus on the cross was true friendship at its practical best.

WHAT GOOD ARE GOOD INTENTIONS?

Where we live, now some automobile license plates display the slogan, "You've Got a Friend in Pennsylvania." It is true! Six years living among the rolling hills of western Pennsylvania have brought me face-to-face with some of the most amiable and neighborly people I have ever known. What's more, Pennsylvania friendship is practical. It is more than lip service. Pennsylvanians are a pragmatic people for the most part.

Not long ago the car parked next to mine in a downtown Pittsburgh parking garage would not start. I could tell from the registration that the driver was from a neighboring state. I was the first to offer help to him, but there was little I could do. My offer of help was not much use since my jumper cables were hanging neatly in my garage at home. As well intended as it was, my friendship was, for that moment at least, just words. It was impractical. It was well intended but finally useless.

The number of other local drivers who in the moments following offered help impressed me. Several had jump-start cables in their car trunks, which they freely made available. That fellow discovered he had a lot of friends in Pennsylvania. I can tell you that I went home that day and put those jumper cables in my car trunk. What use is the right tool if it is twelve miles away?

Friendship that is not practical is ultimately of little use. We have all had fair-weather friends, people who profess comradeship when life runs smoothly but who have a way of being hard to find when the road of life gets rough for a while. We all know people who, though well intentioned, are the bearers of "friendly" advice that is somehow disconnected from reality. By God's grace, we have all also had friends who stick by us in the tough times, whose advice is good and who, like Dickens's Carton, would stand in for us at the place of cruel death if need be. Such people are almost always motivated by a love that goes beyond mere lip service.

Our Best Friend

"A man that hath friends must shew himself friendly: and there is a friend that sticketh closer than a brother" (Prov. 18:24). Wouldn't it be wonderful to know that you have a friend whose very name is an unbreakable promise to be the most loyal and practical companion you could ever hope for? One who says that no matter what your past contains, he will forgive you? One who will always pick you up when your spirits are down? One who always walks in when others walk out? One who will meet you wherever you are and look out for you in truly practical ways? Good news! You already have someone like that! His power energizes everything good about this world we live in and His primary desire for your life is that you should rise to achieve everything good for you. He is the Holy Spirit of God, the Breath of Abundant Life.

Jesus said, "I will pray the Father, and he shall give you another Comforter, that he may abide with you for ever: Even the Spirit of truth; whom the world cannot receive, because it seeth him not, neither knoweth him: but ye know him; for he dwelleth with you, and shall be in you" (John 14:16-17).

When Jesus spoke those words, He was preparing the disciples for a new season in their lives. He knew that He was walking in the shadow of the cross. For us, though not for Christ, the cross was an intensely practical experience. Justice demanded that a penalty be paid for sin. For Christ the cross was, for the first and only time in His life, a journey into sin's darkness. Yet from His darkness rings out the sure voice declaring God's immeasureable, practical love. His love is neither flippant nor capricious. It is neither changeable nor inconsistent. Consistent practicality is a part of Christ's essential nature because His Father never decrees anything that makes no sense. What is more, when we examine the Bible record, we are forced to conclude that God the Son never did anything that was not sensible.

It makes good sense, therefore, that Christ's Holy Spirit in the world today will also act in ways that are intensely practical. Yet no part of the Godhead has suffered more at the hands of inconsistent and impractical theological crackpots than the Holy Spirit. The Bible picture of the Holy Spirit is anything but that. This chapter presents a biblical response to some of the misunderstanding of the person and work of the Holy Spirit in recent times. It demonstrates the scriptural representation of the Holy Spirit as a real personality and as Christ's Comforter and every Christian's Companion.

I remember reading a newspaper column sometime ago by Sidney J. Harris. Harris told of an author whose books were like a breath of fresh air in a putrid chamber. This author was big on things Harris considered important. Family ties were high on his list of priorities. It was his expressed desire to be a good father and role model to his children. Harris was impressed until he learned the real truth about the man. It turned out that his high-sounding words were nothing more than that; they were only high-sounding words. At home that author was a tyrant to his wife and children. He held them accountable to unrealistic ideals of what he thought they should be. They were ideals he had yet to demonstrate in his own life. He showed no patience with his family members' perceived imperfections. Sidney J. Harris wrote that for him that man's message was lost in the quagmire of impractical idealism. We can all understand how Sidney Harris might feel that way.

As tragic as that man's poor example was, it is not as devastating as the witness of some Christians to life in the Holy Spirit. A young woman I know was invited to attend services for renewal led by a regionally well-known evangelist. She was impressed by the man's message of the evening, and when he gave an invitation at the close, she was one of the first people to walk forward and pray for Christ to come into her life. Thus began her walk as a new disciple of Jesus. Unfortunately, it was to be a journey of only a few steps because two weeks later, while she was still in the infancy of her new life, the evangelist took his own life. What that young woman, and many others, did not know was that the evangelist for years had led a secret life. He was a participant in a long-term immoral relationship outside his marriage. When an investigative reporter uncovered this, the news soon spread throughout the region and that young woman, who was for a moment counted as a new convert, fell by the wayside. Today she demonstrates no real evidence of growth in the things of Christ. She seems unable to get past that experience of a false prophet whose message, once so appealing, was undermined by an incompatible lifestyle.

The same is true of others who have heard the Spirit of God described in ways that are just plain hokey. Much that is portrayed as the work of the Spirit is impractical and unrealistic. Neither is it in keeping with the life of Christ nor the message He taught. After receiving a tip-off, television news personality Diane Sawyer carried out an investigative report on the ministry of a widely broadcast television evangelist who closed each of his televised programs with an appeal for viewers to write to him with prayer requests and donations. He assured his would-be correspondents that he would personally pray over every letter. Diane Sawyer discovered something far contrary to what the evangelist promised. Envelopes addressed to that ministry were opened but no prayer requests were read. The evangelist prayed for no one. Neither did anyone else connected to that ministry. Once the money was removed, the remainder of each letter sent was discarded in a garbage can. Meanwhile the evangelist lived a secret life in the lap of luxury with several multi-million dollar homes, expensive cars, and a fine yacht all purchased with donations that were given to advance God's work. People watching that program were reminded of the movie version of such a character in Elmer Gantry.

That is religious quackery of only one kind. There are, however, others. Those who often seem to be motivated by a kind of spiritual one-upmanship have always attributed bizarre acts of supposed Christians to the Spirit of God. They range all the way from the old-time snake-oil salesman to religious revivalists who appear to feel that the work of the Holy Spirit must be demonstrated in ways that seem more in keeping with a circus performance than with the teaching of the Bible. The net result is that those set on undermining Christ's work in the world often find their ammunition provided by the weird demonstrations of those who are part of the family of God. Famous atheist Madelyn Murray O'Haire, for example, used to take great delight in describing the Third Person in the Trinity as "the spook." Webster defines a spook as "a frightening object." When someone thinks of the Holy Spirit in terms like *spook*, that person is acknowledging that God's Holy Spirit is like a scary Halloween ghost. Does your mind picture the Holy Spirit as something or someone mysterious and strange? Is He a weird agent of fear, despair, and doubt? The Bible picture of the Holy Spirit is absolutely unlike any of these images.

A GENERATION RUN AMUCK

Yale Law School professor Stephen Carter, in his book *The Culture of Disbelief,* sets forth the thesis that Christian influence in America is on the decline. Carter concludes that our nation's spiritual future is abysmally ominous. He supports his thesis by documenting various indicators of our declining spiritual national life.

Apart from what Stephen Carter says such indicators are not hard to find. The response of lawmakers and others who seem to want to replace the United States Constitution with the results of the latest popular opinion polls following the revelation of promiscuous sex in the White House Oval

Office is blatant evidence of how far off we are spiritually. The number of Americans who wanted to turn a blind eye to that kind of behavior by the highest elected official in the land because the economy was good at the time may have revealed what really matters in America.

Many books and sermons lend support to Carter's thesis. Both sociologists and theologians struggle to coin new terms that help define what is going on in our society. Some have called this the "post-modern" era. Others have labeled us a "post-Christian" society. I take these labels to mean that their proponents believe that America's moral slide is already so far advanced that there is no hope of reclaiming our spiritual roots. Whether one agrees with this conclusion or not, there can be no doubt that this age is marked by a lack of moral absolutes. This is seen in both the secular and religious realms of our generation.

In the world of the church, for example, we often find that those in positions of church leadership set Scripture's standards aside when what the Bible says does not meet their personal goals or objectives. The result is a series of glaring inconsistencies that testify to a people who have lost their way. For example, *U.S. News and World Report,* on April 4, 1994, reported that even though 80 percent of Americans say they consider the Bible to be God's inspired Word, 48 percent of the population believe that no one set of values is absolute. That, of course, is evidence of a glaring contradiction. In one meeting of Christian leaders where I was present, a veteran Bible teacher declared, "We don't care what the Bible says; we just want to do what we want to do." When that statement was challenged, the person who made it responded, "Then show us from the Bible how we can do what we want to do." She was apparently oblivious to the inherent self-centered paganism revealed in her words.

SHE IS NOT ALONE.

"Where there is no vision, the people perish" (Prov. 29:18). Another way to translate the Hebrew words in that passage is, "Where there are no standards, the people cast off all restraint." When Scripture is not seen for what it is, people set their own limits, make their own rules, and unwittingly finally plot their own paganism.

A quick look at history demonstrates this. From Eden's Gate to Europe's Dark Ages, every time a society dilutes the authority of God's inspired Word, a period of unrestrained godlessness results within a generation or so. This finally culminates in spiritual death. No nation that has locked God out of its public life has survived for long. Nor should we expect God's blessing when His expressed desire has little or no bearing on our private or national life. As we saw in the last chapter, sin entered the human race when Eve overstated God's Word. Much of what is offered in the name of the Holy Spirit today is nothing more than an extension of Eve's actions. In short, the Holy Spirit's name is sometimes used to credit Him with things that are not founded on Scripture.

THE BIBLICAL PORTRAIT OF THE HOLY SPIRIT

My mentor, Sam Heslip, used to say "No one has a monopoly on the Holy Spirit because He is just too big for any of us to handle." That is true. The Bible picture of the Holy Spirit is broader than any one person or any one book, including this one, could ever describe. His ways are past human understanding. When we turn to the Bible, however, we do find some images that help us to grasp something of what He is like and that is what this chapter seeks to do. What does the Bible say about this Breath of Abundant Life?

It says He is like fire! "One mightier than I cometh, the latchet of whose shoes I am not worthy to unloose: he shall baptize you with the Holy Ghost and with fire" (Luke 3:16). When John the Baptist spoke those words, he was telling his hearers that Christ would bring a new understanding of the Holy Spirit to all who would follow Him. We will consider this promise in more detail in a later chapter.

SPIRITUAL COBWEBS!

Another Bible picture of the Holy Spirit is that He is like wind! "The wind bloweth where it listeth, and thou hearest the sound thereof, but canst not tell whence it cometh, and whither it goeth: so is every one that is born of the Spirit" (John 3:8).

This Wind of God, said Jesus, is unpredictable. I'm writing these words in Destin, on the Florida Panhandle. From where I sit, I can look out across some of the whitest sand on planet earth to the splendid emerald green waters of the Gulf of Mexico. It is a beautiful morning. Little children are building castles on the sand. Teenagers and adults are frolicking in the warm Gulf waters. Someone just passed over on a parasail. Out toward the horizon, some fishing boats troll the deeper waters hoping for the catch of the day in this place the locals call "the world's luckiest fishing village."

It is hard to realize on a day like today that Destin is not always so serene. Less than two years ago, this entire building was blown off its moorings by Hurricane Opal's almost 200 miles per hour winds. In the aftermath of that one night of terror, this whole region lay in ruins. Not far away, the sounds of reconstruction are a constant reminder that not long ago this little town looked like ancient ruins. Buildings that construction engineers designed to withstand any storm were reduced to rubble on the sand. Opal's wind was more than they could stand.

We used to live on this coast. We were here for Hurricane Camille's treacherous visit to Mississippi in 1969. Two days after the storm, we drove along the coast road and saw whole sections of a four-lane highway bridge that Camille had picked up and moved over ten feet or so. In some places, the misplaced sections looked as though the bridge might have been designed and constructed that way. At one point near Gulfport, Mississippi, a huge sea-going oil tanker sat dry-docked in the middle of the highway. It, too, had been washed onshore by the wind.

Meteorologists will tell you that almost every time they "miss it," it is because the wind has not followed the predicted pattern. Predicting the direction of the wind is the hardest thing a meterologist does. There is no way to forecast where the wind will go or what it will do. Sometimes it follows a pattern. Sometimes it has a mind of its own. Jesus was right: no one can tell where it might go or even how strong it might become.

In the same way, the Wind of God, the Holy Spirit, can appear to be refreshingly cleansing or terrifyingly rough as it strips away the false shelters we build in our foolish attempts to try to shield parts of our lives from God.

For many years, meteorologists tried to find a way to prevent and control hurricanes. They were persuaded that hurricanes were one form of weather we would be better off without. Plans were devised to prevent them from gaining strength or making landfall. They included such techniques as cloud seeding that would keep hurricanes from fully forming. That strategy is no more. Now weather experts are convinced that hurricanes are necessary for our good. They are part of God's plan to maintain nature's delicate balance. Their high winds help dissipate much of the oppressive heat that builds up around the equator and are responsible for spreading rainfall across America's fruited plains. One meteorologist told me that the current wisdom about hurricanes in his profession is "Don't mess with the wind."

Jesus used that understanding of wind to describe something of the work of the Holy Spirit. The Wind of God can bring refreshment, temporary discomfort, or long-term disruption to our lives as it produces what Paul calls an "eternal weight of glory" (II Cor. 4:17).

HIS STRENGTH IN OUR WEAKNESS

Paul understood the things we often call human handicaps in a different light after he met Christ on the Damascus Road. When that happened, God's wind re-directed his whole life. Later, he reasons that the same wind brings impediments that are an intended normal part of life. He writes, "There was given to me a thorn in the flesh, the messenger of Satan to buffet me, lest I should be exalted above measure. For this thing I besought the Lord thrice, that it might depart from me. And he said unto me, My grace is sufficient for thee: for my strength is made perfect in weakness. Most gladly therefore will I rather glory in my infirmities, that the power of Christ may rest upon me. Therefore I take pleasure in infirmities, in reproaches, in necessities, in persecutions, in distresses for Christ's sake: for when I am weak, then am I strong" (II Cor. 12:7-10).

Paul is saying that some things we count as loss are actually platforms for our growth. Are you thanking God for your thorns in the flesh? Will you open the eyes of your heart and see that in His time God will use the thorns to raise you and others up in wonderfully practical ways to become more than would ever be possible under "perfect" circumstances?

An unknown poet wrote:

> Circumstances! How we pet them;
> How we give them right of way!

But the Master never planned
That we should fall beneath their sway.
For our good they work together,
Though they seem to shroud the day

Paul saw that his thorn, which he once regarded as a setback, was given not to hinder him but to help him grow in his reliance on Christ's great strength. Seen in this light, his bane became a blessing. Yours will too for "we are more than conquerors through him that loved us" (Rom. 8:37). Whether it is impediment of birth, unfair treatment beyond our control, or besetting sin, God's plan is to use all our weaknesses to learn to trust His strength.

How we view our handicaps is in itself evidence of the Spirit's indwelling power. Seen in the Spirit's light, every problem can be a condensed opportunity. Within each problem are the seeds of our salvation, which, although secured for us on Calvary's cross, is always being worked out.

As a pastor, speaker, and student of human nature, I am privileged to meet many fascinating people. They range from the quiet heroes next door in every neighborhood to internationally known religious and political leaders. In each of these relationships, I find there is a consistent thread. Every great pastor I have ever met and every outstanding leader I've ever known stands on a foundation scarred by some personal failure, hurt, or potential hindrance that others have relegated to their emotional file marked "Insurmountable." Those who conquer have chosen to turn their setbacks into comebacks. They have seen their impediments as a special opportunity to demonstrate God's power. Thus, what others see as inextricable thorns in the flesh have become, for them, pearls beyond price. I am unable to think of a single one who has not come face to face with failure and risen above it in God's strength. That is, whether always acknowledged or not, the work of God's Breath of Abundant Life.

How many thousands of Christians each year sing such stalwart faith hymns as "To God Be the Glory, Great Things He Has Done" or "Praise Him! Praise Him! Jesus Our Blessed Redeemer" and know that Fanny Crosby, who wrote these and hundreds of other great hymns was in her childhood blinded by a careless physician? It is said that in her later years she often told her friends, "If I could meet that doctor now, I would say thank you over and over again for making me blind." She "saw" her blindness as a gift from God that forced her reliance on Him. His faithfulness to her was the inspiration behind great hymns that still stir our hearts decades after her death. Fanny Crosby's tragedy made her better instead of bitter.

The same can be true in your life and will be if you will see your handicaps for what they really are. Ask God to help you see them as He sees them and lead you by His Spirit through them all to the victories hidden inside them. That is part of what Christ meant when He said, "The kingdom of God is within you" (Luke 17:21).

So we see in a spiritual sense what meteorological scientists have learned from years of study. Seemingly destructive forces, properly understood, become constructive forces through God's grace.

Each time we visit San Francisco, Barbara and I like to walk across the Golden Gate Bridge. Its construction is a source of wonder for us. However, for Barbara and me, the Golden Gate is more than one of the world's great bridges. It is a place of spiritual wonderment. We always stop for a moment at the halfway point and let the wind blow hard against us. It is a source of constant amazement how that wind refreshes and reinvigorates. It loosens the skin, relieves bodily tensions, brightens the eyes, and brings new freshness to life. If you ever get there, try it. To use an Irish phrase, "It'll blow the cobwebs off you!"

In the same way, the Holy Spirit blows away our spiritual cobwebs. "Suddenly there came a sound from heaven as of a rushing mighty wind, and it filled all the house where they were sitting" (Acts 2:2). When the Holy Spirit came on Pentecost, He did not come merely to have people speak in tongues they had not learned before so that they might impress each other with their new linguistic skills. He came to blow away the spiritual cobwebs from a people whose individual and national spirit felt the crush of Rome's oppressive ways. It was not long before Rome's cruel pagan leaders found out that nothing in their armory could withstand these people in their newfound power. Nothing! Not beatings, imprisonment, facing the lions, or even a Roman cross could dissuade them from moving forward in God's strength. In time, that Roman cross upon which Christ and many of His followers died became the world's ultimate plus sign. That is how God's

Spirit works. Each time someone intentionally makes a good thing out of a "bad" thing, the Wind of God, the Breath of Abundant Life, has blown again. His wind still blows! Let it blow through you.

PEACE AT THE CENTER

More than either fire or wind, the Bible also pictures the Holy Spirit as a dove. "I saw the Spirit descending from heaven like a dove" (John 1:32).

A reporter asked the late president Herbert Hoover, "Mr. President, how do you handle criticism? Do you ever get agitated or tense?" "No," President Hoover said, seemingly surprised at the question, "of course not." "But," the reporter went on, "when I was a boy, you were one of the most popular men in the world. Then for a while you became one of the most unpopular, with nearly everyone against you. Didn't any of this meanness and criticism ever get under your skin?" "No, I knew when I went into politics what I might expect, so when it came I wasn't disappointed or upset," he said. He lowered his familiar bushy eyebrows and looked directly into the reporter's eyes. "Besides, I have peace at the center, you know."

That dove that returned to Noah's ark with an olive branch in his beak gave the world its first peace sign. Since then the dove with the olive branch between its beak has always been an internationally recognized symbol of peace. The dove flew again when Christ was baptized at the River Jordan.

When John, in his gospel, speaks of peace, he is not talking merely about the cessation of conflict. Inner peace comes from inviting God, his Son Jesus, and His Holy Spirit to come into the center of our personality. Peace is the gift of Jesus Christ who, just before leaving His disciples told them, "Peace I leave with you; my peace I give unto you" (John 14:27). Paul adds that this peace comes "because the love of God is shed abroad in our hearts by the Holy Ghost" (Rom. 5:5). The Holy Spirit brings peace at the center of all of life for us.

Fire! Wind! Peace! Each of these beautiful, powerful, and eloquent symbols expresses not only what the Spirit of God is like, each tells us something more about what the Holy Spirit does. Yet as wonderfully descriptive as each one is, they all miss the full vitality of who the Holy Spirit is.

THIS SPIRIT IS NO SPOOK

There is one more vital characteristic about the Holy Spirit we must come to know. It is that the Holy Spirit is a person. The Holy Spirit is not an "it." That is, He is not some inanimate thing but a real personality. The Bible presents a series of personal pronouns that are designed to help us understand this great revelation of the Holy Spirit.

THIS PERSONAL SPIRIT

Not long before Hollywood legend Gene Autry died, he was called an actor by a reporter during an interview. With a kindly, modest smile, the old cowboy placed his hand on the reporter's arm. "Don't call me an actor," he said. "Clark Gable, Errol Flynn, and some of those other fellows were actors. Compared to them, I was never an actor." "What were you?" That reporter quizzed him. "I guess I was more of a personality," Gene Autry replied.

The reporter interpreted Gene Autry's response as a mark of modesty. However, when one looks at Gene Autry's lifetime achievements, to call him an actor would also be to understate who he really was. Any list of his accomplishments would have to include singer, actor, cowboy, movie producer, studio owner, baseball team owner, sharpshooter, horseman, real estate developer, investor, people builder, entrepreneur, and philanthropist. All these titles and some others describe the rich full life Gene Autry, the son of a country preacher, lived. He was much more than an actor. He was a real personality.

The Holy Spirit too is personality. Just about the time we might think we have the Spirit defined, we discover that there is a lot more to be discovered.

He is a personality in another way too, however. The characteristics we use to measure the personal development of people are all present in Him. This makes the Spirit not some impersonal "it" but a "him." John sees this better than any other Old or New Testament writer: "I will pray the Father, and he shall give you another Comforter, that he may abide with you for ever; Even the Spirit of truth; whom the world cannot receive, because it seeth him not, neither knoweth him: but ye know him; for he dwelleth with you, and shall be in you" (John 14:16-17)

These words with which Jesus introduces his disciples to life in the Spirit repeatedly use the personal pronouns *he* and *him* when the impersonal pronoun, *it* would be otherwise sufficient were the Holy Spirit an inanimate being or thing.

In addition, other Scripture writers tell us that the Holy Spirit manifests certain characteristics that inanimate things never do. For example, the Spirit prays: "Likewise the Spirit also helpeth our infirmities: for we know not what we should pray for as we ought: but the Spirit itself maketh intercession for us with groanings which cannot be uttered. And he that searcheth the hearts knoweth what is the mind of the Spirit, because he maketh intercession for the saints according to the will of God" (Rom. 8:26-27). There are times when words fail us. When that happens, the weakest surrendering sigh of a sincere heart is worth more than ten thousand superficial, verbose prayers, for the Spirit of God translates our sigh into a prayer for what is best for us.

Once, when I was an undergraduate student and finances were tight, I could see no way to pay tuition so that I might return to school for another semester. On the very morning that my tuition was due, I made an unplanned stop at the local hardware store to collect some light bulbs that had been specially ordered for our church. Having never met the owner of that business, I did not expect that he even knew my name. As I stood at the counter waiting in line, one of the employees who did know me said, "The boss wants to see you." I could not imagine what he might want with me. When I entered his office, he greeted me warmly and explained that his wife had heard about Barbara and me and, having been unexpectedly blessed a few days before, believed that God had directed them to share the blessing with us. He gave me an envelope that contained a check in the exact amount needed for that semester's tuition. How did that happen? Neither Barbara nor I had confided our need to anyone. It happened because our prayers were bounced off heaven into the hearts of a Christian couple who were looking for a way to thank God for an extra blessing. What a glorious God we serve! What a wonderful Spirit He gives to pray for us when we are not sure where to turn.

This Spirit who prays for us also stays alert to God's bigger plans for us: "The things of God knoweth no man, but the Spirit of God" (I Cor. 2:11). The Greek can be translated to say that the Holy Spirit knows the plan God has for each of our lives.

He speaks! "Men and brethren, this scripture must needs have been fulfilled, which the Holy Ghost by the mouth of David spake before" (Acts 1:16). Every word in the Bible was whispered into the hearts of the writers of Scripture in order that it might be passed on to us. When we realize this, it makes the Bible come alive.

The Spirit possesses the emotional senses with which we all identify: He is capable of love—and puts true love in our hearts (Rom. 15:30). He cries with passion—and yearns for us to know the Father (Gal. 4:6). He grieves—when we persist in our disobedience (Eph. 4:30). He befriends— and invites us to be friends with God (II Cor. 13:14). He can be lied to, though never deceived (Acts 5:3). The Holy Spirit, you see, is not some cosmic force but a personal, compassionate person who is sensitive to who we are and what we need. He feels our joys and sorrows. He hears our unspoken prayers, and He is the source of all our wisdom.

GOD ON OUR SIDE

Best of all for us, the Holy Spirit is an unfailing helper and guide. "I will pray the Father, and he shall give you another Comforter" (John 14:16). The Greek word for this Comforter Jesus promises to send us is *parakletos*. It is a compound of two words, *para,* meaning "to lend support," and *kaleo,* meaning "to call" (we get our English word *call* from *kaleo*). Another translation of this Greek word might be "One who supports the called." Just before He went to the cross, Jesus said that someone else would stand tall with us.

Perhaps as you read these words again, you remember a time when you found extraordinary strength to face a crisis. Temptation loomed large before you, but somehow you found courage to do the right thing, in Robert Frost's words, to choose "the road less traveled." Just as you believed you had reached the end of your rope, you found new strength and determination to carry on. You struggled against doubt and despair and felt unseen arms support you. Each time it was the Holy Spirit giving you some extra special attention just when you needed it.

Then there was that time when you looked back across your life with all its failures and disappointments. You knew that despite your good intentions you were not where you needed to be with God. Depression and hopelessness could have come easily in that moment. Instead, your heart warmed as you heard Jesus whisper, "Come unto me, all ye that labour and are heavy laden, and I will give you rest" (Matt. 11:28). Somehow, despite your failures and sin, you knew those words were meant expressly for you. You answered His invitation by giving Him your life. The weight of your sins shifted from your shoulders to His shoulders on Calvary's cross. You were set free from sin's penalty and found new strength against its power. That, too, was the Holy Spirit. He is more than a spook. He is our friend who brings us to our Best Friend, the one who sticks closer than a brother and who breathed His last at our punishment place. To paraphrase Sydney Carton, "It was a far, far better thing than we could have ever earned or hoped for." Yet it was real, practical, and positive. It changed life for you and changed you for life.

Or perhaps even now you know you never have made an absolute surrender of your life to Christ. As you read these words, a still, small voice within tells you this is what you need to do. That is the voice of your friend the Holy Spirit, the Breath of Abundant Life. Everything He counsels is for your good. You would do well to heed Him now.

PRACTICAL PARACLETE

An old story tells of a former drunk who came to Christ and was gloriously saved. His former cronies did not give up easily. They came by his home one night and urged him to join them out on the town. "I dare not come," he said, "for I am Christ's now." One smirked, "Surely you haven't started all that stuff about changing water into wine and so on?" The redeemed one smiled in response, "I could never prove that He changed water into wine, although I choose to believe it. What I can prove is that in my home, he changed hard liquor into furniture and clothes for my family."

Practical? Yes, intensely practical! And the gospel life Christ calls us to is also practical. When all is said and done, it makes good sense. As we shall see in the chapters that follow, this work of the Holy Spirit has a wonderfully practical application for every area of our lives and every situation we shall ever face, for He is nothing if He is not practical.

4

Older than dirt!
stronger than steel!

A thousand worlds which roll around us brightly,
Thee in their orbits bless;
Ten thousand suns which shine above us nightly,
Proclaim thy righteousness.
Thou didst create the world-'twas thy proud mandate
That woke it unto day;
And the same power that measured, weighed, and spanned it,
Shall bid that world decay.

Sir John Bowring (1792-1872)

Cosmas Ndeti has always liked to run. As a boy, he ran through his little Mount Kenya village of Machakos faster than anybody could remember. Its rolling hills were a natural training ground. Today, having won the Boston Marathon three times, Cosmas Ndeti is a national hero, the inspiration for a new generation of Kenyans. Wherever he goes, the young people of Kenya shout out in Swahili, "Nienda kusemba ta Ndeti," which means, "I want to run like Ndeti." There is a reason Cosmas Ndeti runs the way he does.

GOD III

Two junior high school students, coming out of their Sunday school class, discussed the morning lesson. "I still don't get it," the first one declared. "How can God be one person and three people at the same time? It sounds impossible!" "It is not impossible," said his want-to-be helpful companion. "It's really very simple. It's like this: My name is the same as my dad's and my dad's name is the same as my granddad's name. All three of us have the same name. My granddad is Senior. My dad is Junior. I'm the Third. That's how it is with God. God the Father is the granddad because He was first. Jesus is Junior because He came next. The Holy Spirit was last so He's really God the Third!"

GOD III?

It is really rather remarkable how many Christians subscribe to an understanding of God not far removed from a junior high student's theology of the Holy Trinity. Reasoning that there was no Jesus before the night the angels serenaded field shepherds near Bethlehem nor any Holy Spirit prior to Pentecost, they believe that a kind of hierarchy by birthright exists within the Godhead. Such a notion has no foundation in Scripture, for obviously none of the people within the Godhead were ever born. They simply are. That is, Scripture opens with an assumption that God is: "In the beginning God" (Gen. 1:1). The writer of the epistle to the Hebrews affirms this: "He that cometh to God must believe that he is" (Heb. 11:6). Thus, we are told that God as Father, Son, and Holy Spirit was ever in existence.

In the last chapter, we saw that the Holy Spirit is a real personality, the Third Person in the Trinity, not "it" but a "He." As our advocate, He calls us to a profoundly practical way of life. When we say that He is the Trinity's Third Person, however, we must be careful to understand that this does not diminish him in relation to God the Father and God the Son. Contrary to what that junior high student believed, the Holy Spirit is not "God III."

In this new chapter, we will look at what the Bible says about the continuous ministry of the Holy Spirit. We will look at His existence before time began. We shall see, too, that in every era of human history the Spirit has been active and in every way equal to His counterparts in the Deity.

OLDER THAN DIRT

"In the beginning God created the heaven and the earth. And the earth was without form, and void; and darkness was upon the face of the deep. And the Spirit of God moved upon the face of the waters. And God said, Let there be light: and there was light. And God saw the light, that it was good: and God divided the light from the darkness. And God called the light Day, and the darkness he called Night. And the evening and the morning were the first day. And God said, Let there be a firmament in the midst of the waters, and let it divide the waters from the waters. And God made the firmament, and divided the waters which were under the firmament from the waters which were above the firmament: and it was so. And God called the firmament Heaven. And the evening and the morning were the second day. And God said, Let the waters under the heaven be gathered together unto one place, and let the dry land appear: and it was so. And God called the dry land Earth; and the gathering together of the waters called he Seas: and God saw that it was good" (Gen. 1:1-10).

Look carefully at these verses delineating the creation of the universe. Notice the sequence in which the events of the first three days were ordered. In verse two, the record of Scripture shows, "The Spirit of God moved upon the face of the waters." It is not until verse 9, we read that God said, "Let the dry land appear."

Having traveled and lived through several regions in these United States, we have been blessed with an overview of regional language differences that is at the same time fascinating and delightful. Each region has its own language peculiarities. The rural South is a virtual gold mine of quaint and graphic verbal expressions. One of my favorites describes the age of an elderly person. It goes something like this: At a birthday party for a senior citizen, a well-wisher might inquire, "How old is he?" In good humor the answer is sometimes, "He's older than dirt!"

Just how was the earth created? Heated debates have taken place over that question. Some say it all came into being through a great explosion out of which the whole universe was formed. Others say God started it all then left it to evolve over millions, or even billions, of years. No attempt will be made to resolve these differences here. Suffice it to say that the Bible says God created the heavens and the earth. It goes on to detail the only account of how the universe came into being that finally makes sense. Not only does it make sense, the Bible record of Creation makes all things potentially good and creates a sense of human dignity that is unequalled in the history of the world.

Integral to the Bible's Creation account was the role of the Holy Spirit in the universe's formation. "The Spirit of God moved upon the face of the waters" (Gen. 1:2). The Hebrew imagery of the Holy Spirit moving over the unformed universe is like that of a mother bird caring for her new egg. In Deuteronomy a similar series of Hebrew verbs is used to speak of a mother eagle hovering over her young (see Deut. 32:11). The Hebrew verb used in each of these verses, rachaph, is a wonderful word. It means "to wait patiently for the time of expectation." It can also mean, "to shake" as in to shake something loose.

Ornithologists who specialize in the study of eagles tell us that these magnificent birds choose the place where they will build their nest with greater care than any other birds. Usually eagles select a virtually unreachable ledge high up on a cliff face. There the mother eagle lays her egg. Almost immediately she nurtures her egg patiently until it hatches. Day upon day she waits and broods as though some innate sense is telling her that something wonderful will happen. That picture multiplied many, many times demonstrates the role the Holy Spirit played in the creation of the universe.

Once upon a time, more precisely, once before time, the Spirit of God brooded over a formless mass from which he expected something very special to develop. As He waited, there was neither light nor plant nor land. All that would come later. The Breath of Abundant Life was there before life was abundant. He was present before there was any firmament. He is older than dirt. He was there when there was only sea, before land came into being. He watched over and nurtured the formless void until the time of arrival came.

Now, lest there be a temptation to believe that the Spirit's role was purely passive, it is important to note that the Spirit was never inactive. Just as the mother eagle plans the way of her baby, the Spirit of God also plans the path of his own. The same ornithologists who study eagles have learned that after the egg hatches and the baby eaglet is born, the mother's next role is to shake it loose from the nest. She does this by allowing it to develop sufficiently in order for her to safely push it out of the nest. At first, the baby free-falls through the air and the mother eagle flies down below it to rescue it and carry it back to safety. She does this repeatedly until her baby realizes it too can fly. It is necessary for the mother eagle to shake her babies loose lest they become complacent in the nest and never develop the massive wings with which they soar majestically across the heavens.

Moses, once a shepherd, no doubt observed this happen many times as he tended sheep. He leaves Israel an inspiring song that remembers the eagle's experience: "As an eagle stirreth up her nest, fluttereth over her young, spreadeth abroad her wings, taketh them, beareth them on her wings: so the Lord alone did lead him, and there was no strange god with him. He made him ride on the high places of the earth, that he might eat the increase of the fields" (Deut. 32:11-13).

Since creation God's Spirit has remained with His people and his work has been sometimes more, sometimes less, obvious. When there has been a need, he has always been there. Sometimes His presence has been ignored. At other times, when it was acknowledged, His presence makes the difference at highlight moments. Such examples run like a golden thread woven through the Old Testament. Many illustrations could be given. What follows are but a few that demonstrate the Spirit's constant presence.

SUFFICIENT SUPPLY

In the Pentateuch, He meets the needs of the children of Israel as they journey through the wilderness on the way to the Promised Land. It is soon after the Exodus, which most Bible scholars date between 1450 and 1200 B.C. "The Lord spake unto Moses, saying, See, I have called by name Bezaleel the son of Uri, the son of Hur, of the tribe of Judah: And I have filled him with the spirit of God, in wisdom, and in understanding, and in knowledge, and in all manner of workmanship, to devise cunning works, to work in gold, and in silver, and in brass, and in cutting of stones, to set them, and in carving of timber, to work in all manner of workmanship" (Exod. 31:1-5).

We often are tempted to think that God's Spirit works only through those who are gifted as leaders. Sometimes we are lulled into believing that He is more present with those people who possess particular ministerial abilities than with others who have different abilities. We say of someone that he or she "really has the Holy Spirit." In that context, we are tempted to downplay the importance of our own role in God's work. Believing we are somehow lesser Christians and that some Christians are more important than others, we sell ourselves for a mess of modern-day spiritual pottage. To the contrary, the Bible says each of us has special gifts and talents that God has given.

Imagine a multimillion dollar six-lane freeway leading to a sparsely populated rural community. As you drive along it, you stop for directions and learn that only a few hundred people live there. "How ridiculous," you think. "They could use this far better in some city that has gridlock every morning and evening at rush-hour." It would look absurd. In a similar way, the Lord never displays disproportionate power and grace. He always scales His provision according to a particular need. When a courageous leader was needed to face down the pharaoh and lead the Israelites out of Egyptian bondage, He raised up a Moses. Now, the need was not for a mouthpiece but for skilled workmen; and God, through His Holy Spirit, gave special gifts for the moment. In this case the gifts were artistic craftsmen with the necessary skills to build the temple. No need is ever unmet or oversupplied for Christians.

Is there a need in your life now? Somewhere within your environment God has provided for it. If you do not know where His provision lies, ask Him. He will show you. "Take therefore no thought for the morrow: for the morrow shall take thought for the things of itself. Sufficient unto the day is the evil thereof" (Matt. 6:34).

SPECIAL LEADERS FOR SPECIAL TIMES

In the historical books we see another example: "The spirit of the Lord came upon him, and he judged Israel, and went out to war: and the Lord delivered Chushanrishathaim king of Mesopotamia into his hand; and his hand prevailed against Chushanrishathaim" (Judg. 3:10).

History is replete with examples of how God raises up special leaders for special times. Whether the name is Washington, Jefferson, Lincoln, or Churchill, God is always preparing people for such times. To meet the need of the hour, He endows them with courage and wisdom above their normal limits and brings His blessings through them.

Here it was Othniel, the first of Israel's hero-rulers known as judges, who lived approximately 1,300 years before Christ or about 1,330 years before Pentecost. Othniel, a true national champion for a special hour in Israel's history, not only ruled wisely but, like Moses, he was endowed by the Holy Spirit to be God's appointed leader who would free the Israelites from the grip of the dictator Chushanrishathaim.

The words "The spirit of the LORD came upon him" are given about other judges of the time too. They testify to the Holy Spirit's ongoing work of raising leaders according to the need. Each time we read those words in sequence in the Book of Judges, they connect a seemingly ordinary person to a spontaneous measure of extraordinary power. On each occasion this supernatural anointing prepared someone God had chosen for a special mission.

On a national level as well as in a personal sense, that has not changed. The Holy Spirit still comes upon ordinary people in uncommon ways to prepare them for special tasks. He will do it for you. When we face particularly difficult experiences, the Spirit, just as He did at creation, broods over us and then endows us with whatever is needed for that occasion.

Are you facing a crisis? Do not be cast down by its potential for evil. Instead, keep on believing in Christ who saved you and whose promises never fail. Rest all your weight on God's promises. Just when it seems that heart and flesh are about to fail, God, by His Holy Spirit, the Breath of Abundant Life, will provide a new infusion of strength in your life and you will come through the victor.

THE SUPERINTENDENT OF RECURRING NEWNESS

In the Old Testament poetic books, evidence of the Spirit's presence is seen repeatedly. The psalms, written between the time of Moses and the time of the Babylonian captivity (from approximately 1440 to 586 B.C.), are filled with testimonies of His activity. None is more telling than this: "Thou sendest forth thy spirit, they are created: and thou renewest the face of the earth" (Ps. 104:30). Another way to translate the original Hebrew text is "You send your Spirit and life becomes new all over again."

The anonymous author of this psalm begins with a poetic summary delineating the order of creation we have already discussed in this chapter. Against that backdrop, he goes on to note that not only did God create the earth, He also sustains and renews His creation by the ongoing work of His Spirit. If the earth is God's garden, part of the Holy Spirit's work is to keep it looking fresh. It is the Spirit who supervises the colors of the leaves each autumn, the fresh leaves each spring, and the flowers that follow.

Little Mikey went fishing and camping with his grandfather. As they floated in the middle of a lake, the youngster was greatly impressed by the amazing blue sky above with its fleecy white clouds drifting lazily along. As Mikey lowered his eyes, he began to see for the first time in his brief life the splendor of the autumn leaves and the shimmering surface of the water on which he and his grandpa floated. The sights to which he was just coming alive filled the little fellow with a thousand questions. "Grandpa," Mikey asked finally, "who made all these things?" "God did," the elderly gentleman replied. "Grandpa," the youngster responded, "who keeps them?" "God does, Son," the old man replied once more. "Grandpa," the lad asked a third time, "can anybody see God?" "Son," the old man said thoughtfully, "when I sit in the midst of all this splendor and look at you on an afternoon like this, I can't see anything but God."

Have you ever seen God? "No man hath seen God at any time," you say quoting the Scriptures. You are right, of course. Still, there is a sense in which all who are willing to open their eyes to the ever revolving splendor, design, order, variety, complexity, and power in nature, year after year, human lifetime after human lifetime, cannot help but see the evidence of His hand at work everywhere. Who sustains all this? Why, the Holy Spirit of God, the Breath of Abundant Life, does. He who once supervised the formless void still watches over the recurring newness of the universe. So we see that not only is the Spirit older than dirt, He still renews the dirt with the nutrients that are good for this year's growth.

What is true for nature is also true for human life. A social worker told her associates about visiting an urban ghetto and seeing a young boy who had been struck by a car several months before. A victim of poor medical treatment, his legs were little more than a painful mass of twisted flesh. He lay helpless when it came to moving himself or getting around. Despite the fact that he was not one of her charges, something about that young fellow's pitiful condition touched the social worker's heart and she arranged to take him to an orthopedic surgeon friend on her next day off. The surgeon volunteered his services to perform a series of surgeries to straighten the lad's twisted limbs. A year to the day from when they had first met, that boy walked into the social worker's office unaided. His recovery was complete. The two of them embraced, and she thought, "If I achieve nothing else in my life, I have made a real difference in this case."

Some years later, that social worker spoke at a conference and recounted the experience. She asked as she closed her speech, "Can you imagine where that young man is today?" Some asked aloud if perhaps he had gone on to become a social worker or doctor himself. Others asked if he was perhaps a teacher or minister. "No," said that social worker, "he's in the penitentiary serving life with no possibility of parole for committing some of the most heinous crimes any human being could ever commit." Then she added, "I could help bring renewal to his legs, but there was no one near to help bring renewal to his soul."

Soul renewal is the work of every Christian. All of us are called to be witnesses for Jesus. However, our best efforts achieve nothing without the gracious renewing power of God's Breath of Abundant Life. Wherever God sends His Spirit, new life comes. It was true when the psalmist, hundreds of years before Pentecost, wrote this hymn of praise for creation's renewal that we have come to know as Psalm 104. It is still true today.

THE POWER BEHIND THE PROPHETS

The Holy Spirit's presence in the times of the prophets is also clearly and repeatedly evidenced. Over seven hundred years before Pentecost, Isaiah asks, "Who hath directed the Spirit of the Lord, or being his counsellor hath taught him?" (Isa. 40:13).

Bible scholars sometimes call Isaiah's prophecy "The fifth gospel." In this passage, Isaiah, the leading prophet of his time, who became God's spokesman in 740 B.C., marvels at God's creative power, His sustaining provision, and his supporting presence. His message is echoed later in approximately 520 B.C. by Haggai as he recalls that the Holy Spirit sustained, guided, and cared for the Israelites during their Egyptian bondage and throughout their journey to the Promised Land: "According to the word that I covenanted with you when ye came out of Egypt, so my spirit remaineth among you: fear ye not" (Hag. 2:5).

HOW TO MAKE A SUCCESS

Go to any major bookstore and see shelf after shelf lined with self-help books. Hundreds of authors have written their formulas and "success secrets." Many say that to succeed in this world a person must be hardy and harsh in both business and private relationships. Their measure of success usually calls for someone to win and someone to lose. Zechariah's prophecy, written around 500 B.C., sums up Israel's reason for success in a way that is altogether different. Success by God's standard does not call for aggressive hostility or one-upmanship but for trust: "Not by might, nor by power, but by my spirit, saith the Lord of hosts" (Zech. 4:6).

Success with God is not based on conquering external forces such as other people but on controlling our internal forces. As the individual spirit of a person is yielded to the Holy Spirit, says Zechariah, God brings forth that which is best for us. That message was true for the citizens of Jerusalem half a millennium before Christ was born. It is true for us today.

So we see that God's Holy Spirit is not some later addition to the Godhead. He is not, as the junior high Sunday school student thought, God III. He was not first born at Pentecost. Nor is He something or someone added occasionally to produce a finer, more elegant, or more enthusiastic type of Christian. He has been a part of God's dealings with His world in every generation, and He is a pure necessity in every Christian's life. He is older than dirt. What is more, He is stronger than steel.

STRONGER THAN STEEL

Before time, God lived alone. There was no heaven where angels sang His glory, for there were no angels. There was no earth. There was only a formless void where earth would come to exist. There were no other planets either, for God had called none of these things into being.

There was only God. So the Scripture record begins, "In the beginning God." There was, as a wonderful gospel song says, only God alone. The Hebrew word for God in this instance is *elohim*. The *im* on the end indicates that it is plural. This gives it not so much a hint of the Trinity as some people have said as it speaks of God's amazing multifaceted power. When there was no sun, God was present in three persons, Father, Son (not Jr.), and Holy Spirit (not III). He demonstrated His power by calling the sun into existence; "God said, Let there be light: and there was light" (Gen. 1:3). He made the sun to give the light that would separate day from night.

He is the sea's God too. You will remember his unequalled art of walking on it when He took a notion and of calling it to calm and it did. Then there was that time He ordered its fish to gather in a certain spot so that His disciples could net them quickly after a fruitless night of fishing and get about their more important business of fishing for people (see and compare Matthew 14:25; Mark 4:37-39; Luke 5:4-7). When He does these things, He demonstrates that He is the God whose power not only covers the land but also saturates the sea and all its creatures.

The Glory That Already Was

All of this is part of being *elohim*. When Moses, inspired by the Holy Spirit, chooses *elohim* as the Bible's first name for God, he is saying, in effect, that God is God. That is a way of declaring quietly that God does not need anybody else. Creation made Him neither more God nor more glorious. It simply revealed a glory that already was and that is why the psalmist David sings, "The heavens declare the glory of God; and the firmament sheweth his handiwork" (Ps. 19:1).

The story is told that during the French Revolution many leaders were determined to destroy Christianity. One beautiful clear night one boastfully proclaimed, "Every evidence of your God will be abolished. We will destroy it all. We will tear down your churches and burn all your Bibles. We will kill all your clergy and remove everything that you say testifies to God's existence." One old man could not resist the temptation to laugh out loud. "Why are you laughing," ranted the speaker. The old man pointed toward the stars and said, "I'm just trying to imagine how you and your cronies will ever get those down!"

Here is the wonder of it all: This God who hung the stars when he created all things and keeps the earth in constant renewal cares for each of us so much He has given His Spirit the assignment of looking out for our best interests. No matter what happens with us, He will still be God. Whatever problems we encounter, He is the Lord over them. Whatever struggles we face, He walks through them with us. He was our God before we were born. He is our God now, and He will be our God forever and ever.

SPIRIT AND PLOD

"Let mount Zion rejoice, let the daughters of Judah be glad, because of thy judgments. Walk about Zion, and go round about her: tell the towers thereof. Mark ye well her bulwarks, consider her palaces; that ye may tell it to the generation following. For this God is our God for ever and ever: he will be our guide even unto death" (Ps. 48:11-14).

What possessed seventy-five-year-old Abram to leave the security of his birthplace with his sickly, elderly wife and move to a region he had never seen before, believing it would benefit their as yet unborn children?

What made Moses, Moses? What possessed a man with a stammering tongue who was wanted for murder to re-enter the land where he committed his crime and stand fearlessly before its supreme leader and declare, "Thus saith the Lord God of Israel, Let my people go, that they may hold a feast unto me in the wilderness" (Exod. 5:1).

Do you ever wonder how Elijah could throw down the gauntlet before a nation of spiritual adulterers and declare, "How long halt ye between two opinions? if the Lord be God, follow him: but if Baal, then follow him" (I Kings 18:21)?

What overcame the spirit of fear in Peter's life so that he would fearlessly declare salvation to all on the Day of Pentecost?

Why would a Martin Luther risk life and reputation by standing against corrupt church leaders and declare, "My conscience is held captive by the Word of God. Here I stand. I can do no other. God help me."

What possessed Bishop Hugh Latimer to believe he could get away with calling King Henry VIII of England into account for his immoral lifestyle, and that in the king's own palace? Such a risk could have easily cost him a long time in the dungeon or worse. Yet he did it. What is more, when he did it a second time, King Henry commended Latimer's forthrightness.

What is it that makes Cosmas Ndeti run the way he does? It is, in Cosmas Ndeti's wife Jane's words, "Since Cosmas found Jesus Christ, he is a different person. Now he wants to run like Jesus. When he feels he is getting tired in a race, he says he asks Jesus to give him the strength to finish and always feels more energy. He knows that every victory belongs to Jesus." Once his career was threatened by a raucous lifestyle. Today his life is renewed and Cosmas Ndeti is almost as well known for his inspirational messages, which he gives at every opportunity, as for his running. Cosmas has experienced renewed life in the power of the Holy Spirit. He runs with God's wind behind him.

THE SECRET OF SUCCESS

Do you want to know the secret of success? It is the same thing that brought each of these people renown? It is that in every case they were, and are, filled with God's Spirit. They knew, and know, that God's strength and power surround them and determined to move forward in his strength. I call that determination to move forward in God's strength "Spirit and plod." It is more than spirit alone. It is a willingness to commit yourself to an ideal and to work hard to achieve it. They knew that "as the body without the spirit is dead, so faith without works is dead also" (James 2:26).

Their success with God is not founded on always being perfect and possessing faith that never wavers. The greatest Christians who have ever lived have at times wavered. Every one of them has faced a difficult situation and tried to work it out his own way only to fail. What makes us honor the lives of Abram, Moses, Elijah, Peter, Luther, and Latimer is that despite their failures they finally believed something about this Lord of creation that many people in our generation do not seem to accept. They believed in God's Godness. That is, they believed that if God is truly God He will do anything He wants to do, and they worked with their hand in His to achieve great things. Cosmas Ndeti believes that too, and so he both prays and works out. He knows that prayer by itself will not make a champion.

"Hear, O heavens, and give ear, O earth: for the Lord hath spoken, I have nourished and brought up children, and they have rebelled against me. The ox knoweth his owner, and the ass his master's crib: but Israel doth not know, my people doth not consider. Ah sinful nation, a people laden with iniquity, a seed of evildoers, children that are corrupters: they have forsaken the Lord, they have provoked the Holy One of Israel unto anger, they are gone away backward. Why should ye be stricken any more? ye will revolt more and more: the whole head is sick, and the whole heart faint. From the sole of the foot even unto the head there is no soundness in it; but wounds, and bruises, and putrifying sores: they have not been closed, neither bound up, neither mollified with ointment. Your country is desolate, your cities are burned with fire: your land, strangers devour it in your presence, and it is desolate, as overthrown by strangers" (Isa. 1:2-7).

By contrast, what makes a society such as ours foolishly imagine that it can successfully legislate God out of world affairs through foolish politically correct decrees that are not far removed from those of Elijah's day? We have forgotten, "The Spirit of truth; whom the world cannot receive, because it seeth him not, neither knoweth him" (John 14:17). He is older than dirt and stronger than steel, and He will demonstrate His power in your life when you yield your will to Him.

THE WONDER OF GRACE

The wonder of grace is that "He hath not dealt with us after our sins; nor rewarded us according to our iniquities" (Ps. 103:10). Rather, He extends to us in every generation a new opportunity for renewal. The wonder of grace is that He still sends His Spirit and new life comes and meets us at our point of deepest need.

"Is any thing too hard for the Lord?" (Gen. 18:14). God's famous question to Abraham is also for us. The answer is, of course not. There is nothing He cannot do. There is no addiction He cannot break in us. There is no experience in our lives that is too hard for Him. There is no sin that He through Christ will not forgive. When we, in the Spirit's power, put our trust in Him for all our needs, we find that nothing is too hard for us. Jesus says, "All things are possible to him that believeth" (Mark 9:23). "Faith," said St.

Augustine, "is to believe what we do not yet see; and the reward of faith is to see what we believe."

HE STILL HOVERS

After over a quarter century as a pastor and student of people, I believe that two spirits reside within each of us. One is the Spirit of God, the Breath of Abundant Life. He hovers over us with all of heaven's powers of protection and purpose. The second spirit is the spirit of one whose ambition is to bring about our ruination or to render our lives ineffective in Christ's service. His highest desire is to direct our lives toward evil. Failing that, his secondary goal is to make us lethargic about the great eternal realities of life. We ultimately choose which spirit will have his way with us. We decide whether to hear within our hearts the voice of God who ever calls us to a higher good for all humanity.

"Stir up the gift of God, which is in thee by the putting on of my hands. For God hath not given us the spirit of fear; but of power, and of love, and of a sound mind. Be not thou therefore ashamed of the testimony of our Lord, nor of me his prisoner: but be thou partaker of the afflictions of the gospel according to the power of God; Who hath saved us, and called us with an holy calling, not according to our works, but according to his own purpose and grace, which was given us in Christ Jesus before the world began, but is now made manifest by the appearing of our Saviour Jesus Christ, who hath abolished death, and hath brought life and immortality to light through the gospel: Whereunto I am appointed a preacher, and an apostle, and a teacher of the Gentiles" (II Tim. 1:6-11).

Timothy, the young preacher to whom Paul wrote these challenging words, faced opposition. His options in such a setting were to surrender to his enemies and become like them, to become docile and timidly allow them to have their way, or to make up his mind to rise above them trusting ability, strength, and authority beyond himself. Paul reminded him that gifts lay dormant within him, which, if he stepped out boldly in power, love, and self-control, would bring him victory over all his enemies. God gives gifts to every Christian. If you belong to Him, there are powers in your life that go far beyond natural abilities.

What holds you back? What keeps you from being all God desires for you to be? Choose now to give it over to God. Recommit your life to serving Him fully. Believe Him to have overcome every opposing force and walk forward boldly in the love of Christ and in the power of the Holy Spirit. When you do, you will have joined a great parade of saints who once also wavered. Ahead of you in this parade is one called Abraham, one called Moses, one called Elijah, one called Peter, one called Luther, and one called Latimer. Each of them knew many moments of doubt that led to hesitancy, adultery, murder, deep depression, drunkenness, despair, and denial. Out of those backgrounds they found new power to overcome and made up their minds to rise on the wings of victory.

You can do it too. Make up your mind to rise on the wings of him who lives within you. Nothing is too hard for Jesus whose Spirit lives in every Christian.

"Is anything too hard for the Lord?" When God first asked His question, Sarah had just laughed at the possibility that she and Abraham would become parents together. Everything they thought they knew said it was impossible. Some long-term medical condition had prevented her from conceiving a child before. Age was against them. How could it ever be? But it happened.

Just as remarkable is this: The same one who made Abraham and Sarah parents can make a bad person good and a dead person live again. The God of creation is still in the life-renewing business. He offers new life to all who surrender their old life to Him. He invites us in amazing ways to come and experience life on a higher plane, as we shall see in the next chapter.

5

It's time you lost control!

An adventuresome fellow from a remote rural community planned his trip of a lifetime to New York City. Arriving at the airport, he hailed a cab and asked to be taken to a hotel in the heart of Manhattan. Unknown to the enterprising visitor, this was the cab driver's first day at work. What is more, a recent immigrant, the cabby knew almost no English. Nevertheless, with great enthusiasm, the driver set out to impress his fare by showing off his driving skills. With great daring, he sped through the heavy traffic through the streets of Manhattan and around Times Square. He made bold turns, barely missing other cars and came to jarring stops at several intersections. At other intersections, however, the man did not stop but speedily barreled through traffic lights that were turning red. At the same time, he kept looking over his shoulder and attempted to engage his back seat passenger with a happy pidgin-English conversation. The longer the trip lasted, the less certain the out-of-town adventurer was that he would survive it. Finally, he mustered the courage to order the driver to slow down, heed the signs, and keep his eyes on the road. In his broken accent the driver responded, "Trust me, Boss. I'm in charge. It's all under control."

"Trust me. I'm in charge." Somewhere deep inside every emotionally healthy adult, whether timid or outgoing, there lingers a need to be in control. We become nervous, tense, scared, and neurotic when we feel we are no longer in charge of our lives. The fact is, however, that there are times when we need to relinquish that control. There are occasions when it is wise to surrender to the authority of another.

A wise medical school professor once told her students, "A doctor who doctors himself has a fool for a patient." She was telling them that when they needed medical care it would be wise to put themselves in the charge of another.

65

WHO'S IN CHARGE HERE?

A certain Pharisee planned his trip of a lifetime to come and see Jesus one night. His need to surrender control is demonstrated in one of the best known conversations in the entire Bible:

There was a man of the Pharisees, named Nicodemus, a ruler of the Jews: The same came to Jesus by night, and said unto him, Rabbi, we know that thou art a teacher come from God: for no man can do these miracles that thou doest, except God be with him. Jesus answered and said unto him, Verily, verily, I say unto thee, Except a man be born again, he cannot see the kingdom of God. Nicodemus saith unto him, How can a man be born when he is old? Can he enter the second time into his mother's womb, and be born? Jesus answered, Verily, verily, I say unto thee, Except a man be born of water and of the Spirit, he cannot enter into the kingdom of God. That which is born of the flesh is flesh; and that which is born of the Spirit is spirit. Marvel not that I said unto thee, Ye must be born again. The wind bloweth where it listeth, and thou hearest the sound thereof, but canst not tell whence it cometh, and whither it goeth: so is every one that is born of the Spirit. Nicodemus answered and said unto him, How can these things be? Jesus answered and said unto him, Art thou a master of Israel, and knowest not these things? Verily, verily, I say unto thee, We speak that we do know, and testify that we have seen; and ye receive not our witness. If I have told you earthly things, and ye believe not, how shall ye believe, if I tell you of heavenly things? And no man hath ascended up to heaven, but he that came down from heaven, even the Son of man which is in heaven. And as Moses lifted up the serpent in the wilderness, even so must the Son of man be lifted up: that whosoever believeth in him should not perish, but have eternal life. For God so loved the world, that he gave his only begotten Son, that whosoever believeth in him should not perish, but have everlasting life. For God sent not his Son into the world to condemn the world; but that the world through him might be saved (John 3:1-17).

THE ONE VITAL NECESSITY OF ALL ETERNITY

It is hard to imagine anything more foreign to the thinking of a Pharisee and "a ruler of the Jews" than that he must surrender control. Pharisees, by their very nature, were take charge people. That was basic to the requirements for being admitted to the Pharisaic sect. Pharisees, to be Pharisees, first had to have demonstrated that they liked to control things. On a national level, the daily presence of occupying Roman forces both offended and humiliated them. Yet there was Nicodemus with Jesus telling him it was time for him to surrender control to yet another force by allowing God's Spirit to take charge of his life: "Marvel not that I said unto thee, Ye must be born again. The wind bloweth where it listeth, and thou hearest the sound thereof, but canst not tell whence it cometh, and whither it goeth: so is every one that is born of the Spirit."

ALMOST BUT NOT ALTOGETHER!

Christ's ministry in Jerusalem, it would seem, had already impressed Nicodemus, for he called Jesus "Rabbi." Among the Jews, no title conveyed greater respect than that. The rabbi was the professor of the academic world. It came from the Hebrew meaning "my great leader." By opening their interview with this term, Nicodemus acknowledged that he already accepted Christ as a spiritual teacher whose understanding was far above his own. At the same time, Nicodemus also betrayed something of his own need to retain certain controls over his life. He came to see Jesus at night. The mention of the time in the text indicates that Nicodemus likely had carefully chosen to take advantage of the cover of darkness. Believing in Jesus was one thing. Publicly acknowledging that belief was something quite different; therefore, Nicodemus came secretly in the darkness. If he would unite with Jesus, it would have to be on his own terms. Perhaps he enjoyed his position as a leader among the Jews and feared that openly professing faith in Jesus would mean he had to give it up. Whatever it was, Nicodemus almost belonged to Jesus but he was not yet altogether committed to following him. Like King Agrippa he was almost persuaded but not altogether (Acts 26:28).

"Almost" surrender was not enough to satisfy Christ. It never will be. To convince Nicodemus of the inadequacy of partial surrender and of the uselessness of mere intellectual commitment, which his secret journey implied, Jesus invited Nicodemus to a radical new way of life that is impossible without God's help. "Verily, verily, I say unto thee, Except a man be born again, he cannot see the kingdom of God." That was it. There would be, could be, no other way. No one can get to heaven on his or her own merit. One vital necessity forces every human being to the same level as every other. If we would see God in eternity, we need to be born again.

FROM THE TOP

What follows is a fascinating opportunity for us to eavesdrop on a conversation between the Son of God and a scholar of the Jewish religion. Jesus points out to Nicodemus the foundation for new life. He uses a powerful Greek word, *anothen.*

This word literally means "from the top down." Nicodemus was not puzzled by the idea of birth from above. Foundational to his Jewish understanding of life was the idea that birth is a gift from God. What he failed to understand was how birth could occur twice in one human life. What Nicodemus could not see initially was that Jesus was inviting him to experience a higher understanding of life. It was an awareness of life so far removed from Nicodemus's present understanding of life that it called for him to set aside everything he believed he understood until now and be born all over again.

That is what the new birth is. Birth is a beginning. It is not a reconstruction, reprogramming, or renovation of something already in existence. It is a commencement, a dawning, a genesis of something that has not existed before. It begins for each of us individually. It cannot be inherited. It is a once for each lifetime decisive moment when we become one-on-one with God. Human beings can simulate newness of life. In this generation, science has even learned to clone it. Yet faced with the challenge of making something out of nothing, we are helpless. Recognizing that helplessness is necessary to being part of the greatest miracle any human being can experience, a brand-new you. No wonder Nicodemus had difficulty fathoming such an idea. It ran counter to everything he had ever heard before.

Recognizing his friend's dilemma, Jesus uses a foundational teaching principle. He finds common ground by stating a life principle everyone knows. "That which is born of the flesh is flesh," He says. Nicodemus would understand that. Bloodlines were a high priority issue among the Pharisees. To maintain the narrow prejudices of their order, it was important that no one of uncertain heritage was permitted to join them.

Like begets like. If you want apples, don't plant oranges. If you want roses, don't plant daffodil bulbs. If you want to breed dogs, don't mate horses or cats. Biology cannot create. It merely reproduces whatever was there at the beginning. Education, even the high quality instruction of the Pharisees, cannot create. Its best hope is to disseminate what is already known. Its highest hope is to modify what is.

Nicodemus understood. Now Jesus switches his attention away from the physical to the realm of the spirit by adding, "And that which is born of the Spirit is spirit."

As Freeing as the Wind!

We have already seen that the Holy Spirit, as part of the Trinity, is an agent in the creation of the universe. Now we see the Holy Spirit as God's specific agent in creating new life. Having begun to describe the Spirit's role in recreating human lives from biology, Jesus now turns to the laws of another branch of science, meteorology, to help Nicodemus further grasp the Spirit's work. "The wind bloweth where it listeth, and thou hearest the sound thereof, but canst not tell whence it cometh, and whither it goeth: so is every one that is born of the Spirit."

Many children who watch the program *Mr. Rogers's Neighborhood* do not know that Fred Rogers is actually, "The Reverend Fred Rogers." He is an ordained Presbyterian minister. He tells a story from his days as a seminary student that illustrates this point. One Sunday he and some friends attended a small church. Since he was studying preaching at the time, Fred Rogers found himself more interested in the content and delivery of the elderly preacher's sermon than in its spirit. As he listened and observed, Fred Rogers mentally checked off each mistake the old man made. As the old preacher waxed on, Fred Rogers became increasingly critical and judgmental. When the sermon ended, young Fred Rogers turned to his friends, intending to comment negatively on the old man and his message. The tears rolling down one friend's cheeks arrested him as she looked at Fred and whispered, "He said just what I needed to hear today." Fred Rogers, stopped in his tracks by what he saw, said nothing. Sometime later, Fred Rogers told some friends that he learned that day that good preaching is not always well ordered and articulate. Good preaching is Bible truth that touches people where they need to be touched.

"Not by might, nor by power, but by my spirit, saith the Lord of hosts" (Zech. 4:6). What is true of preaching is universally true of the Spirit of God. He blows in ways human beings cannot chart beforehand. He truly is as free as the wind. If Nicodemus would ever know new life in all its fullness, he must first be prepared to set aside his own preconceived notions and accept the fact that God's Spirit knows no boundaries and will blow wherever He chooses. Nicodemus is invited to sweep away his old Jewish notions of who God is and what he can do in order to be raised to life's higher level.

LIMITATION VERSUS LIBERATION

"Buy your son a motorcycle for his last birthday!" That sign on the wall of the orthopedic surgery wing of a hospital came back to my mind not long ago when I heard about an ironic turn of events that changed the direction of a group of Michigan motorcyclists. They were riding together to their state capitol building to demonstrate against a proposed motorcycle law they deemed prohibitive. They had invited the press to join them there as they made speeches and symbolically smashed motorcycle helmets in protest. On the way to the protest, however, a tragedy occurred when one member of the group lost control of his motorbike and crashed. He suffered near fatal head and facial injuries that doctors agreed would not have happened had he been wearing a helmet.

Similarly, there are many people who believe that becoming a Christian is to take on a narrow, prohibiting, restrictive lifestyle. They buy into the shallow media hype that portrays life in Christ as a dismal, negative hopelessness that delights to put people down. It is hard to imagine any more radical misrepresentation of the truth.

"The angel said unto them, Fear not: for, behold, I bring you good tidings of great joy, which shall be to all people" (Luke 2:10). The word from the angel the night Jesus was born was news so good that some people still refuse to believe it is true. "Fear not!" "Good tidings!" Great joy!" "All people!" New life in Christ is not a limiting experience but a liberating one. It is not a new set of restrictive principles but freedom to be what God made us to be. Every law God gives is ultimately for His glory and our good. The things Christ calls us to abandon for the sake of the gospel are always things that finally enslave us and do us harm. That is why the Bible tells us, "Where the Spirit of the Lord is, there is liberty" (II Cor. 3:17).

Nicodemus failed to see that. Believing himself to be a ruler among the Jews, he failed to see that he was, in fact, a slave to unseen forces. A fence composed of manmade religious traditions hindered his life. He awoke every day behind a barrier of religious dictates that had nothing to do with God's plan for Nicodemus's life. A far greater tragedy is that two thousand years later there are still many people living out their lives behind invisible iron curtains.

CHOOSING THE HIGHER LIFE

Life without the Holy Spirit is never life the way God intended us to live it. Life without Him is always dysfunctional. It is broken and it needs to be fixed. No, it cannot be fixed. It needs to be replaced. The old life has to be done away with in order for this new life God wants for us and sends His Spirit to give us can take its place.

The old life is a slave of every spiritual dictator it has ever known. Call them addictions, obsessions, fixations, bad habits; but finally they are always sin, for they keep us from God. Often we do not recognize the self-defeating behavior patterns that enslave us. Bill, a young man who came to see me a long time ago, was held captive for years to a habit that would, at the end, kill him. He bragged, "I can quit anytime I want." The truth, however, was that he could not break the habit for it had already broken him. It had him like a horse with a bit in its mouth, for that is how sin enslaves its victims. One of Satan's primary ways of binding his followers is to make them believe that a life of obedience to Christ is too hard, demands too much, is too straight-laced and a prohibition against things they enjoy. They do not realize Christ's own promise, "My yoke is easy, and my burden is light" (Matt. 11:30). His ways are always best for us.

CAUGHT BY THE WIND

Along the sea front near Bangor, County Down, I watched a young boy try out his new kite on a windless day. He ran across a long grassy knoll near the beach, pulling the kite string behind him. As he ran, the kite climbed into the air. It looked for a moment as though it might rise above the rooftops. Alas, all too soon, he reached the end of the grass and was forced to stop by a fence. As he stopped, the kite fluttered lifeless to the ground. He adjusted the tail and tried again. He got the same results as before. For a moment the kite looked as though it might fly. Alas, the spirit-less flatness of a lifeless kite lying on the ground became a reality again. He checked the cross pieces and tried a third time. It made no difference. "It must be the guide string," he reasoned and modified the guide string. Modifying the guide string made no difference either. Finally, after his fourth futile attempt, his friend who was watching called out to him from the edge of the grassy knoll, "You cannot soar without the wind."

Now, there's a truth that we all need to hear and heed: Whether it is a paper kite or a besetting sin you are trying to manage, you will not soar without the wind.

HOW DO I CATCH THE WIND?

I was a grown man with a family before I understood the eternal spiritual reality of this concept. Like Nicodemus, I had grown up in religious circles. All my life I attended church. I liked church. I have always enjoyed good oratory and our family ministers had always been friendly toward me. In spite of that, I failed to hear the gospel. It was not because it had not been taught. It had been preached in my presence many times and offered to me personally more than once. I even thought I knew it. All I understood, however, were some intellectual concepts that, even though I tried many times to follow them in my own life, I was unable to uphold. What always followed was a gnawing sense of guilt, failure, and confusion. In truth, while I understood the words, I had somehow failed to grasp one vital part. When I finally realized that one part, however, it changed the whole direction of my life in ways I never would have imagined.

The reason Jesus told Nicodemus, the religious Jew, he needed to be born again was that Nicodemus, for all his religion, was spiritually dead. That is true of everyone who is without a personal relationship with Christ.

The Reality of Mortality!

Barbara and I had not been long in the United States when I approached my uncle Sam Heslip with some questions about Christianity. Sam was also our pastor and had been very instrumental in helping us come to the United States. Sunday by Sunday we had sat under his preaching. As I reasoned through some things he said from his pulpit, questions that demanded answers arose within my mind.

At the time I brought my questions to him, Sam had just returned from receiving training in a new evangelism method called Evangelism Explosion. I suppose I might have been the first person to whom he presented this new method now that he was back home. Whether I was first or not, the Holy Spirit had prepared me for that moment.

"Leslie, have you reached that point in your spiritual life where you know for certain that if you died today you would spend eternity with God in His heaven?" Uncle Sam's words gripped me because they were direct and because I felt they begged for only one acceptable answer. For me that answer was "No." It seemed to me that for anyone to "know for certain" was presumptuous and egotistical.

I replied, "I don't think anybody can know that for sure."

God Wants You to Know

"Really?" Uncle Sam opined, "Suppose I could show you that God actually wants you to know? What would you say?"

I said, "If that was the case, I'd say that I need to know."

73

Without saying a word, he opened one of the Bibles on his desk and pointed out these words: "These things have I written unto you that believe on the name of the Son of God; that ye may know that ye have eternal life, and that ye may believe on the name of the Son of God" (I John 5:13).

Uncle Sam continued, "If God's wants you to know that you have eternal life, shouldn't pursuing that become one of your life's main goals?" His words made sense. Somewhere within me there was a rapidly growing desire to listen carefully. It was God's Holy Spirit prompting me to take careful stock of what I was being told.

Uncle Sam asked me another question, "Suppose you were to die today and God asked you, 'Why should I let you into my heaven?' What would you say to Him?"

VIRTUE IS A BAD THING!

I do not recall the exact words of my answer, but something about this question brought me face to face with the reality of mortality. I knew that I could die today. None of us will leave this life alive and most of us will have no control of when we do die. I was at the same time realizing that I could die at any moment and recognizing that it was clearly foolish for me not to have made preparation for that possibility and trying to frame what would be my best answer in words God might find acceptable. What would I say to God? What could I say to God?

To the best of my recollection, my answer went something like this: "I would say that I had not committed any big sins like murder or adultery and I had attended church and I pray sometimes."

I was caught! The twinkle in my uncle Sam's eye told me he knew already exactly where I was with God. He said, "Leslie, there's nothing worse than good works that think they can satisfy a sinner's need of God!"

He proceeded at that point to tell me his own story of coming to faith. He began with a reassurance that there was a time in his own life when he would have answered as I had just done. "I needed to learn," he said, "that all my good works together could never save my soul. One day I read in Isaiah, 'We are all as an unclean thing, and all our righteousnesses are as filthy rags' (64:6)." "Then," he said, "I made the most amazingly wonderful discovery of my entire life. I learned that heaven is a free gift. Would you like to learn what I did?" I said I would and he invited me to draw my chair over to his desk where we could look together at his Bible.

WAGES AND GIFTS

He pointed out these words: "For the wages of sin is death; but the gift of God is eternal life through Jesus Christ our Lord" (Rom. 6:23). I had seen these words before. I remembered that they were painted on the side of a barn along the coast near where I had grown up.

"Do you realize what this tells us?" he asked. Quickly he added, "What, in your opinion, is the difference between wages and a gift?" "The difference between wages and a gift," I answered, "is that wages are something we earn and a gift is something someone gives us for nothing."

"Exactly," he said. "Now think about your answer a moment ago when I asked what you would tell God if you were asked why you should get into heaven. Were you describing wages or a gift?"

I realized immediately that my answer was all about wages. It spoke about what I might have earned by what I had done and not done. I had done what I considered to be some commendable things and I had not committed what I called, "big sins." Here was God's own Word telling me that all the wages I had ever earned could never total enough to make me fit for heaven. I thought of that barn sign again and realized that as many times as I had read it I had never thought about what it was telling me.

Uncle Sam said, "Let me show you something else." Opening his Bible at another place, he pointed out these words: "For by grace are ye saved through faith; and that not of yourselves: it is the gift of God: Not of works, lest any man should boast. For we are his workmanship, created in Christ Jesus unto good works, which God hath before ordained that we should walk in them" (Eph. 2:8-10).

I knew these words too. I remembered preachers reciting them in sermons. I had read them in the Bible previously, but they seemed to have no particular meaning to me.

"It's not that works are a bad thing," Uncle Sam said. "It is just that works by themselves cannot earn heaven. It takes something more. That something more is called grace. 'For by grace are ye saved.'"

He paused as I pondered his words before saying, "We need grace because we cannot save ourselves and we need grace because we are sinners."

SINNERS UNANIMOUS

He opened his Bible at another place and showed me these words, "There is none righteous, no, not one: There is none that understandeth, there is none that seeketh after God. They are all gone out of the way, they are together become unprofitable; there is none that doeth good, no, not one" (Rom. 3:10-12) "For all have sinned, and come short of the glory of God" (Rom. 3:23).

"Do you see our human predicament?" he asked me. "All of us are stained by the same thing; you and me and everybody else in the world. We have all fallen short of God's glory. We are unanimous in our guilt."

He paused again before adding, "God, however, is holy. Look at what the Bible says here, 'Be ye holy; for I am holy' (I Pet. 1:16). He is also righteous. 'The Lord our God is righteous in all his works' (Dan. 9:14). He always does the right things. Because God is holy and righteous, He must keep His Word and His Word says, 'The soul that sinneth, it shall die'; and this, of course, 'For the wages of sin is death' (Ezek. 18:4; Rom. 6:23). This means that we have an impossible predicament. We have sinned and our death sentence has already been pronounced."

I could see it clearly. For a moment I felt as though I was a prisoner on death row.

Uncle Sam added, "What is more, we cannot save ourselves." I knew that, for already I had resolved more times than I could remember to do better than I had done and I had failed every time. Like that kite on a windless day, I kept falling. I lacked the necessary power.

WHAT LOVE DID

Uncle Sam spoke again, "God not only is holy; He is love. Out of His amazing love He has done something for sinners." He opened his Bible to two verses from Christ's interview with Nicodemus that I remembered memorizing as a child, "For God so loved the world, that he gave his only begotten Son, that whosoever believeth in him should not perish, but have everlasting life. For God sent not his Son into the world to condemn the world; but that the world through him might be saved" (John 3:16-17).

"Now, substitute your name for 'the world,'" I heard my uncle say. I did and now the verse began, "God so loved Leslie Holmes that he gave his only begotten Son." Those words memorized in childhood became, in that instant, personal and direct. I knew for the first time that God sent Christ into the world and to the cross for me.

Uncle Sam asked me, "What would it take to make you give up your son?" Uncle Sam knew what it was to lose a son, for his first son, Tom, who was born soon after I was born, had died in infancy. Over twenty years had passed since Tom died, yet that loss still brought daily pain to Sam and to my aunt Pauline. I grew up hearing about Tom's death from other members of our family too. The grief of losing him had taken its toll on many of them. I thought at that moment of our own son, Gary. We would soon celebrate Gary's first birthday. It was then that I realized as never before the amazing love God had. I could think then, and after over a quarter century as a pastor I can think today, of no more costly painful grief than that which comes from a child's death. Yet God did not lose His Son to death. He voluntarily gave Jesus over to death because He loved me. When I realized that God's sacrifice of Jesus was made for sinners like me, I was stunned by how deep God's love for me runs. I could not imagine giving my son up for anything in the world. Yet God gave His Son up for me.

My uncle explained that Jesus, God's Son, is our only Savior. He pointed out that the Bible confirms this in Acts 4:12: "Neither is there salvation in any other: for there is none other name under heaven given among men, whereby we must be saved." Then Uncle Sam reinforced this by pointing out Christ's own claim, "I am the way, the truth, and the life: no man cometh unto the Father, but by me" (John 14:6).

Con Artist or Christ of God?

"When you think about it," Sam added, "anyone who makes that claim for himself must be a liar or a lunatic, or he is Lord. Which will you call Christ? The Bible tells us which He is, for it says, 'God hath made that same Jesus, whom ye have crucified, both Lord and Christ.'" He was quoting from Acts 2:36.

Jesus did something for us we could never do for ourselves. He took away our sins. Peter says that Jesus "his own self bare our sins in his own body on the tree" (I Pet. 2:24)." Isaiah in the Old Testament saw this and prophesied seven centuries before Christ was born, "All we like sheep have gone astray; we have turned every one to his own way; and the Lord hath laid on him the iniquity of us all" (Isa. 53:6).

RSVP

Which is it? Was Jesus a confidence man or God's own Christ? Each of us has the urgent and compelling call of all eternity imploring us to answer this question. No one else in the entire world can answer it for us. We must each answer it for ourselves. For reasonable people there can be no doubt. Christ, who died on Calvary's cross out of love for us and who promised to send His Holy Spirit to us, was God's only begotten Son. In spite of that, He made the most amazing sacrifice the world will ever know. Now He invites sinners to become sons and daughters. Like an invitation to a significant event with "RSVP", the Bible brings God's invitation to new life to us and asks us to RSVP. How will we reply to such a magnificent invitation?

Perhaps a better question is how God wants us to respond. The Bible says, "The Lord is not slack concerning his promise, as some men count slackness; but is longsuffering to us-ward, not willing that any should perish, but that all should come to repentance" (II Pet. 3:9). It is God's desire that we be saved. We are saved John 3:16 says when we "believe on" Christ. Belief in this sense is more than mere intellectual assent. When Jesus called Nicodemus to belief, He was calling him to full surrender of his will in an act of faith.

FORSAKING ALL I TRUST HIM

What is faith? Faith, according to the Bible, is absolute confidence, conviction, trust, and reliance that Jesus is who He said He is and that He will always do what He says He will do. Human beings exercise faith every day. How many of us wonder each time we sit on a chair whether it will hold our weight or not? Most of us assume the chair will hold us and sit on it without calculating the possibility of failure. That is an act of faith in the chair. In a similar way, when we drive our cars at high rates of speed on the interstate, we do not question the likelihood that our brakes will stop us when we press the brake pedal. That, too, is an act of faith.

Chairs and cars are inanimate objects. When the apostle Paul writes, "By grace are ye saved through faith," he is telling us that placing our faith on a living Person, the Lord Jesus Christ, saves us. Just as we trust the chair to hold us, saving faith trusts Christ to sustain us through life. Similarly, as we trust the car brakes to stop when we need to, so we also trust God's Son, Jesus, to usher us into a glorious and unending eternity in heaven when we die.

Faith as an acrostic can stand for Forsaking All I Trust Him. That is what saving faith is. It is giving up all the other things we have ever relied on to save us and trusting the only One who can save us, God's Son, Jesus. That takes an act of the will on our part and, says Paul, that act of the will is a "gift of God." In other words, God gives us the faith. How? Through his Breath of Abundant Life, the Holy Spirit.

The Breath of Abundant Life, who brooded over the creation of the world when life as we know it first began, is present every time a genuine conversion to Christian faith takes place. "Thou sendest forth thy spirit, they are created: and thou renewest the face of the earth" (Ps. 104:30). It was the Holy Spirit who made the difference that day my uncle Sam set the gospel I had grown up hearing, but never understood, before me. My life's direction was changed completely as a result. With time's passing, things that once were of primary importance were replaced with other far more important things.

I had arrived in America seeking my fortune through financial riches, but now God had endowed me with all the riches of His grace, riches no bank can contain. Previously I had envisioned entering into a successful business venture, but now God raised an insatiable desire to spend the rest of my life doing business with and for Him. What once seemed vitally necessary lost all its attraction. Now I knew somehow that God's intention was for me to invest my life in telling anyone who would listen that God loves him and that his Son, Jesus, presents a plan for a new life more wonderful than any human being could ever imagine without Him.

LIFE'S MOST COMPELLING QUESTION

"What shall I do then with Jesus which is called Christ?" (Matt. 27:22). These words framed by Pontius Pilate only hours before our Lord's crucifixion constitute the most compelling question we shall ever answer. One thing we cannot do is ignore Him, for Jesus Christ will not go away. One day each of us shall stand before Him to give account of how we answered it. Therefore, answer it we must, either here or there before His judgment seat. We must either take Him for who He says He is or classify Him as a phony.

When I realized this, I knew that I would be foolish not to cast my lot with Christ. Under my uncle Sam's guidance, I prayed this prayer, "Lord Jesus Christ, I admit that I am a sinner and that I cannot save myself. I have no hope of salvation except by your sovereign mercy and grace. I repent of my sins. Please forgive me for them and come into my life. Live in me as Savior and Lord for the rest of my life. In your name I pray. Amen."

For me, there were no flashing, blinding lights, like the ones Paul experienced on the Damascus Road. I felt no surge of electricity inside. In fact, it took four days for the reality of what had happened to possess me. There was only the heart assuring, quiet confidence of God's Word. "He that believeth on the Son hath everlasting life" (John 3:36). "All that the Father giveth me shall come to me; and him that cometh to me I will in no wise cast out" (John 6:37). Those words that came to me through a human hand were protected and inspired by God's Breath of Abundant Life. Now the same Breath brought them to life in my heart. I was born again. New life had begun. All my sins were forgiven. All my guilt was taken away by Jesus on the cross. Everything about me had a brand new start. This was the greatest news I would ever hear in my life. It was the greatest news any person could ever know.

I heard and saw nothing the day I asked Christ to forgive my sins and make me new but in heaven the angels rejoiced for the Wind of God chose to blow into a little church in Moss Point, Mississippi, and bring a sinner home. A lost sheep was found. An unclean pagan became a child of God for all eternity. A man who was dead was born again. It was the beginning of a whole new direction for my life.

WHAT WILL YOU DO?

The Lord Jesus Christ has done all that is necessary for your salvation. What will you do with him? If you have not committed your life to Jesus before, you can do it now before you turn this page. Confess you are a sinner. Repent from your sin. Ask Christ to save you and He will. Having done that, tell someone about your decision. Begin to pray and read the Bible every day and unite this week with a church that worships Christ and teaches God's Word.

Nicodemus that night, so far as we know, did not substitute his name for "the world." The Bible does not say the leader of the Jews came to faith in Jesus during that meeting. So we are left with a great uncertainty as to whether Nicodemus's life was maximized for God's great good.

Our hope for Nicodemus's salvation lies in later passages where he defended Jesus before the Sanhedrin and where he donated the mixture of myrrh and aloes to be used to prepare Christ's body for burial. Even that is not certain evidence of discipleship, however. The Scripture plainly says, "Not by works of righteousness which we have done, but according to his mercy he saved us, by the washing of regeneration, and renewing of the Holy Ghost; Which he shed on us abundantly through Jesus Christ our Saviour" (Titus 3:5-6).

What a tragedy it must have been if having left Christ with no firm commitment being made that secret night long before, Nicodemus finally realized who Christ was only at the Master's last hour, when it was too late to save Jesus or promote His cause. Imagine what he might have done as a born-again leader. Could he have persuaded the other leaders among the Jews to look at who Christ was in light of their Old Testament prophecies? Jesus Himself said, "Whosoever therefore shall confess me before men, him will I confess also before my Father which is in heaven. But whosoever shall deny me before men, him will I also deny before my Father which is in heaven" (Matt. 10:32-33). We will never know this side of glory.

Or suppose Nicodemus had died in the meantime, would he have gone out into an eternity lost without Christ? What a difference his life might have made if only he had surrendered to Christ that evening!

What a difference Christ makes to our lives and what a difference one life wholly committed can make for Him! There is no telling how far Christ, in the power of His Spirit, plans to take and use a man or woman until they take the first step of trust. As Lloyd Ogilvie says, "Give your life to Christ and you'll surprise even you!"

BETTER THAN NICODEMUS

We have a splendid opportunity to do better than Nicodemus by receiving Christ now and declaring His Lordship over our lives by word and deed from this day forward. Perhaps you now sense a call within your heart to come to the Lord of Calvary in absolute surrender. Listen to that call. It comes through the Breath of Abundant Life. "To day, if ye will hear his voice, harden not your hearts" (Heb. 4:7). This can be the start of something wonderful for you and the people you love. Open the windows of your heart and let God's Wind blow through you.

Make your commitment to begin anew with Christ now. Then read on, for you have only just begun to live the most exciting adventure possible for any human being. In chapter six you will learn more about what God has in store for you.

6

Heaven's down payment

After many prayers and two fierce days of house-hunting, we agreed that the English Tudor in Pittsburgh's rolling North Hills was the right home for us. We made an offer through our realtor. At that point the question was raised, "How much earnest money do you want to pay?"

Earnest money! The term is an everyday one in the real estate industry. It did not matter that the local press had already noted that I was the newly elected senior minister of a world-renowned church in the heart of Pittsburgh's Golden Triangle. It was not important to the company that owned the house that our church was the oldest incorporated entity in the city or that we had been doing business for Christ for over one hundred years before they were founded. Nor did it seem to matter that our new congregation, through their leaders, had indicated a willingness to guarantee the mortgage on the home of our choice in an effort to expedite our move to the city. At that moment, no one asked where I had gone to school or how much experience I brought to my new position in the heart of the city. The principle concern of the people involved in assisting us to find a new home was earnest money.

What is earnest money? Earnest money is a deposit that signifies the beginning of a process that usually results in a change of ownership for a piece of real estate. It is a potential buyer's way of saying, "I guarantee my earnestness with this collateral."

Having previously discussed the matter with Barbara, I wrote a check for an amount we believed sufficient to prove our sincerity. In the bottom left corner I scribbled, "Earnest money." Later we would redeem the transaction by signing the appropriate legal papers and paying the balance due to transfer the title. In the meantime, our earnest money signified to the present owner that we meant business.

From that moment, so far as we were concerned, our house-hunting expedition was over and our new address was settled. With the passing of time, our furniture in those rooms, our pictures hanging on those walls, and our clothes hanging in those closets would make that house our home. None of that, however, could happen without the earnest.

At the right time, after the transaction was consummated, the former owners removed their possessions. Well almost, for, immediately after we moved into our new abiding place we found some of their belongings in our attic and, of all places, in our refrigerator. That's right! The day we moved in we found a credit card belonging to the former owner stuck in the door of the refrigerator.

Nor did our findings stop there. Not long ago I was attempting to catch a field mouse that thought it had found free lodging for the winter in our basement. The little varmint ran behind the hot water heater to escape. In trying to reach it there, I discovered a Frisbee with the last owner's name inscribed upon it. Unbeknownst to us, that Frisbee had stayed behind our hot water heater for over five years.

GOD'S DOWN PAYMENT

"Ye were sealed with that Holy Spirit of promise, Which is the earnest of our inheritance" (Eph. 1:13-14). Paul reaches into the legal lexicon of Graeco-Roman real estate and borrows a word that describes God's serious intentions in saving us. That word is arrhabon, meaning "an earnest pledge to complete a transaction." The Holy Spirit is God's earnest, Paul writes. The Spirit signifies God's intention to occupy us.

When I confessed my sins and invited Jesus to take up residence in my life, my body became a house for God to live in. At that moment, the Breath of Abundant Life came alive in me. That does not mean the Devil willingly agreed to transfer ownership. In fact, he has consistently refused to move out willingly. He has not yet fully evacuated the premises, for I continue to find his things in my spiritual attic and in some of the still-cold places of my heart. Like that credit card in our refrigerator and the Frisbee behind the water heater, he keeps showing up in unexpected ways and places. Yet the fact remains that God in Christ has "put His money" on me.

84

The Scriptures warn, however, that while Satan can never again hold title to the life purchased by Christ, he will not surrender that territory without a fight. The result is a lifelong struggle between the Holy Spirit and the spirit of the old man. That struggle and how we overcome it forms the backdrop for much of this chapter. To fully digest that conflict, we need to think about salvation in Christ as Paul knows it.

SIN AND SINS

The fullness of our salvation in Christ is frequently not understood even by Christians. Part of the reason for that is that many of us do not fully understand the Bible's message about sin. Grasping the impact of sin is a vital part of realizing what salvation entails. We must know we are sinners before we can be saved.

The Bible speaks of "sin" (singular) and of "sins" (plural). The New Testament Greek word for sin is *hamartia.* It comes out of the world of sports and means "to miss the target." When we sin, we miss God's target. Paul tells the Romans that sin is a problem for every person ever born: "As it is written, There is none righteous, no, not one" (Rom. 3:10). "For all have sinned, and come short of the glory of God" (Rom. 3:23). "By one man sin entered into the world, and death by sin; and so death passed upon all men, for that all have sinned" (Rom. 5:12).

HANDS AND HEART

A watchmaker I know has a clock on his wall that is obviously wrong. People leaving off a broken watch on their lunch break are likely to hear the clock strike thirteen times. It does that approximately once every ten minutes all day long. Customers also notice that the hands on that clock are permanently set at twenty minutes after four. Below the clock the watchmaker placed a sign that reads, "Don't blame my hands! My problem lies much deeper!" Obviously it does.

The same is true about sin when the Bible uses the word in its singular form. Sin goes deeper than my hands. Sin is in my heart. It is a principle and not merely an act. It entices me to do wrong in defiance against God. The forbidden fruit of sin is knowing better than I do. Adam and Eve, the original sinners knew that God told them not to eat the forbidden fruit, but they did it anyway. Sin can be the self-centered screaming of a child who has learned that if he screams long enough his parents will always give in and he will get his own way. It can be the internal struggles that beckon a great saint back to the self-defeating habits of his life before Christ.

The Bible concept of sins, in a plural sense, is not about what I am but about what I do. The relationship between the two is easy to see: I do what I do because I am what I am. That is why all my previous efforts to turn over a new leaf—which I wrote about in the last chapter—ended with frustrating failure. The only way to successfully get over what we are is to be born all over again. "Except a man be born again, he cannot see the kingdom of God" (John 3:3). Nothing we can do or be can solve this universal human problem. Only God can fix it. He did that through the death and resurrection of His Son, Jesus.

SALVATION IN THREE SETTINGS

The Bible understanding of our salvation is so comprehensive that it speaks of it in three tenses. The first is that we were saved. Paul writes, "We also joy in God through our Lord Jesus Christ, by whom we have now received the atonement" (Rom. 5:11). Salvation has a past tense dimension.

Salvation Past—We Were Saved from Sin's Penalty

Not long ago a man who had just been tried and acquitted admitted outside the courtroom that he was in fact guilty of the crime with which he had been charged. His confession made many people angry and there were calls to try him again. That could not happen because of a principle in American jurisprudence called "double jeopardy." Double jeopardy protects a person from being prosecuted more than once for the same offense.

Double jeopardy is also a basic principle of divine justice. Because of God's gracious salvation, we who are in Christ, though we are guilty of all kinds of sin, are beyond the bounds of punishment. Every sin we've ever committed or will commit was prosecuted and its penalty was given to God's Son, Jesus, at Calvary.

The idea of past tense salvation was demonstrated by the annual Jewish ceremony of atonement. "We have now received the atonement," Paul writes. He uses the Greek aorist tense of the verb to signify a completed action. The aorist tense captures past action like a snapshot. That is, it "freezes" it in time. It is neither continuous nor repetitious. Atonement, says Paul, is like a photograph, frozen in time. It happened. It is accomplished. Nothing can change it. When the Bible says, "We have received the atonement," it means the penalty for our sins was paid in full. It need never be paid again.

In the Old Testament, the annual atonement ceremony signified the cleansing of all Israel from the highest high priest to the lowest tribesman who repented of sin and offered satisfactory sacrifice. That ceremony declared every sinner "at-one" with God. It said all the sins of the past year were forgiven. It was the annual day of "At-one-ment."

For Christians, our Day of Atonement does not come once in a year but once for all eternity. The day of our conversion to faith in Christ is our once in a lifetime Day of Atonement. On that day the Breath of Abundant Life breathes into us a recognition not only that we have sinned but also that Jesus paid our sin penalty in full on the cross. We are forgiven, not for a year, but forever. He convinces us, in light of that, to repent and believe the gospel. In an instant we are forgiven from every sin we ever committed. We are declared to be "at-one" with God. As quick as a flash, God forgives us for all our sins and wipes them out completely. "I will forgive their iniquity, and I will remember their sin no more" (Jer. 31:34).

God will not bring our old sins and their penalty before us ever again. This is important because when properly understood it helps us forgive ourselves and delivers us from the tyranny of self-imposed guilt.

Sometimes this verse is interpreted as teaching that God forgets sin. That is not accurate. Forgetfulness is a characteristic of human frailty. God has no inclination to absent-mindedness. He does not forget as we do but chooses, rather, to remember no more. That is, He models what we are to do with the sins of one another. He intentionally makes a choice to never bring our sins up again.

THE GRACE WE FIND IN CHRIST

A great bell hung silently in the belfry of an old church. One day some visitors decided to sound it out again. They tugged on the bell-pull rope, but there was no noise. They climbed the bell tower to investigate the silence. There they discovered that the old bell bore a large crack. Some unknown person realizing that this blemish would make its once proud sound seem dingy and hollow had carefully wrapped the bell's hammer in cloth so thick it was impossible for it to strike the side of the bell with enough force to ring out and advertise its giant flaw.

Similarly, the Bible tells us that God does not advertise our flaws for the world to hear. He works, rather, to allow our best side to be seen. The message of His love is not that we have sinned but that we have hope. "God was in Christ, reconciling the world unto himself, not imputing their trespasses unto them" (II Cor. 5:19). Christ did not come to hound us or to keep us in guilt bondage for what happened long ago. "For God sent not his Son into the world to condemn the world; but that the world through him might be saved" (John 3:17). Christ came to put sin behind us once and for all. This is the essence of Paul's letter to the church in Ephesus. He opens by presenting a speedy synopsis of God's redeeming work in Jesus. God has done what only God can do in giving His Son to serve the sentence our sin demands.

This is the necessary beginning point of the salvation experience, but it is not the end of it. Yet this is as far as some Christians go in their salvation experience. They stake their whole eternity on a decision they made at one time and believe that is all there is to it. Failing to recognize the rest of the process of salvation, they miss the best Christ has for them. This short sighted understanding of salvation often places an emphasis on what the sinner did instead of recognizing what God has done and is doing. Thus, it slights the Holy Spirit. It is inclined to speak of salvation in self-serving terms such as "I made a decision" or "I walked forward when the invitation was given." In that life the earnest of the Spirit has been given but God has often not been welcomed to consummate what has been begun. Salvation past saves us from the penalty of sin forevermore. It is a once-in-a-lifetime step.

SALVATION PRESENT—WE ARE BEING SAVED FROM SIN'S POWER

"Go ye therefore, and teach all nations, baptizing them in the name of the Father, and of the Son, and of the Holy Ghost" (Matt. 28:19). Another way to translate the Greek is "Go therefore and make disciples of all the nations, baptizing them in the name of the Father and of the Son and of the Holy Spirit" (New King James Version). Becoming a convert is different from becoming a disciple. No one can become a disciple apart from the Holy Spirit, the Breath of Abundant Life. The Greek word for disciple means "to be saddle-broken." It finds its origins in the world of horses. A newly captured horse is not a saddle-broken one. Saddle-breaking a horse takes time and training. It is a contest of the wills between the horse and the trainer, so also becoming a disciple of Jesus is a contest between the wills of the old man and Christ. Becoming a disciple, or to be "saddle-broken" to Christ, also takes time and training. Obedience is not natural to us; rebellion is. Even when we first admit our sin and receive Christ as Lord, we have a way to go.

Tom Dowling knew that progress often comes slowly and with great effort and personal sacrifice. The chairman of the Board of a major Pittsburgh corporation retired not long ago after a stellar rise through the company. Raised in a poor working class section of our city, he started out as an errand boy. His first job was to take things from one executive office to another. He was paid less than anybody else in the company. He was drafted into the army during World War II. After the war, he rejoined the company and went to night school to further his education. He was the first person in his family to graduate from college. After completing his degree, he climbed steadily up the corporate ladder. Fifty-two years after first joining the company, Tom retired from the top position within the company. Last year his salary and stock options earned him multiplied millions of dollars. "I decided in the trenches in Europe that if I lived through the war I was coming back to Pittsburgh to do everything in my power to take over this company one day," Tom Dowling said. "There were times," he added, "when I wondered if it was worthwhile. Often the money was tight and the hours were long. One time, while I was working all day and going to night school, my wife, Jean, and I literally had to shake the sofa to see if there was any change we could use to buy enough baby food to get us through to payday. At times like that I remembered the sacrifice some of my army buddies paid in those trenches and knew I had to do this for them."

Discipleship growth is not unlike that. It calls for self-sacrifice, determination, and submission of the will to a higher ideal. There are times when quitting would be easier, but we remember that blood was shed for us and we carry on. We also know that quitters never win. Jesus says, "No man, having put his hand to the plough, and looking back, is fit for the kingdom of God" (Luke 9:62).

WORK IN PROGRESS

"The preaching of the cross is to them that perish foolishness; but unto us which are saved it is the power of God" (1 Cor. 1:18). The Greek tense signals a work that is still in progress. Salvation past is an entry-level once-in-a-lifetime experience, but its present is a daily process of working our way through the ranks of faith. Day by day we choose between two paths, the one good and the other evil. Jesus says, "Strait is the gate, and narrow is the way, which leadeth unto life, and few there be that find it" (Matt. 7:14).

Just as top-of-the-corporate-ladder success did not come to Tom Dowling the day he joined the company, so salvation in all its fullness does not come at the moment we enlist with Christ. Salvation fully understood is a process. This evidence of our being saved is not that we once decided to follow Jesus but that we are changing our attitude, which in turn leads to changed behavior. "Be renewed in the spirit of your mind" (Eph. 4:23). Old habits die hard, and the reason they die hard is that in spite of God's earnest our old owner fights to retain control.

"Christianity," said media mogul Ted Turner, "is a religion for losers." He went on to say that Christian faith is a crutch for weaklings. On the surface, that may seem true. In reality being a Christian is very difficult. It requires admitting failure, commitment, perseverance, and inward resolve to follow Jesus every day. It demands a shift from self-centered thinking to Christ-directed thinking, "Bringing into captivity every thought to the obedience of Christ" (II Cor. 10:5). It involves being willing to be vulnerable, for people do not always understand the changed ways that come with new life in Christ. It calls for self-sacrifice. Jesus said, "Whosoever shall lose his life for my sake and the gospel's, the same shall save it" (Mark 8:35). Thus, being saved takes a lifetime.

Following Jesus is not for wimps. Peter found this out the hard way when, after having walked three years with Jesus, he fell back to his old habits of lying and swearing when he was put under pressure the night before that ominous cock crowed.

Paul knew from firsthand experience that sin is a monster that does not give up easily. "I delight in the law of God after the inward man: but I see another law in my members, warring against the law of my mind, and bringing me into captivity to the law of sin which is in my members. O wretched man that I am! Who shall deliver me from the body of this death?" (Rom. 7:22-24).

Growing in Christ taught Paul life lessons that nobody ever learned at the feet of his old teacher Gamaliel.

The first lesson was about the insufficiency of his intellect. As brilliant a student as Paul was he had to learn that his intellect was insufficient: "I was alive without the law once: but when the commandment came, sin revived, and I died. And the commandment, which was ordained to life, I found to be unto death. For sin, taking occasion by the commandment, deceived me, and by it slew me" (Romans 7:9-11). Nothing he could learn in all his formal years of study would bring him the salvation he needed.

The second lesson Paul had learned was about the insufficiency of self-sufficiency. His words have something to say to any of us who think we can be saved by self-determination: "What I would, that do I not; but what I hate, that do I" (Rom. 7:15).

When the Darkness Comes Back Again

Some years ago when Gary and Erin were still children, we spent one week on vacation on Fripp Island. As we unloaded a week's worth of groceries from the trunk of our car, a friendly raccoon appeared, seemingly

91

from out of nowhere. Gary and Erin were enamoured of him from the start. They had seen raccoons before but only from a distance. There were lots of wild raccoons near where we lived in Mississippi. Unlike them, however, this one obviously was tame. It came right up beside them and extended raccoon friendship. An attractively studded, red leather collar around his neck indicated he was someone's pet. His name, according to the brass tab on the collar, was Ben. Ben was docile and playful.

Early the next morning the streets and gardens around our formerly pristine vacation neighborhood bore the evidence of a nighttime rampage. Everywhere we looked, garbage cans were overturned, garbage bags were burst open, and their contents were strewn across roads and gardens that were tidy the last time we saw them. A nearby resident observed Ben doing all the damage. Despite his daytime friendliness, when darkness fell again, Ben's native instincts took over with their entire sinister behavior patterns. He was proving out the inspired observation of the psalmist: "It is night: wherein all the beasts of the forest do creep forth" (Ps. 104:20).

The same is true of us. Even though God takes title to our lives when the Holy Spirit enters in, the darkness of our old fallen human nature lingers not far away awaiting an opportunity to undo Christ's work in us to the best of its ability. The dark side of our lower sinful nature keeps on sneaking to the fore of our personalities. When that happens, we do things none of us could be proud of. Call it by some pseudo-polite mitigating metaphor, if you like, but the fact remains that every one of us is a sinner. We are each capable of making a lot of garbage.

THE ENEMY WITHIN

In his first Thanksgiving proclamation, Abraham Lincoln spoke of "the enemy who is of our own household." President Lincoln too recognized that our greatest enemy lies within. Seeing the truth in this, Paul acknowledges to the Romans that he has learned he cannot be a Christian on his own strength. Sin lurks near the surface of his life and would control him completely were it not for the grace of God and his reliance on the Holy Spirit. His greatest adversary is himself, just as I am my own greatest adversary and you are yours. The only good thing about any of us is Jesus.

THE GREATEST SINNER

Let's think about the same principle from another angle: If you were asked to name the worst sinner you can think of, what would you answer? Adolf Hitler? Idi Amin? Is it some despot from another place and time? Would it be someone close to where you live who has done you a great wrong? Are you ready to acknowledge that you are capable of doing the worst thing that person has done? "Sin lieth at the door. And unto thee shall be his desire" (Gen. 4:7). "Let him that thinketh he standeth take heed lest he fall" (I Cor. 10:12).

DYING TO LIVE FOR JESUS

Paul walked a great while with Christ before he could acknowledge openly that one of the clear and present dangers of the Christian life is supposing that we are somehow better than other people are or that we are sinners emeritus. As Paul progressed in his life with Christ, he saw that from one perspective the Christian life is a dying life.

This becomes especially clear in a close study of Paul's writing in the context of his life. In his first church letter, for example, he signs on as, "Paul, an apostle, (not of men, neither by man, but by Jesus Christ, and God the Father, who raised him from the dead)" (Gal. 1:1). He lays claim to the highest office in the church of his day. Seven years later he describes himself as "the least of the apostles, that am not meet to be called an apostle, because I persecuted the church of God" (I Cor. 15:9). Eight years after that he makes no claim of apostlicity. Instead, he writes that he is "less than the least of all saints" (Eph. 3:8). Finally, near the end of his life he writes, "Christ Jesus came into the world to save sinners; of whom I am chief" (I Tim. 1:15).

Christianity, as Paul came to understand it, includes a descending view of self and an ascending view of Christ's grace. In John the Baptist's words, "He must increase, but I must decrease" (John 3:30). The evidence of the Holy Spirit's presence in us is that we die to ourselves and Christ becomes more alive in us.

Paul's third lesson was that Satan, the monster who makes his life inside us, is a monster who is slow to surrender. He abdicates his authority grudgingly in our lives. It took only a few minutes for me to become a

93

Christian that day I prayed to receive Christ in my uncle Sam's study. In those few minutes the Breath of Abundant Life came alive in me. By leading me through repentance and faith in Christ, He did His work of conversion. Thirty-one years later, however, I must admit that becoming like Christ is taking a lot longer than that. The battle is not won all the way. It seems to be taking a lifetime. The longer I walk with the Lord and the closer I grow to Him, the more I understand why Paul compares the Christian life to a long-time civil war. It is a war I cannot win alone. I need to recall the earnest of the Spirit every day.

God's Holy Spirit comes to every new believer like a down payment, guaranteeing and validating His intention to live in us. The presence of the Breath of Abundant Life in us evidences God's genuine pledge to make us His own. He commits His gift of eternal life to us day by day. With time's passing He will put the furniture of new habits in our rooms and hang His pictures on the walls of our imagination, and we will slowly be transformed into the home He wants us to be. The Devil's belongings will continue to show up in us, but we must resolve in the Spirit's strength to do whatever is necessary to evict Satan and all his belongings so that all our neighbors will know that Christ lives here.

LINGERING IN FAITH'S LOBBY

Salvation's second tense recognizes that the earnest, or down payment, of the Spirit is but the beginning point of a process. Process, by its very nature, demands movement. Spiritually, we are all on the move every day. We are going in one direction or another. What direction are you moving? Are you closer to Christ than you were one year ago? One month ago? Yesterday?

To not move, to linger in one place, is deadly. That night he denied Jesus, Peter lingered on the porch the Bible says (see Matt. 26:71). Instead of ascending the steps of faith that Christ had laid out before him, Peter descended into some of his old ways. He lingered on the porch, and his old monster came alive again in the darkness.

"God hath from the beginning chosen you to salvation through sanctification of the Spirit and belief of the truth" (II Thess. 2:13). "Sanctifica-

94

tion," says an old catechism in recognition of that statement and others like it, "is the work of God's free grace." Salvation, the first step in this process which saves us from sin's penalty, is a gift. Sanctification is a work. Saving us from sin's penalty took a cross. Saving us from sin's power takes a lifetime. "If any man will come after me, let him deny himself, and take up his cross daily" (Luke 9:23).

FORTY SOLDIERS WRESTLING FOR CHRIST

Legend says that as Christian faith spread through the early church and reached the very heart of Rome's army, Nero, the weak-kneed Roman emperor became increasingly paranoid. Fearing that the Christians might soon outnumber their non-Christian counterparts, Nero passed an edict demanding that every soldier be called upon to renounce Christ and bow to himself. He could not imagine that their loyalty to Christ made some of his soldiers more loyal to their emperor than they might have ever been before.

Not long before that order was passed down through the ranks, one platoon of one hundred Roman soldiers stood shoulder-to-shoulder through an especially fierce and bloody battle. That experience built a bond between those soldiers that only men who have been in war together understand. Forty Christians were among the men of that platoon. Brave and true, these followers of Jesus were noted for their high standards of morality and personal grace. Their platoon leader, a centurion called Vespasian, had seen the difference Christ made in them. Having worn the uniform a while, Vespasian prided himself in knowing a good soldier when he saw one.

One by one the defenders of Rome in every platoon filed past Nero's statue and pledged their faithfulness to him alone. As each of the forty Christians stepped before the statue, he declared, "I will defend Rome and the emperor with my life, but I bow my knee to none but Christ Jesus my Lord." Having refused to bow, each Christian received Nero's mandatory death sentence. Heartsick, Vespasian knew Rome left him no choice but to march those men toward an iceberg that rose like a small, frozen mountain just offshore. Once there, they would be stripped of their heavy, protective tunics and left naked to freeze to death. Vespasian carried out this duty personally, hoping that along the way he might persuade at least some of them to compromise their faith and return to the platoon. Instead, he heard them cite Scripture passages that tell of a perfect Master who rather than demand that His soldiers die had given His own life for them on a cross near Jerusalem. They encouraged each other with reassuring promises of Christ's offer of eternal life. Vespasian listened as together they raised their voices in a marching song as they inched nearer to Nero's cruel, needless death. It touched Vespasian more deeply than anything he had experienced before:

Forty soldiers wrestling for Thee, O Christ.
Forty soldiers wrestling for Thee.
We claim for Thee the victory;
And from Thee the crown of life that never fades away.

As nighttime fell, Vespasian and his men arrived near the shoreline. Together, with Vespasian standing over them, they the cast off their uniforms and walked naked through the waves to the iceberg that would mark their death place. He knew that if they chose to, they had the power to overcome him, take his life, and walk away to freedom. He made a roaring fire on the edge of the shore and watched and waited, his heart heavy with sadness. These men had faced death with him before. He remembered that they had not shown fear then either. He stayed through the night and his heart begged an unknown God that even yet these men might change their minds in the bitter cold. His pagan prayer was interrupted by their haunting chant in the darkness:

Forty soldiers wrestling for Thee, O Christ.
Forty soldiers wrestling for Thee.
We claim for Thee the victory
And from Thee the crown of life that never fades away.

As dawn broke on the new day, one solitary soldier jumped off the iceberg and plodded through the cold water up to the shore. Only one!

He tramped, shivering, toward Vespasian's roaring fire. Lips blue and shivering, the soldier saluted Vespasian and said he would turn his back on Christ and obey the imperial decree.

Vespasian beckoned the turncoat to move closer to the fire. He also noticed that the uniforms these men had taken off the night before now lay on the snow, stiffened with the cold of the night. Slowly Vespasian began to unbutton his own tunic, one button at a time. He took off his heavy topcoat and each garment underneath it. As he took off each piece, Vespasian reached it to the defector and helped him put it on. Now naked, Vespasian walked toward the shoreline. He plodded through the icy water to the iceberg. Once there, Vespasian became their leader once again. This time, however, he did not lead them for Nero. With loud bold voice he led their singing:

> Forty soldiers wrestling for Thee, O Christ.
> Forty soldiers wrestling for Thee.
> We claim for Thee the victory
> And from Thee the crown of life that never fades away.

The determined witness of his men about what Christ had done for him left the repentant Vespasian with no choice but to enlist in the army of that one King of all kings. He knew a good soldier, and he knew a good leader when he saw one.

The second tense of our salvation takes time and committed consistency. It calls for dedication, and it bears results because it is finally and always the work of Christ through His Holy Spirit. "God hath from the beginning chosen you to salvation through sanctification of the Spirit and belief of the truth: Whereunto he called you by our gospel, to the obtaining of the glory of our Lord Jesus Christ. Therefore, brethren, stand fast, and hold the traditions which ye have been taught, whether by word, or our epistle" (II Thess. 2:13-15).

Salvation in this tense is a progressive word. It is like a journey. It is a journey. It is a journey to heaven.

SALVATION—FUTURE: WE SHALL BE SAVED

"Being now justified by his blood, we shall be saved from wrath through him" (Rom. 5:9). Salvation past is an accomplished fact. We were saved from sin's penalty through Christ's death on the cross. Salvation present is a progression. We are being saved from sin's power day by day.

Paul turns to an unusual Greek verb tense that speaks of something that is not yet but which is as sure as though it has already happened. "We shall be saved," he declares with certainty. We shall be saved from sin's presence when we go to be with God in heaven.

Jesus also speaks of salvation in this context: "He that endureth to the end shall be saved" (Matt. 10:22).

THE SPIRIT'S PARTNER

How can anyone know this marvelous salvation in all its tenses? John writes, "The Spirit and the bride say, Come" (Rev. 22:17). It is a myth to believe that we can achieve salvation alone. The "bride" is God's partner with the Holy Spirit in calling us to experience it all. The bride, in this instance, is the bride of Christ, the church. The church, that is the called out people of Christ, is not an optional extra for Christian growth, nor is the church an appendage to God's plans for us. The church is at the core of what God is doing in the world, and God gives the church for us.

The Bible clearly teaches that the church was God's idea from the very beginning. The best of churches have their faults, but that does not excuse us from participation in them, for the church is given as the Holy Spirit's partner in calling us to salvation in all its senses. Martin Luther, even after the church dispossessed him for his failure to recant his Ninety-five Theseis, was often heard to say, "The church, though she acts like a whore, is still my mother." Luther acknowledged that even though the church in his time was far from perfect, it was the means by which he had come to be nurtured in Christ and the gospel. The church is still God's only idea for the world. To the church alone has He entrusted His plan of saving lost people. "The Lord added to the church daily such as should be saved" (Acts 2:47).

The term *sacred discontent* has taken on new meaning in our generation. To have a critical spirit about the church is seen in some circles as a mark of elevated spirituality. Those who criticize the church seem often to forget that by her very nature she has a dual nature. She is at the same time Christ's and ours. The bride is His, but she is composed of sinners. The danger of sacred discontent, however, is that it subtly becomes self-serving. What happened between Palm Sunday and Calvary Friday demonstrates how easily we human beings can forget good works and become harsh critics. Before we criticize the church, let us first take into account who owns her and the price He paid for her. Moreover, we need to ask what we ourselves have done and are doing to rectify her wrongs. He who sealed us with His Holy Spirit as the earnest of His good plans for us designed the church for our benefit. Do we really believe we can build a better church than He has done? Charles Haddon Spurgeon urged his students to never preach on hell without tears. We do well to apply the same rule to criticizing the church and to remember nothing is wrong with the church that God is incapable of fixing in His time and with our cooperation. That takes time plus patience plus grace like His.

PLODDING TOWARD THE PRIZE

Aesop in one of his best-known fables told about the hare and the tortoise. Perhaps you remember the story from your youth. The cocky hare bragged before the other animals about his racing ability. Finally, he challenged any of them who thought they might beat him to a race. The tortoise, the least likely of all the animals, accepted the hare's challenge. "What a joke!" the saucy hare responded. "Why, I could dance around you all day long and still win." The tortoise, unmoved and unafraid, made ready for the race. A course was fixed and a starting place was established. The signal was given, and the hare, as might be expected, darted rapidly out of sight. The tortoise plodded forward, doing the best he could. Soon, however, the hare stopped and looked back. The tortoise was nowhere in sight, and the hare, chuckling with self-confidence, lay down to have a nap. Meanwhile, the tortoise plodded on steadily. He was slow, but he was sure. Finally, the hare awoke from his nap just in time to see the tortoise crossing the finish line off in the distance. He was too late but not too hard of hearing to hear the cheers of the other animals as the tortoise claimed the victory, "Plodding wins the day!"

To endure demands fortitude, patience, stick-to-it-iveness, and holding out against suffering. To endure calls, finally, for victory and "a crown of glory that fadeth not away" (I Pet. 5:4).

"We shall be saved." The salvation that began on the cross of Christ with conversion goes on working within us through the continuous act of sanctification. That sanctification will be completed when God calls us out of this sin-filled world to live in His presence and in the presence of those we love and have lost.

This is salvation in three tenses, as Paul understands it. It is full and it is complete. Best of all, it does not rest upon who we are or what we can do. It all rests upon the finished work of Christ on the cross at Calvary. Its message is conferred upon us and confirmed in us by His Spirit, the Breath of Abundant Life.

In the meantime, our journey with Christ and the Breath of Abundant Life continues on. In the next chapter we will consider more biblical evidences of the transforming work of the Holy Spirit in the life of the Christian.

7

Our cutting companion

Fort Benning, Georgia, is perhaps the largest southern command post of the United States Army. Located near the city of Columbus, Fort Benning is the principal employment center for that part of southwestern Georgia and the nearby small towns across the border in Alabama. As one enters the base, one becomes aware that this is far more than some barracks square where soldiers come to practice marching and strut their stuff. Fort Benning is, in fact, a city unto itself, and what one encounters of the United States Army in the surrounding area is largely Fort Benning's overflow. Think of anything that you might expect to find in a city of approximately 150,000 people. You will find it on Fort Benning. Included on the base are five full-scale dental clinics, each staffed by as many as ten dentists. The United States Army knows that good dental care is important to military readiness. There is also a well-equipped hospital where a host of medical specialists practice their craft.

It was a pleasant Saturday evening when our son Gary's pager sounded as we paid for our meal at one of those fine barbecue places that dot the Southland. Gary, a graduate of the Dental School at the Medical College of Georgia, now in private practice, was, at that time, a civilian subcontractor who practiced alongside army dentists at one of the dental clinics on base. The screen on top of his pager told him he was needed at the base hospital emergency room. This was Gary's weekend to take calls from soldiers whose dental needs could not wait until the dental clinics opened again on Monday morning. After calling the hospital to confirm that he had received the page and ascertaining that this was indeed a genuine need, Gary invited me to make the trip on base to the emergency room at the hospital.

It was not hard to figure out which patient in the waiting area needed emergency dental treatment. A red, swollen jaw on a grimaced mug, even when it is carefully cupped in the large hand of its owner, is not hard to detect. It looks different from the broken bones and bandaged heads and most of the more common ailments one encounters in a place like that. If I may be so bold to say so, the patient's oversized countenance brought to mind some cartoon pictures I have seen of sufferers in dentist offices. The uniform of a Special Forces master sergeant does not hide the humorous look in such situations for mildly sadistic observers like me. Gary took one look at the chart that was waiting for him at the nurses' station and stepped into a back room to scrub and put on his surgical suit. A nurse beckoned the swollen-faced soldier, "Come on back, Sergeant. Dr. Holmes is ready to see you." The soldier, chin in his hand, followed her meekly. I thought, "There's something very leveling about a severe toothache that brings all ranks together."

Some time elapsed before the sergeant, his jaw diminished in size, returned to the waiting room. He stopped by the nurses' station to wait for the medication that was prescribed for him. As he waited, Gary also reappeared, now in civilian clothes once more. The soldier took one look at Gary, smiled, and said, "Doc, you have got to be the best dentist in the whole United States Army." It was a moment to make a father proud.

As we drove back home that evening, I asked Gary what was wrong with the sergeant's jaw that made it swell so much. He explained that his patient had first noticed his toothache a week before but, being afraid of dentists, had attempted to treat it through some self-administered non-conventional ways. Some of these had only served to worsen the situation with the result that a huge pocket of poisonous pus developed below the gum line. Now the potential existed for that infection to enter the bloodstream and spread throughout the body. This would likely result in severe illness and, in extreme cases, could be fatal. In response to my follow-up question about treatment for the condition, Gary told me that he had to surgically open the gum, clean out the infected pocket as much as possible, provide a means of drainage, and prescribe a strong antibiotic. I know Gary. I've watched him grow since the day he was born, and I know very well his innate reticence to hurt any living thing. I asked him if cutting open the master sergeant's gum was not a procedure he found difficult. His reply stays with me, for Gary also has a quick-witted side to his personality: "Nope. Sometimes you've gotta cut 'em to cure 'em!"

YOU'VE GOTTA CUT 'EM TO CURE 'EM!

"Every branch in me that beareth not fruit he taketh away: and every branch that beareth fruit, he purgeth it, that it may bring forth more fruit" (John 15:2). Jesus says that His Father is the gardener who cares for the branches that are connected to the true vine. Our job, having been engrafted to Christ at conversion, is to bring forth fruit. That was the Father's intention from the very beginning. So those who make only a superficial commitment will be separated completely while others will be pruned. This cutting is a necessary thing. In Gary's words, "You gotta cut 'em to cure 'em!" To leave fruitless branches does more than accommodate worthlessness. It also risks allowing the growth inhibitor, whatever it may be, in those branches to infect the rest of the vine. If that is allowed to happen, the whole vine may be lost or permanently damaged.

God's instrument in promoting the growth of His vineyard in this necessary manner is the Holy Spirit, the Breath of Abundant Life. Jesus distinguishes between two kinds of cutting. There is a cut that cures and a cut that enhances strength.

The first is the cutting that results in complete separation. The Greek used is *airo*. It conveys the sense of cutting loose and removing. Branches that are completely fruitless are cut off at the trunk because there is something seriously wrong and irredeemable about them.

The second cut Christ speaks about is encompassed in the Greek word *kathairo,* which means "to purge." The idea here is to promote strength. This word comes from the same Greek root as the idea of atonement. This is not the cutting of separation but the cutting that strengthens, the cut that cures.

Even though I have lived in rural Mississippi, California, and Pennsylvania, three areas where grapevines grow and grapes are produced for jelly and wine production, I must confess that I do not know much about how to

103

grow healthy grapevines. My father, however, was for many years a rose fancier, and I learned much about the growth principles for roses from him. What he taught me from roses served later to enhance my understanding of the covenantal concept of our engrafting into Christ. It also helps me to better understand what Christ is speaking about in John 15.

My dad spent a lot of time with his roses when I was a boy. Some of my best childhood memories come from those hours when I followed him through his rose patch. Sometimes Dad did what looked like brutal surgery with his sharp rose clippers. He pruned away branches that were obviously decayed. He also, on occasion, pruned away branches that were still green and looked alive and well to my untrained eye. As he did, he patiently answered my inquisitive nature by explaining that what he was doing was good, for the whole bush. The branches that were green looked good but they had no bud beginnings on them. They would produce no flowers, he told me. They would eventually rot and send their poison through the entire system. He was making the cut that cures.

Another day, Dad explained why he was cutting away branches that had buds on them. "Why not leave them there and get more flowers?" I asked him. He explained that if he allowed every rosebush to bear all the flowers it could, none would ever reach their full potential for beauty. The result would be a lot of scrawny roses. On the other hand, by concentrating all the strength of the plant in a few blooms, he would produce finer quality, full-bodied roses that would make us all proud. "If you want the best roses," he said, "you must be content with fewer blooms on each rose bush. It's quality we want, not quantity." Dad was right. I do not doubt that what is true for roses is true for other kinds of plants and vines as well. I have seen it work in vegetable gardens.

It is also true for us. If we will grow into the full measure of spiritual maturity God has in mind for us, the pruning must happen. "Leaving the principles of the doctrine of Christ, let us go on unto perfection" (Heb. 6:1). "Let us go on unto perfection" is a call to progressive spiritual maturity. It is a call to spiritual advancement.

THE SPIRIT OF JUDGMENT AND FIRE

God's Spirit has many different ways of promoting that advancement. Not all of them seem initially pleasant. Isaiah speaks of this work of the Holy Spirit in terms of judgment and fire: "The Lord shall ... have purged the blood of Jerusalem from the midst thereof by the spirit of judgment, and by the spirit of burning" (Isa. 4:4).

There is a time coming when Messiah will rule the earth and evil will be no more. The distinctive mark of His citizens in that new day will be their righteousness. This is the time of preparation for that. The preparation is taking place now in the lives of each of His true followers.

In the Authorized King James Version of the Bible, the word spirit begins with a lowercase letter s. Some newer translations follow this pattern as well. This might cause one reading the passage to assume that the "spirit" referred to is not the Holy Spirit. It is important to remember, however, that the original Hebrew language in which Isaiah writes makes no distinction between uppercase and lowercase letters. As a result, when our English translations use the small s as a preference over a capital S, that is purely the decision of the translators. The same Hebrew word is employed here as in Genesis 1:2, "The Spirit of God moved upon the face of the waters." Thus, I believe that the capital S belongs here because the Spirit referred to is the same Holy Spirit, the Breath of Abundant Life. What is more, the New Testament appears to reinforce this opinion, as we shall see presently. I am not alone in this conclusion. The late Dr. R.A. Torrey first brought it to my attention some years ago in a sermon of his I was reading at that time.

THE SPIRIT OF JUDGMENT

We live in a time that is in many ways similar to that of Elijah in ancient Israel. In fact, in other places I have called this era of American history "These Elijah times." It is an era of many Baals, or false gods; a time of spiritual fog and of amazingly rapid moral decay that has taken place in a very short period of our national life. In such times, there is no fixed moral or spiritual code. Our society's limitations on human behavior and sin, if there are any at all, are often self-determined. Sometimes, socially acceptable moral standards are prescribed by popular opinion polls.

The evidence of this was seen clearly when the Monica Lewinsky scandal made news. The behavior attached to that scandal, and admitted to by both parties, was such that it would have repulsed almost any earlier generation of Americans and caused any public figure guilty of such sins to leave office in disgrace. However, given that the opinion polls indicated that President Bill Clinton was very popular, many Americans decided that he should be allowed to remain in office. The United States Senate, which only a year or so before had forced one of its own members from office for similar behavior that was not even proved at the time, could not muster the necessary votes to impeach the president. Such times, you see, make it unpopular for public figures to judge or condemn immoral behavior. The result is that the people we elect to lead us become followers of what they believe to be the opinion of the masses.

JUDGMENT AND TOLERATION

"Let us not judge! This is the age of toleration! Live and let live!" These statements are representative of the kinds of declarations uttered in many quarters in the United States today. On the surface they sound appealing, even to some Christians. It is easy to be tolerant of the improper principles and behavior of other people only when you have no convictions of your own. Don Shula, former coach of the Miami Dolphins, in his book *Everyone's a Coach* says, "The problem with most leaders today is that they don't stand for anything. Leadership implies movement toward something, and convictions provide that direction. If you don't stand for something, you'll fall for anything."

UNCHANGING STANDARDS

God the Holy Spirit does not have that problem. His holy standards are not subject to whims because they do not consider popular opinion, no matter how strong the polls. His judgments are neither changed nor changeable. The Spirit's judgments are set for all time. "The grass withereth, the flower fadeth: but the word of our God shall stand for ever" (Isa. 40:8).

When Isaiah speaks about "the Spirit of judgment," his thoughts are in line with what Jesus had in mind when He said of the Holy Spirit, "When he is come, he will reprove the world of sin, and of righteousness, and of judgment: Of sin, because they believe not on me; Of righteousness, because I go to my Father, and ye see me no more; Of judgment, because the prince of this world is judged" (John 16:8-11).

Dr. Karl Menninger, whose book *Whatever Became of Sin?* first drew my attention some years ago to this Baal spirit in our generation, tells about a fellow who stood on a busy corner of the Chicago Loop one evening at rush hour. As people hurried by, he would point at one after another and intone rather loudly the single word, "Guilty!" He did this repeatedly and was ignored by many passers-by. Perhaps they thought that was the best way to respond to such a fellow. Perhaps some thought he must have been speaking to someone else. One man to whom he pointed, however, immediately turned to his companion and asked, "But how did he know?"

In the same way, the Holy Spirit is standing near and whispering a similar judgment on each of us. The Lord, through His Spirit, is calling to acknowledge that we are wrong. He does it not with malice but with amazing love. I know because Scripture says so, and I know because I speak from personal experience. There have been many times in my own life when the Spirit has whispered such a warning to my heart.

A Talking Machine

There was one time in particular—As the minister of a large congregation in a major southern city, I was in great demand as a preacher and conference speaker, but in my own soul I felt continually dry and barren. I felt I had nothing left to give, but addicted to the popularity of the moment and blinded by personal ambition, vanity, and pride, I kept on accepting invitations to speak and preach anyway. A critical spirit, self-centered anger, fear of failure, and love of praise took control of me. It never struck me as odd that while I was a popular speaker with other ministers and conference organizers, there was no evidence of lasting fruit from my ministry. More important, the fruits of the Spirit, "love, joy, peace, longsuffering, gentleness, goodness, faith, meekness, temperance" (Gal. 5:22-23), were either non-existent or so scarce that they were nearly impossible to find. I was tired all the time. My preaching deteriorated. Inside, I felt as though I was no longer a preacher of the gospel but some kind of talking machine. My attitude, especially near those closest to me, deteriorated rapidly. I became increasingly tense and did not respond well in any number of situations that called for patience and calm. I was lacking any sense of the abundant life Christ had come to give me (John 10:10).

Believing "a change is as good as a rest," I thought a new pastorate might revive my spirit. It was not hard to find one. In fact, one came looking for me. Not only did the change not prove restful; it compounded the pressure I was feeling because it was a situation for which I was not a good match. Even then I determined I could "make it work" and set about working even more feverishly. I could not see that I was like a laboratory rat on a wheel. I could run faster, but I was not going anywhere. The tension within me mounted almost daily. Instead of trusting God, I began to try to work things out my own way. One mistake seemed to aggravate another one until soon, largely in anger, I initiated the process that led to my resignation. I seriously contemplated leaving the ministry of the church altogether and re-entering the business world. There was no peace in that idea either.

After a while I sought the counsel of a much-trusted Christian friend, Dr. Jim Mallory. He said, "I could prescribe medication for someone in your condition, but it will alleviate only the symptoms. What you really need is to find the inner peace I've heard you preach about many times."

At first, his words cut me to the core. He was prescribing my own medicine. In my consciousness I heard his words saying, in effect, "Physician heal thyself!" What an indictment to hand down against someone convinced that his popularity on the speaking circuit was sure evidence he was one of God's choicest servants! My initial response was to reject Dr. Mallory's counsel. However, as time passed I was drawn increasingly to recognize he was right. I was guilty as charged. His was a cut that began the healing process.

In the months following, I begged the Holy Spirit in prayer to show me what was wrong in my life and how it might be corrected. Soon the invitations to speak and to travel dried up somehow and allowed time, in God's grace, to tap again into Jesus as the joy of life and spring of living water that never goes dry. I had forgotten Him in the rat race of my own Christian busyness.

As I read the Bible, listened to and sang great hymns of praise during long mountain walks, prayed, and confessed my sins to Christ, a renewed sense of His forgiving, loving grace welled up within me. I realized there were things in my life that needed to be cut out (the cutting of separation) and there were others that needed to be cut back to allow me to focus on what God wants me to do for Him (the pruning that strengthens). I made myself accountable to a group of Christian friends. For at least the time being, they would have the final say in any assignments I accepted. Slowly, but surely, I came anew to see the truth of His wonderful promise: "He that believeth on me, as the scripture hath said, out of his belly shall flow rivers of living water. (But this spake he of the Spirit, which they that believe on him should receive" (John 7:38-39). I know the convicting, judging power of the Holy Spirit and can attest that it comes for our good. I know out of personal experience that he is the Breath of Abundant Life.

THE BURNING SPIRIT

Isaiah also speaks of him as "the spirit of burning" (Isa. 4:4). What does he mean? Matthew helps us see the answer: "He shall baptize you with the Holy Ghost, and with fire" (Matt. 3:11). On Pentecost, "there appeared unto them cloven tongues like as of fire, and it sat upon each of them" (Acts 2:3).

Gary Lombard is a big man by any standard of measurement you want to apply. For years before he retired, Gary made his living working for the railroad. He and Helen, his wife, still live in Mobile, Alabama. Gary knows more than trains. He knows a lot about gold too, for you see Gary's hobby is goldsmithing. Give him your old gold and tell him what you want to make of it and Gary can do it. Once Barbara and I gathered up all our old gold—it was not a lot—and took it to him. There was gold from jewelry we had grown tired of and a part from an old watch that didn't keep time anymore. There was even a piece of gold from a gold filling a dentist had removed from my

109

mouth once. We asked Gary what it might become. He showed us some ideas, and we chose a new ring for Barbara. Would there be enough? Gary thought there would but said he would not know for certain until the gold was refined. He allowed us to watch the refining process. All our old gold was put in a crucible and subjected to a fire whose heat ran all the way to seventeen hundred degrees Fahrenheit. At that heat the gold melted into a liquid. Soon tiny black and gray specks of dross appeared floating on the surface of the melted gold. The heating process, Gary explained, causes the dross to rise to the top where the goldsmith can clean it away.

"He shall sit as a refiner and purifier of silver: and he shall purify ... them as gold and silver, that they may offer unto the Lord an offering in righteousness" (Mal. 3:3). Job says in the face of his friends' misunderstanding and false accusations, "When he hath tried me, I shall come forth as gold" (Job 23:10).

The Holy Spirit of God, the Breath of Abundant Life, brings fire into our lives to remove the dross in our character and make us more like we were meant to be. Job understands that if we are believers all our sins are forgiven because God's forgiving and purifying are sufficient. If, like Job, we sincerely seek to know God and do His will, we can withstand false accusations. Eventually, in the power of the Holy Spirit, we will be vindicated and restored.

MEN LIKE GOLD

Not far from here there are still remnants of the old steel mills that once dotted the edges of the Monongahela River. The biggest name in Pittsburgh steel was Andrew Carnegie. Carnegie, a Scotch Presbyterian from Dunfermline, came to live near Pittsburgh as a twelve-year-old immigrant lad. He took a job that paid him $1.20 a week. From there he took a variety of jobs, often two or three at one time, and invested his money in railroad cars, bridge building, gold, and steel. He built up one of the world's great steel companies. Fifty years later, he was giving away a third of a billion dollars of his own money.

Andrew Carnegie had a reputation for expecting those who worked for him to work hard too. When they did, he rewarded them generously. At one point he had 43 millionaires working for him. A newspaper reporter from Chicago once asked him why he had hired so many millionaires. Andrew Carnegie corrected that misperception. He said that none of those men was a millionaire when they started working for him. Rather, he explained, they became millionaires by working for him. The reporter's follow-up question was, "How did you develop these men into persons of such value that you made them millionaires?" The canny Scot, with a trace of the Dunfermline burr still in his voice, replied, "I realized early on that there are certain important similarities between developing men and processing gold. When gold is mined, it is found in great amounts of dirt. Often a lot of dirt has to be removed just to capture a little bit of gold, but it is well worth while. One does not go out mining for dirt, however. One goes out searching for the gold, and when he finds it, he knows the dirt must be burned away if the gold's true value will ever be appreciated."

"The Spirit of fire" is God's instrument for mining the gold in us. He does not go out looking for the dirt, but He knows the dirt must be burned away if our gold will ever shine. He permits our dirt to be removed in a variety of forms, including hardship, brokenness, suffering, illness, trials, and testings of many kinds. Accept the fire when it is turned toward you and come to appreciate it. It will burn away the dirt so that your shining beauty might be revealed. No one ever grew into the man or woman he or she was made to be without going through the fire.

FIRE RE-ENERGIZES!

"Stir up the gift of God, which is in thee" (II Tim. 1:6). For "stir up" the Greek is *anazopureo,* a verb meaning "re-kindle." This, too, speaks of the Holy Spirit's fire. General William Booth, founder of the Salvation Army, called together a few of his fellow workers on one occasion and charged them in these words, "Young men, take heed of the fire in your own hearts, for it has a tendency to go out."

When I first heard that report about General Booth, my mind drifted to that part of Bunyan', *The Pilgrim's Progres,* where Interpreter shows Christian a small fire burning against a wall. Although a man continually douses the fire with water, the fire is not extinguished. In fact, it only burns hotter. Interpreter says to Christian that the man pouring the water is the Devil. Then he reveals why the fire will not be doused. On the other side of the same wall stands another man who pours a continuous stream of oil on it feeding the flame. "This is Christ," explains Interpreter. "The oil of his grace continually sustains the work that has already begun in our hearts." The Spirit is Christ's fireman. He it is who stirs up the flame in us that will go out all too easily if left unattended.

THE GREAT EXPOSITION!

Fire does something else. Gary Lombard demonstrated it for us that day in his goldsmithing workshop. Fire exposes falsity. Its heat enables the goldsmith to separate real gold from imitation gold. The "Spirit of fire" quickly determines what about our relationship with Christ might be unreal. "Every man's work shall be made manifest: for the day shall declare it, because it shall be revealed by fire; and the fire shall try every man's work of what sort it is" (I Cor. 3:13). Paul says that when Christ returns as judge of all the earth, His fire shall test the work of every person in the world. What Christ will do when He returns, God's "Spirit of fire," the Breath of Abundant Life, is doing now with each of us. Exposing us to ourselves, He reveals our true nature, showing us sides of our personality we have often not been aware of before. There is an insincerity and phoniness about all of us that needs to be revealed in the fire. That revelation may be a painful experience, but it is a necessary one if we are ever to achieve genuine glory. When fire comes your way, avoid the temptation to run away too quickly. Ask yourself rather why the fire might have come your way. Perhaps it is permitted to enter your life so that you may be made better for Christ's service.

During those long mountain walks that I took alone with God's Spirit, He showed me elements to my own personality and style that needed to be done away with. I saw my unrighteous anger and ego in a new light. I realized I was self-centered in a way that a minister of the gospel ought never to be. It was not easy to accept these truths at first, but I wanted above all else to be honest with myself and with God. Jesus had said, "If ye continue in my word, then are ye my disciples indeed; And ye shall know the truth, and the truth shall make you free" (John 8:31-32). I needed to be set free from whatever it was within me that kept me from knowing the joy Christ promised and which I had not known in some time. What I did not expect to find was that the same truth that sets us free often first breaks our hearts. My heart was broken at the way my life had been headed.

Sometimes, as hard as it may be, even heartbreak is for our good. Sometimes God must allow it or direct it our way because He loves us. "For whom the Lord loveth he chasteneth, and scourgeth every son whom he receiveth" (Heb. 12:6). Difficulty is a hard schoolmaster but a good one. When God wants to use someone, He prescribes a course of preparation that usually includes some bitter lessons. He sends us through the school of hard knocks. Because of this experience, I am convinced today that though the Spirit's fire can be hard for us, it is easier to go through the fire now than it will be on that terrible and wonderful day when God's final fire will "try every man's work of what sort it is" (I Cor. 3:13).

PENTECOST AGAIN

So far I have been dealing with the Spirit's fire from what may be perceived to be an initially negative manner. So we turn now to consider, as it were, the impact of the other side of the Spirit's fire in us.

FIRE POWER!

Fire produces power. "There appeared unto them cloven tongues like as of fire, and it sat upon each of them. And they were all filled with the Holy Ghost" (Acts 2:3-4).

A preacher, according to an old story, got really roused preaching about the Second Coming. He cried out, "Lord, come down through the roof tonight and I'll pay for the shingles." Many a preacher, if he has not prayed that prayer, has harbored the sentiments of it in his heart. Real Pentecostal power, however, produces something more than momentary excitement. That day the disciples were all filled with the fire of the Holy Spirit they were empowered to witness more boldly than ever before. Just imagine! Three thousand people were converted in one day! We need to experience that kind of Pentecost again. It will happen when we invite the

Holy Spirit into our lives and into our churches with fire and we avail our-selves to burn out for the Lord of the church, Jesus.

FIRE HEATS

When I was a lad of about seven years, our family moved to a new housing development not far south of Belfast. We were among the first fam-ilies to locate there, and a great deal of construction work was still in process. Some of it was located directly across the road from our new home, and on some cold winter nights I would go and visit with the night watchman in his hut. I would gaze in wonderment as he drank his tea from a billycan that he heated on his fire. One night, I slipped away from our house with an old tin cup one of my uncles had brought back from the Second World War. In my imagination that night, I became the watchman's partner. When he poured his tea, I asked him if I might drink some with him. He poured some from his billycan into my tin cup. I could feel the heat of it travel into the cup's tin handle. When he took a sip, I took one too. It was the hottest tea I've ever tasted. As I think about it now, I can still feel it scalding the tip of my tongue. What made it so hot? It is no secret. He heated it the same way he always did on the coke fire that burned just out-side the door of that hut where he spent long hours alone each night.

FIRE RENEWS OLD THINGS

You stand in a blacksmith's forge. He takes a piece of scrap iron from a rusted pile of metal stacked on his floor. To the untrained eye, it looks dirty and worthless. What good could ever come of it, you find yourself wondering. He plunges the iron into his fire, and with his bellows he makes the flame blaze with new heat. Soon the rusted iron takes on a new color. It begins to glow, first a dull red then a bright glowing crimson. He with-draws it, and with his tools he shapes it into something new and useful.

See yourself in that useless piece of iron. How coarse and cold we can be by nature. Then Christ throughHis loving grace thrusts us into the furnace of His Spirit and our old rust burns away as we start to glow anew.

The greatest need of the church in our generation is for us to be thrust anew into the furnace where the Spirit sets us on fire. Perhaps this is never truer than in preaching. People speak of how great their preacher is, but in fact there are no converts under his ministry. How can that be? It can only be because the fire of God has not been given freedom to melt cold hearts and burn away their dross. May God give us a new day of spiritual glowing that we may experience spiritual renewal in this generation.

Fire Illuminates and Enlightens!

Benjamin Franklin gets credit for many things, but not many people know how he initiated a program for lighting the streets of Philadelphia. In order to convince the people of his potholed, rough stony road neighborhood about the advantages of good street lighting, Ben Franklin bought an attractive lantern. After carrying it home, he polished the lens and placed the lamp on a specially made bracket in front of his house. Each evening at sundown, Ben lit the wick. Its flame, enlarged in brightness by the sparkling lens through which it gave off light, impressed his neighbors. It created a sense of warm glow in front of the Franklin house. Moreover, its light made potholes and rough spots on the street easier to see in the darkness with the result that fewer people or horses stumbled. Soon a neighbor purchased a lantern and followed Ben Franklin's example. Now there were two. A third did the same thing. Soon there was a fourth, and a fifth, and a sixth. It was not long before the whole street where Ben Franklin lived was illuminated. It was the pride of the city. Residents from other districts came by to see and soon copied Ben Franklin's idea. It was not long before the whole City of Brotherly Love was known across America as the first city to have streetlights. It all happened because one man allowed his light to shine.

"He was a burning and a shining light" (John 5:35). Jesus is speaking about the radiant light of John the Baptist and its impact on other people who became Christian disciples because of it. Every bit of light in the world finds its origin in fire. In John's case, that fire was the fire of the Spirit in him. When a Christian welcomes God's Holy Spirit, the Breath of Abundant Life, and gives Him free reign in his or her heart, amazing things come to light. Dark burdens become easier to carry in the light of Christ's love. Dark thoughts are exposed and brought into the light where they can be recognized and dealt with in the Spirit's fire. Dark deeds are unveiled that we might be delivered from them and redeemed from the scrap heap of life. The formerly dull sentences of the Bible come to life in new and won- derful ways as the firelight of the Spirit shines through every page. People who live in darkness see the difference He makes in us and are attracted to the light of life. "Let your light so shine before men, that they may see your good works, and glorify your Father which is in heaven" (Matt. 5:16).

On the outer banks of North Carolina not long ago, we made a tour of lighthouses. We heard the tales of the lighthouse keepers whose little lights, made more brilliant by the magnifying glass behind which they shine, had saved the lives of thousands of sailors from shipwreck and helped direct them to safety. In a sense we who belong to Christ and have received His Holy Spirit, the Breath of Abundant Life, are God's lighthouse keepers for our generation. All around us there are many people—men, women, and youngsters too—who spend their lives foundering like ships on a storm-tossed sea. It is entrusted to us to carry the fire of the Spirit in our own lives that they may be directed to the one and only Light of Life, Jesus Christ.

Perhaps you are reading this book because you are now where I once was. It may well be that you sense Christ's abundance is missing from your life. I have learned that none of us walks so close to Christ that we are immune to that happening in us. "Let him that thinketh he standeth take heed lest he fall" (I Cor. 10:12). If you are there now, or if at some point in the future you drift off in that direction, allow me to tell you what made the difference in my life.

UNCONDITIONAL SURRENDER

The first step is a renewed total and unconditional surrender to Christ. You cannot, will not, resolve your situation in your own strength. The great likelihood is that you got here because your relationship with Him is not now, and perhaps never was, where it needs to be. You must come back to Him and give Him as much of yourself as you know. This calls for repentance. Biblical repentance has four components to it. The first is regret: I need to acknowledge where I am in my relationship with

God. The second is remorse: I need to see that the blame for where I am belongs to me alone. The third is restitution: I need, so far as possible, to make right the wrongs I have done. The fourth is recommitment: I need to return my life to God completely.

FAMILIAR FRIENDS

The second step calls for a renewed determination to spend time regularly in God's Word. That will not happen unless you resolutely determine to do it. If need be, take your schedule book and block off time to be with Him. Begin to read the Bible systematically. For me it was helpful to start with "old friends," the old basic truths of the gospel whose words were so familiar that I could quote them from memory. Reciting them has value, but for me it was important that I go back and read them again. "Ask for the old paths, where is the good way, and walk therein, and ye shall find rest for your souls" (Jer. 6:16). Read them and take them to heart. Those grand old promises are given for your good as well as for God's glory.

PRAYER: THE CATPIE FORMULA

Prayer is the third step. Prayer is much more than merely coming to God with a glib, self-focused spiritual grocery list. A determined life of prayer calls for six components. They are confession, adoration, thanksgiving, petition, intercession, and examination. Using the initials of each of these prayer components, C-A-T-P-I-E, I call this the "Catpie formula." Confession means acknowledging our sin before God. Adoration allows a time in prayer to praise God for who He is. In thanksgiving we express our gratitude to God for His care and provision. Petition means we bring Him requests that relate personally and directly to us. Intercession means we pray on behalf of others. Examination comes at the end of prayer because only as we have spent meaningful time with God in the other components of prayer are we able to examine ourselves in the light of His Word and the knowledge of ourselves we carry in our hearts. I find that the best way to do this is to pray through a brief passage of Scripture and then ask God to help me to see how I might bring my life into compliance with what it teaches. "Thy word is a lamp unto my feet, and a light unto my path. I have sworn, and I will perform it, that I will keep thy righteous judgments. I am afflicted very much: quicken me, O Lord, according unto thy word. Accept, I beseech thee, the freewill offerings of my mouth, O Lord, and teach me thy judgments" (Ps. 119:105-108).

SONGS THAT MAKE SOULS SOAR

Finally, make music a regular part of your journey back to God. For me the great faith hymns I grew up with have always provided a meaningful expression of the message of Scripture. Just as they have inspired saints down through the decades and centuries, they have both stirred and challenged my soul. Listen to them on tape and learn to sing along.

I bring these steps to you because they helped me find my way back to Christ in the power of His great Breath of Abundant Life. It is not important that you follow a particular order in doing these things. It is important that you either do these or create your own formula for regular fellowship alone with God. They come with my prayer that His Holy Spirit, the Breath of Abundant Life, will multiply their usefulness in the lives of many others.

What is the evidence that we have the Spirit? Does it even matter that we do? In the next chapter we will clarify a popular misperception and examine some ways that help us to determine whether the Holy Spirit's life is being lived in us.

8

Do you have the Holy Spirit?

Ted challenged the authenticity of Eleanor's relationship to Christ one afternoon while they discussed religion at the office. "The big difference between your Christianity and mine," he said, "is that I belong to a full gospel church. Only people who have the Holy Spirit can join our church." He paused and drew a deep breath before continuing, "Frankly, El, the people in your church need to get the Holy Spirit before they can understand what Christianity is really all about." Ted paused again and, as if to soften his words, added, "Don't get me wrong. I'm not saying the people in your church are not Christians. It's kind of like taking a trip on an airplane. Some people go first class and some ride coach. They all get there, but some just kind of get there better. Christians who have the Holy Spirit in their lives ride to heaven first class."

Is that true? Are there two classes of Christians? Are there Christians that have the Holy Spirit and Christians that do not? Does God play favorites? Are there grades of Christians? This chapter will explore these and other issues related to believers and the Holy Spirit.

"Paul having passed through the upper coasts came to Ephesus: and finding certain disciples, he said unto them, Have ye received the Holy Ghost since ye believed? And they said unto him, We have not so much as heard whether there be any Holy Ghost. And he said unto them, Unto what then were ye baptized? And they said, Unto John's baptism. Then said Paul, John verily baptized with the baptism of repentance, saying unto the people, that they should believe on him which should come after him, that is, on Christ Jesus. When they heard this, they were baptized in the name of the Lord Jesus. And when Paul had laid his hands upon them, the Holy Ghost came on them; and they spake with tongues, and prophesied" (Acts 19:1-6).

Some people make much more of these verses than what they say when they are understood in the context of the verses and chapters surrounding them. Ephesus, a part of modern Turkey, was an elite, cosmopolitan port city and a leading center for business, much like London or New York are today. It was a crossroads of the oceans. People journeyed through Ephesus to get to places all across the known world. That is no doubt why Paul made Ephesus the center of his third missionary journey and why it plays such an important part in his life's total ministry. The gospel had reached there in part through Paul's previous trips. He was the founding father of the Ephesian church. Yet a misunderstanding of Christ's message and fullness caused some Ephesian Christians to be stunted in their understanding of faith's fullness.

HAVE YOU RECEIVED THE SPIRIT?

These Ephesian Christians who claim they do not know the Holy Spirit may have come to Christ under Apollos, who also had a fruitful preaching trip to Ephesus. Yesterday, we attended the Pittsburgh Home and Garden Show. We marveled at the success of one salesman as we observed the number of people who walked around the show carrying his wares. Some people have amazing natural oratory skills. Give them a product and a platform and they can move a crowd to action. The old saying is that they could sell snow to Alaskans or sun to Floridians. Apollos was one like that. He arrived in Ephesus soon after Paul's previous visit and his well-chosen words, spoken with passion, found a ready audience. However, all was not well. Acts 18 notes that there were limitations to Apollos's preaching and teaching: "A certain Jew named Apollos, born at Alexandria, an eloquent man, and mighty in the scriptures, came to Ephesus. This man was instructed in the way of the Lord; and being fervent in the spirit, he spake and taught diligently the things of the Lord, knowing only the baptism of John" (vv. 24-25).

Apollos's preaching was solidly philosophical. He could argue a case for Christ against the devotees of other religions. He explained the gospel as best he understood it and called people to repentance and faith. It made sense. Paul's preaching, on the other hand, combined phi-

120

losophy and experience. Paul's leading question as to whether these Ephesians had received the Holy Spirit was directed toward their experience in Christ as opposed to their intellectual assent to his message. It was not a question about whether they possessed the Holy Spirit so much as whether they understood the ministry of the Spirit. They knew for sure that they had done everything Apollos had told them. They had heard the gospel and repented of their sins. Apollos spoke of John the Baptist to them and called them to be baptized, as John baptized, upon belief. Apollos's preaching resulted in people repenting and receiving forgiveness for their sins. When they confessed that, he baptized them with water. That was a symbol that their sins were washed away and that they believed in Jesus. This was, and is today, what the Scriptures call the washing of regeneration. It is a bona fide work of the Holy Spirit.

The Ephesians were believers in Christ. They were baptized Christians. Since belief comes also by the Holy Spirit, they must have received the Holy Spirit. Our Lord Himself taught, "Verily, verily, I say unto thee, Except a man be born of water and of the Spirit, he cannot enter into the kingdom of God" (John 3:5). The Ephesians who responded positively to Apollos's invitation had entered the kingdom. Yet there was another side to faith of which they were not aware.

The Greek text gives us a further clue to their situation: "Have ye received the Holy Ghost since ye believed?" "Believed" is in the Greek aorist tense. That indicates, as we saw in a previous chapter, an ended action, an accomplished fact, and a finished move. Another way to ask the same question is, "After your belief was completed, did you receive the Holy Spirit?" Paul's question is directed not toward conversion itself but towards a post conversion relationship that gives conversion ongoing life. This idea is suggested often in the book of Acts. There is a second baptism. It is not the baptism of belief but the baptism by the Holy Spirit. The second baptism for these Ephesian converts took place when Paul laid his hands on them: "When Paul had laid his hands upon them, the Holy Ghost came on them; and they spake with tongues, and prophesied" (Acts 19:6).

DOES GOD PLAY FAVORITES?

Does God play favorites? Peter says, "Of a truth I perceive that God is no respecter of persons: but in every nation he that feareth him, and worketh righteousness, is accepted with him" (Acts 10:34-35).

One story tells of a simple fruit laborer who came to America to make a better future for his family. As a believer, it was normal that he would start off on the right foot and go to church. He asked a new friend, who recommended a church that had an impressive looking building in the heart of the community. The minister there had a reputation as a great orator. The choir was well known for its musical ability. It sounded like a good place for a newcomer to serve Christ and grow in faith. When Sunday came, the new immigrant led his family there. Despite some language difficulties, they sang the hymns, joined their hearts to the prayers, and listened attentively to the preaching. Yet when the service was over, no one stopped to greet them and no one invited them to come again. Despite that, they returned the following week and for several weeks after that. They participated enthusiastically in the Sunday school, and the immigrant's wife offered to teach the children, although her offer received no response. They extended friendship toward those that were there but were quietly ignored. Several times as they left the service, the fruit laborer told the pastor of his desire to join the congregation and become more involved. Yet the pastor never called them and gave no indication of any pleasure at this prospective new addition to the church roll. Meanwhile, occasionally other new members were introduced to the congregation from the pulpit. The fruit laborer observed that each time a new member was introduced the pastor seemed to relish telling the congregation about the position each new member held in the business world or in the community. Finally, the laborer told the Lord about his frustrations in trying to connect permanently with that congregation. That night, in a dream, he imagined he heard the Lord tell him, "Don't be concerned, dear child. You are not alone. My Son and I have been trying to get into that church for a long time, but they don't want us either."

Does God play favorites? The answer is both yes and no. The Bible teaches us that God has favored human beings ever since creation. He has allowed us a relationship with Him and given us dominion over all the earth. We have favored status over everything else God called into being. Yet when it comes to the human race, the Scripture says, "The Lord is not slack concerning his promise, as some men count slackness; but is long-suffering to us-ward, not willing that any should perish, but that all should come to repentance" (II Pet. 3:9). God accepts all who come in response to His call and who revere Him and do His will.

Well, then, was Ted correct when he told Eleanor that some Christians ride first class while others ride "in the back of the plane"? No, he was not. Ted's words betray a common misperception in the ranks even of Christians about life in the Holy Spirit. Some people in the camp of Christ believe that some Christians have the Holy Spirit and some do not. Thus, they perceive that the worldwide family of believers is divided into two main groups. That is a false dichotomy. Sometimes it has led to a kind of spiritual one-upmanship in which some believers see themselves as better than others. Taken to extremes, this view has contributed to divisions within Christ's body. Yet such a position has no solid biblical foundation. When it comes to the Holy Spirit, the Bible plainly teaches that every believer in Christ has Him: "If any man have not the Spirit of Christ, he is none of his" (Rom. 8:9).

Nowhere does the Bible teach that the Holy Spirit will ever divide Christ's disciples. Nowhere does it say that there are two classes of Christians. Nowhere does it convey the notion that some Christians have the Holy Spirit while others do not. Among His people, God does not play favorites. The standard is the same for us all, "Repent, and be baptized every one of you in the name of Jesus Christ for the remission of sins, and ye shall receive the gift of the Holy Ghost" (Acts 2:38). The Holy Spirit is God's gift to us. He is not something we earn but someone God gives us when we confess our sins and turn away from them. Therefore, the vital question for Christians is not "Do you have the Holy Spirit?" The question that really matters is "Does the Holy Spirit have you?" That question, along with its answer, becomes the focal point of our next chapter.

GEOFF'S STORY

Geoff was a fine businessman I met soon after we arrived in a new church on the West Coast. He had an idea that he said, God gave him. He took that idea and, in time, developed a multi-million dollar company around it. He loved to tell the story of starting out first in his basement and watching his small business grow into a large corporation with several thousand employees. Geoff was a noted leader in his field and in our community. His peers elected him president of their national organization. God blessed Geoff's hard work both numerically and financially, and Geoff never hesitated to give God the credit for his success.

A number of Christian organizations benefited financially from Geoff's business blessings. As his pastor, I knew that he was quietly generous toward the Lord's work in a variety of ways. He was the sole supporter of several overseas missionaries. Out of his wealth, he made seminary education possible for a number of Third World ministers who could not have afforded it otherwise. He bought expensive hospital equipment and had it installed in a hospital in East Africa. As a result, children who might have died are alive today and their quality of life is enhanced immeasurably because of Geoff's inconspicuous generosity. So it was a bit surprising when Geoff dropped by the church one day and admitted to me that he was not sure if he was really a Christian. Someone who challenged him a few months before had caused Geoff to doubt his salvation because he didn't speak in tongues. "How can I know I have the Holy Spirit?" Geoff asked me.

"Sometimes I lie awake in bed at nights afraid to go asleep because I don't know," Geoff confessed. I asked him about his relationship with Christ. "Do you trust Jesus as your only Lord and Savior?" "Sure I do," he replied with a tone that indicated surprise at my question. I followed up with another one like it: "Geoff, are you living out your life fully in obedience to Christ with what He has given you materially and otherwise?" He said, as I suspected he would, that he was. Finally, I asked him, "Do you trust any of the things you have done for others to save you?" He said, "No way!"

124

"Then I have good news for you, Geoff" I said. "You have the Holy Spirit and He has gifted you and is using you to advance God's work." I went on to explain to him that speaking in tongues is only one gift the Bible says the Holy Spirit has given to believers.

Relax! Remember! Rejoice!

Have you been in Eleanor's place? Or maybe even Ted's? Has your commitment to Christ been questioned on the basis of whether or not someone else thinks you are a good enough Christian? The reverse side of that question must also be asked here: Have you challenged the authenticity of another believer's commitment to Christ? Have you faced Geoff's uncertainty? Do questions about the validity of your faith in Christ ever come to your mind? My advice to you is threefold: Relax in Christ. Remember who has saved you. Rejoice in His Holy Spirit.

Grace Saved His Soul and Sanity

It is said of Martin Luther that even in the aftermath of the Protestant Reformation when many of his devotees surrounded him with effusion, he, frequently doubted his salvation. Luther was overcome by his sense of his unworthiness and his personal failures and sins. The result was bouts of deep despair when he would repeatedly attempt to reassure himself by muttering quietly, "But I am baptized, I am baptized." Only a growing understanding of the biblical doctrine of grace brought peace to Luther's tormented mind. That grace that saved his soul also saved his sanity.

Almost every great Christian leader I know acknowledges that he or she has faced similar doubts. Some have told me they still face them. The reason we face such uncertainty is that we focus too much on our own shortcomings and too little on the sufficiency of Christ's grace.

A Painstaking Inside Perusal

Some years ago it was my privilege to meet and, for a brief time, minister to Mrs. Marjorie Redpath, the widow of Dr. Alan Redpath. The Redpath's daughter, Meryl, was a member of the First Presbyterian Church in San Mateo, California, where I was ministering. Mrs. Redpath had come to visit Meryl and her family. During that visit, she told me of an experience in the life of her husband, who has long been one of my faith heroes and ministry role models. I tell it here with Mrs. Redpath's permission.

Alan Redpath was a powerful expositor of the Bible. Although I had never met him, his writings have taught me a great deal about God's Word. His widow related that after a serious illness, her husband went through a lengthy period of doubting his faith. It was beyond his imagination how he could ever be a Christian. He knew he could never be good enough for heaven, or even to be a preacher. As time wore on, he found himself thinking the kinds of vile thoughts he had not thought in years. His thoughts so discouraged him that he prayed for God to end his life. At that low point he sensed God telling him that this experience was allowed into his life for two reasons. God's first purpose was to remind him that this was the kind of person—with all his potential for sinful thoughts and temptations that he thought were things of his past—he was and would always be but for God's grace. Second, God was using the experience to say, "I want you to replace every part of you with me, for the only good thing about Alan Redpath is Jesus."

The pain of this inside look was different from the pain of his illness for the great preacher, but it was a pain that brought cleansing and renewal. By God's grace, he came through his illness to some of the most fruitful years of his ministry. He was a physically healed man and a spiritually empowered man. His weakness was made strong in Jesus.

THE HARDEST PRAYER IN THE BIBLE

"Search me, O God, and know my heart: try me, and know my thoughts: And see if there be any wicked way in me, and lead me in the way everlasting" (Ps. 139:23-24).

These words constitute the hardest prayer in the entire Bible. When we get serious with Christ, they form a painful and necessary prayer for our lives. It is always easier to be honest about other people's sins than about our own. Self-searching is a necessary, yet powerfully painful, part of each of our lives. It always leads us to the same conclusion Alan Redpath reached.

The only good thing about us is Jesus! That was the truth for Alan Redpath. It is the truth for Leslie Holmes. It was the truth for Paul: "I know that in me (that is, in my flesh,) dwelleth no good thing" (Rom. 7:18). It is the truth for you, dear reader. It is the truth for all of us. The only good thing, the only thing about us that is of any lasting value, is Jesus.

LIVING IN THE FACE OF SIN

Paul writes his words to the Romans about having the Spirit of Christ as evidence that we belong to Christ almost immediately after confessing his own faith struggles (see Romans 7:14-24). He concludes that his salvation is not sealed by his good works but by Christ's sacrifice on Calvary. "There is therefore now no condemnation to them which are in Christ Jesus, who walk not after the flesh, but after the Spirit" (Rom. 8:1). His use of "therefore" designates his desire that we not skip hastily over the preceding confession that reminds us that even one so great as Paul lived in the face of sinful tendencies.

What about your life? What is there about you that makes you useful to God? Is it not true that without Christ there is nothing? The only good thing about any of us is that God by His grace has put the Breath of Abundant Life, the Spirit of Jesus, within us. This is the secret to Geoff's security as a Christian and of Alan Redpath and of Paul the Apostle and of each of us. Our sufficiency as Christians is not measured by any spiritual prowess, great wealth, or influential relationships we possess but by the completeness of Christ's amazing grace.

At the termination point of the renowned Burma Road in China's Yunnan Provinces it is hard to miss the splendid carvings of the Dragon's Gate Shrine. The images peer across the magnificent Dianchi Lake from near the top of a steep cliff. One of the sculptures is of Wenchang, China's god of prose and poetry. Legend says that the craftsman assigned to complete that particular image was a disciple of Wenchang. For years, the artist labored with painstaking care to create a perfect likeness of his master. It seemed to be working. Passersby often marveled at the emerging masterpiece until, finally, just before the image was completed one slip of the craftsman's chisel created a tiny blemish. No one else could see it, but the artist knew it was there. For the perfectionist artisan, that tiny flaw ruined the entire masterpiece. Overcome by self-blame, inward condemnation,

127

and remorse about having failed his master, the gifted craftsman stabbed himself in the heart with the offending tool and fell off the edge of the cliff to his death.

Such self-condemnation is no foreigner to Christians. Who among us has not made an erroneous slip? We all fail our Master, Jesus, time and time again. His Holy Spirit shows us the ways that we fail Him for that is part of His job. Then just about the time remorse and shame would take us down, the same Spirit reminds us that the splendor of Christ's love is such that He is the one who is creating the masterpiece in us and not we ourselves. Our God is the one who died and who demands no death from us, for His own death was all-sufficient to cover every flaw we will ever make. He is the Lord of new beginnings every time our chisel slips, for He waits with arms outstretched to forgive us and empower us to start over again.

Two Wings to Fly

Having said this, it is important also to say that Christ is not satisfied when we willfully continue in sin. The issue of human responsibility comes into the picture and gives the lie to the notion of carnal Christianity. We are saved fully by Christ. Gratitude, however, demands our cooperation with him that we may grow in grace. As surely as an eagle will never fly on one wing, so we shall never soar with Christ if we rest only on him. The heart of Christian living is submission, trust, and active obedience. By active obedience, I mean forward momentum in Christian growth. Salvation is a solo performance. Christ alone saves us. Growth in Christ, on the other hand, is like riding a tandem bicycle. It takes two to really get it going.

The whole notion of carnal Christianity is built on a false premise that fails to recognize this. Its defective foundation may seem to accommodate the pluralistic mindset and even the creeping universalism of our generation, but it will never take us to heaven.

Sin Free Living

Not long ago, at one of the Tuesday services of our church, I asked the congregation, "Does anyone here live a sin free life?" Then I added, "If you do, please come forward that I may shake your hand and congratulate you. You are the first person in history outside of Christ to accomplish this." Nobody came forward to shake my hand.

I was not disappointed. It was not news to me. Nor did I feel as though my ministry in Pittsburgh had been a failure. I believe we all knew that none of us could ever live sinlessly on this planet. "If we say that we have no sin, we deceive ourselves, and the truth is not in us" (I John 1:8). On the other hand, intentionally and uncaringly continuing in sinful behavior, to trample all over God's Commandments with no remorse, indicates that Christ is not our Master. The same is true when we settle for passive sinfulness such as that which says, "We all have our little sins." To be a follower of Jesus demands forward momentum. If we do not have that, then we simply are not disciples. That forward momentum is not natural. It comes only with the aid of the Holy Spirit.

CHILDREN OF HIS PROMISE

I am a covenant child. By that, I mean that I was born into a family that was grafted into the tree of God's covenant. As a child, unable to speak for myself, my parents made some promises on my behalf. One of those vows called for them to commit to bring me up in the nurture and admonition of the Lord. More important, they acknowledged that they relied on God to keep His promise to save me and that they knew I was helpless without that. As a result, even though I did not surrender to Christ until manhood, I was nurtured in the Christian faith as I grew toward adulthood. All through my life, in ways I failed to recognize until later, God was keeping His promise. That act by my parents did not make me a Christian, but it certainly gave me a head start in understanding something of what it means to be a disciple of Jesus. In fact, I rather suspect that in some ways it was a factor that kept me back from praying to receive Christ earlier than I did. You see, I understood from the teachings of my childhood that asking Christ into my life was no lightweight momentary experience. It demanded making some lifestyle changes that I was unwilling to make earlier.

That engrafting into the covenant happened for our family when a man I shall meet for the first time in heaven, my maternal grandfather, Willie Ferguson, came to Christ. That happened a few years before he died and many years before I was born. My grandfather was a convert when the W. P. Nicholson revival swept through Northern Ireland. His surrender to the Savior impacted his life and mine for all eternity.

DYING TO LIVE

William Patteson Nicholson, sometimes called "A tornado in the pulpit," took my homeland by storm in a Holy Spirit inspired revival early in the twentieth century. He preached Christ in plain language that working people could understand. Stories about him and his preaching style are legend among the people of Ulster. Thousands of people, men and women, young and old, trusted Christ and repented of their sins. It is said that so many employees of the Harland and Wolff Shipyard, where the *Titanic* was built, repented of their sins by returning tools and equipment they had stolen that that company finally was forced to declare an amnesty. With all their warehouses filled to capacity with this unexpected booty of repentance, there was no place else they could store the unanticipated bounties from penitent thieves. Such is the work of the Spirit when true revival comes.

My grandfather did not work at the shipyard, but he came solidly to Christ under Nicholson's preaching. His conversion changed the whole direction of our family. What Nicholson preached from the Bible, he illustrated out of his own experience. He would say, "One day W. P. Nicholson died. He died to his old self-will and pride in all his accomplishments." Nicholson reported how on that vital day he was walking along a street when he encountered a small Salvation Army band holding an open-air meeting. Nicholson felt the Spirit of God nudge him to encourage that band of Christian warriors. It was not Nicholson's idea of spiritual growth. He protested, "Lord, I'm an upstanding, conservative Ulster Presbyterian. As serious as these people are, many of my friends think they are fanatics. Lord, do not ask a quiet, decent churchman like myself to identify publicly with them! Sure and I'd be the laughingstock if it ever was told." All his arguing was to no avail. The Spirit of eternal life within him told W. P. Nicholson that God was unrepentant about the idea. Sheepishly, Nicholson made his availability known to the leader of the band. The Salvationist bandleader handed Nicholson a tambourine with a terse response, "Here. Play this." Nicholson dropped his head in hopes that any acquaintances of his who happened by might not recognize him. Alas, shortly thereafter the bandleader commanded, "Heads up! Forward march!" Now one man stronger, they began to march along the street playing hymns. W. P. Nicholson's hands were beating out a Salvation Army hymn, but his heart was raising a hallelujah chorus. The old W. P. Nicholson and his pride were put to death that day and the new W. P. Nicholson was born in the power of the Spirit, the Breath of Abundant Life. He had died to live.

That was the beginning of a new day not only for Nicholson but also for tens of thousands of others, including my granddad, who would surrender to Christ through his preaching. "For ye are dead, and your life is hid with Christ in God. When Christ, who is our life, shall appear, then shall ye also appear with him in glory. Mortify therefore your members which are upon the earth; fornication, uncleanness, inordinate affection, evil concupiscence, and covetousness, which is idolatry: For which things' sake the wrath of God cometh on the children of disobedience" (Col. 3:3-6).

The transformational power of the Holy Spirit through W. P. Nicholson still lives on years after the old preacher and just about all his converts entered heaven. It made its impact on my life, although I did not realize it until after I left Ulster and moved to the United States. I suspect his influence is still felt throughout the world as other sons of Ulster have gone forth to populate the earth with the good news of salvation by grace through faith. That, too, is how the Spirit works. From generation to generation He breathes out his abundant life. "Thou sendest forth thy spirit, they are created: and thou renewest the face of the earth. The glory of the LORD shall endure for ever: the LORD shall rejoice in his works" (Ps. 104:30-31).

Don't Let God!

Christ alone secures our salvation on Calvary's cross. He alone did all that was needed to pay the penalty our sins demanded. However, when it comes to the matter of our growth in Christ, mutual commitment is needed. Without W. P. Nicholson's surrender all that I have just told you would not have happened. Spiritual growth is not a one-sided effort coming to us like some bolt from the wild blue yonder. The seeking God is met by a searching soul. There is a human responsibility to developing the fruit of the Spirit as much as there is the divine initiative.

Before he prayed to receive Christ under the guidance of one of the partners in his medical practice, Jack drank heavily and lived an immoral life. For a while his lifestyle changed. People close to Jack noticed the difference. Some even asked him what had happened and he replied, perhaps somewhat flippantly, "I've let go and let God."

A few months later, however, Jack fell back into his old ways. He had to learn that "letting go and letting God" does not make a disciple. Some of Jack's new friends cared enough to pursue him. They showed him Paul's admonition to some easy believers in Colossae: "Mortify therefore your members which are upon the earth; fornication, uncleanness, inordinate affection, evil concupiscence, and covetousness, which is idolatry: for which things' sake the wrath of God cometh on the children of disobedience: in the which ye also walked some time, when ye lived in them. But now ye also put off all these; anger, wrath, malice, blasphemy, filthy communication out of your mouth. Lie not one to another, seeing that ye have put off the old man with his deeds; and have put on the new man, which is renewed in knowledge after the image of him that created him: where there is neither Greek nor Jew, circumcision nor uncircumcision, Barbarian, Scythian, bond nor free: but Christ is all, and in all. Put on therefore, as the elect of God, holy and beloved, bowels of mercies, kindness, humbleness of mind, meekness, long-suffering; forbearing one another, and forgiving one another, if any man have a quarrel against any: even as Christ forgave you, so also do ye. And above all these things put on charity, which is the bond of perfectness. And let the peace of God rule in your hearts, to the which also ye are called in one body; and be ye thankful. Let the word of Christ dwell in you richly in all wisdom; teaching and admonishing one another in psalms and hymns and spiritual songs, singing with grace in your hearts to the Lord. And whatsoever ye do in word or deed, do all in the name of the Lord Jesus, giving thanks to God and the Father by him" (Col. 3:5-17).

Like W. P. Nicholson, Jack too needed to die that he might live. He had to learn that overcoming sin requires determination on our part. We must be determined to live for Christ and be inflexible where the corrupt old ways are concerned for there is no room for them in our new life. We do not abdicate all responsibility for what we are becoming, leaving it to God alone to overcome our sins. We partner with God in the Spirit's power to intentionally put them to death. "Put off concerning the former conversation the old man, which is corrupt according to the deceitful lusts; And be renewed in the spirit of your mind; And that ye put on the new man, which after God is created in righteousness and true holiness" (Eph. 4:22-24).

Jesus said it was to be this way: "My sheep hear my voice, and I know them, and they follow me: and I give unto them eternal life; and they shall never perish, neither shall any man pluck them out of my hand" (John 10:27-28). The key phrase that many Christians somehow miss in this statement is the third one. The first phrase tells us that the sheep hear Christ. That is, we become aware that He is calling us. The second phrase says that He knows us. In other words, Christ is intimately familiar with who we are and what we are about. However, the evidence that we are now His is found in this third part of the sentence: "And they follow me."

FOLLOWING JESUS

The conjunction *and* is of incalculable significance in this context, for it challenges the whole notion of carnal Christianity. Carnal Christianity is the idea that one can call Jesus Savior without also making Him Lord. I recall many years ago a televised interview between a well-known Hollywood personality and Barbara Walters. The actor's marriage to an academy award-winning actress was the subject of many magazine articles. He and his wife made a handsome cover picture. One reporter described their relationship as idyllic. By show-business standards the marriage was long and regarded as an exciting example of the kind of love and wealth show-business couples could achieve together. The marriage broke up, however, when the wife fell in love with another man with whom she soon established a live-in relationship even before her former marriage was dissolved. That event, coupled with the announcement of their impending divorce, made news in many papers. In that interview, however, the man assured Ms. Walters that he and his now ex-wife were, in his words, "still the best of friends." He went on to say, "We will always be friends. She is a fantastic lady and can call on me anytime. In fact, she does call. We talk once or twice a month. Sometimes I call her too just to check on how she is doing and to keep her spirits up. And we end every call by saying to each other,'I love you.'"

On the surface, his comments sound like a mature response to an unpleasant circumstance. However, scratch the Pollyanna veneer of that situation and you quickly realize the falsity of it. It is built on an unsound premise that saying "I love you" while failing to demonstrate faithfulness and commitment is sound behavior. In short, that position lacks integrity.

SHEEP WHO ARE NOT SHEEP

There are people who call themselves Christians who describe their relationship with Christ in positive terms. They talk about loving Jesus. Their words sound good. Just below the surface, however, something is missing that makes their testimony weightless. "My sheep ... follow me," Jesus says.

"What if the sheep do not follow?" we may ask. The only sensible answer is, "What if they are not sheep!"

How do we know we are Christ's sheep? The answer is very simple: We know because we follow Him. We obey His Word. And the world knows because the product of our lives goes along with our words. "A good tree cannot bring forth evil fruit, neither can a corrupt tree bring forth good fruit....Not every one that saith unto me, Lord, Lord, shall enter into the kingdom of heaven; but he that doeth the will of my Father which is in heaven" (Matt. 7:18, 21).

JUDGING OR FRUIT INSPECTING?

It is important to note that Jesus gave us these words about bearing fruit soon after saying, "Judge not, that ye be not judged" (Matt. 7:1). On the surface His message sounds contradictory. A closer look at the context of the two statements shows that they are in line with one another.

Our Lord was telling His disciples that before they make any decisions about others they should first take a look at themselves, for they would be judged by the same standards they set for others. He means, "Clean up your own act first!" Having done that, we are equipped to examine the fruit of others but not to judge them. We can evaluate people but always remember that the final judgment of every life belongs to God alone. "Therefore judge nothing before the time, until the Lord come, who both will bring to light the hidden things of darkness, and will make manifest the counsels of the hearts" (I Cor. 4:5). In the meantime, we can, and should, be discerning about false testimony by examining the fruit that goes with it.

The Fruit that Tells Our Story

Not far from where I grew up is apple country. County Armagh soil, combined with the climate of that area, makes it ideal for growing apples. There are many other types of trees there too. A legend from that part of the world speaks of a leprechaun walking through a forest on a windy day and arriving at a fence that divided the forest from an apple orchard. Having climbed the fence, the leprechaun sat down to rest and listen for awhile to the rustle of the wind among the trees. As he relaxed there, he imagined he heard the trees conversing across the fence. A proud maple spoke first, "If your leaves rustled gently in the wind as ours do, you apple trees could make beautiful music like us and attract attention to yourself." The challenged apple responded, "We don't need to make noise to attract attention to ourselves for our fruit tells our story."

Some years ago, after I preached in a church in London, a man came up to me and said, "I've heard that Christianity in America is about three thousand miles wide and half-an-inch deep." He went on to explain that what he meant was that we Americans testify on our coins that we trust in God. Yet our depth of spiritual fervor, being rather shallow, gives the lie to what our money professes. Does what we believe have any effect on our behavior? Recent polls conducted by the Gallup organization indicate that there is little, if any, relationship between Christian belief and behavior in today's America. Professions of faith in Christ often are not followed by ethical performance in the business world or factory floor.

Is our fruit telling our story? Those findings are not a supportive witness to "In God we trust." When our Lord says, "Ye shall know them by their fruits," He is saying that the testimony of John and Jane Christian is told more by how they live than by what they say. "The fruit of the Spirit is love, joy, peace, longsuffering, gentleness, goodness, faith, meekness, temperance" (Gal. 5:22-23). The fruit becomes a checklist against which we can measure how well we are connected to the vine who gives us life and whose name is Jesus. Knowing that we cannot consistently bear it in our own strength, God has put the Holy Spirit in us in order that we may live it out. In the next chapter, we will learn more about it.

9

Does the Holy Spirit have you?

The last chapter and this one have at least one thing in common: They each have a question for a title. Chapter eight discussed the gift of the Holy Spirit, God's favor to all who believe in Christ. "Repent, and be baptized every one of you in the name of Jesus Christ for the remission of sins, and ye shall receive the gift of the Holy Ghost" (Acts 2:38). Notice, "Shall receive." For Peter there was no doubt, nor should there be for us. Paul had no doubt either: "If any man have not the Spirit of Christ, he is none of his" (Rom. 8:9). The "if" is a negative conditional certainty. If the Holy Spirit is not there, it is because Christ is not Lord.

This chapter is not about the gift but about the fruit of the Holy Spirit. Notice immediately the singularity of the subject; it is "fruit" and not fruits. The gifts of the Spirit are many, but there is only one fruit. Search the shelves of your local bookstore or any seminary library and you discover that much more has been written in recent years about the gifts of the Spirit than about the Spirit's fruit. That in itself may be telling about where we are spiritually in the church today, for the fruit of the Spirit is the warp and woof of what it means to live life in obedience to Jesus Christ. When someone comes to Christ sincerely and completely, that person begins to manifest changed behavior. That is the evidence of what God is doing inside that person. "They took knowledge of them, that they had been with Jesus" (Acts 4:13). Even the Sanhedrin had to acknowledge that something was different about Peter and John. That something was the evidence of changed lives.

Many years ago, my wife, Barbara, was involved in a minor fender-bender accident. It happened when a speeding driver made an illegal pass over a double yellow line. In the process of returning to the proper lane, the other driver misjudged her turn and collided with the car Barbara was driving. Although no one was injured, both cars received some damage. The other driver, even though her car was still mostly on the wrong side of the road, stopped and blocked the oncoming traffic. Despite repeated requests she refused to move her car. Someone called the local sheriff, and a deputy was dispatched to the scene. When he arrived, the deputy immediately recognized that the offending driver was in the wrong. Since her car was still straddling the double line, there could be no doubt who caused the crash. After confirming that no one was injured, the deputy sheriff took out his pad and moved toward the offending car, presumably to write a citation. He immediately recognized and greeted the offending driver and put his pad away. In a moment, he declared, "Both cars can be driven. Everyone can leave now." There was no citation written and no official report. Witnesses to the accident, recognizing that something was not proper, protested his instruction. It was not so much that they wanted to see someone cited for the accident as that they believed that proper procedure was not being followed. In response to their objections, he explained that the woman's father was a prominent local politician. "If I cite her," he said, "the judge would likely dismiss the charges because of her connections. It might even end up costing me my job." It was a clear case of the intimidation and abuse of political power. We had the damage to our car repaired at a local body shop. The damage was several hundred dollars and was covered by the uninsured driver provision of our insurance policy. We, of course, had to pay that portion of the repair costs the policy refers to as deductible.

Imagine our surprise when over two years later we received a check reimbursing us for that amount. It came from our insurance company with a letter explaining that they too had been reimbursed for their expenses. We learned later that the offending driver had come to Christ and was doing an act of repentance. Such is the work of the Holy Spirit. Things change when He enters our lives.

The Bible calls those changes "the fruit of the Spirit" (Gal. 5:22). The fruit, though one, has many facets. These facets are evidenced by a variety of positive and progressive character traits. Paul lists them in Galatians

5:22-23: "The fruit of the Spirit is love, joy, peace, longsuffering, gentleness, goodness, faith, meekness, temperance."

What Paul means is that when the Holy Spirit takes up residence in our lives there will be evidence that He is there. How can I get this fruit of the Spirit and how can I help its facets develop in my life? In this chapter, we will look at each facet in turn, using the order of Paul's list. At the end of each facet we will consider some helpful and practical ways that we can develop it in our lives. We begin now with the first one mentioned on Paul's list.

The Fruit of the Spirit Is Love

The Bible never defines love nor tries to grade it like eggs by its size. Four Greek words help to broaden our understanding of love. One signifies love that is centered on self-satisfaction. It is principally sexual in nature. Another word for love describes brotherly love. It carries the idea of reciprocity. A third Greek word describes familial love. It describes the special bond of love that exists between a parent and a child.

The love that the Bible speaks of in this verse is described in a far grander idea than all these words convey. It is suzerain love, which means it is the love of a greater for a lesser. This love says, in effect, "I love no matter what happens. "

BIGGER THAN PEGGY'S PAST

Peggy, a young woman I know, came to Christ out of a sordid relationship. She suffered physical and sexual abuse at the hands of her live-in boyfriend. As a new Christian, she knew she could no longer stay in that sinful circumstance. She moved in with some new Christian friends until she could find an apartment of her own. Her former boyfriend was outraged by her decision.

Three years later, Peggy sat in my study discussing her wedding plans to Ken, a fine Christian young man she first met at a church singles' retreat. She told me that when her former boyfriend learned she was engaged to Ken, he called and threatened her. He reminded her that he had once sworn that if she did not marry him she would marry no one. True to at least that one promise, he did call Ken and tried to tell him sordid details from the past he once shared with Peggy. Ken tried to politely end the conversation but finally believed he had no option but to hang up. When Ken drove up to Peggy's apartment that evening, she thought he had probably come to break off their engagement and end their relationship. No, that was not why he came. He came to check that Peggy was all right and assure her that all was well between them. Ken took Peggy in his arms and said, "I will always love you." "What about my past?" Peggy quizzed him. "You have no past with me, except what has made you the most wonderful woman I know." Ken's love was bigger than Peggy's past. As she told this experience to me, tears of joy filled Peggy's eyes. She knew that she had found someone who really loved her.

The love God demonstrates for us through Christ is like that. "God commendeth his love toward us, in that, while we were yet sinners, Christ died for us" (Rom. 5:8). The only parts of our past God holds on to are those He can redeem for His glory and our good.

This love not only loves despite the past, it looks out for the highest interests of its beloved. It is prepared to love both that which is beautiful and that which is not. It gives up its own and makes that which is not good better. It expresses itself without soupy sentimentality and considers others above itself.

This love of the Spirit, sometimes called "charity" in the King James Version of the Bible, is foundational evidence that the Holy Spirit has us. In Jonathan Edwards words, "more insisted on than any other virtue."[1]

Paul's first Corinthian letter provides a checklist of this love's qualities. From the list below, check how many of the qualities of this fruit you possess. Recognize, too, the ones you need to work on: __Charity suffereth long, __and is kind; __charity envieth not; __charity vaunteth not itself, __is not puffed up, __Doth not behave itself unseemly, __seeketh not her own, __is not easily provoked, __thinketh no evil; __Rejoiceth not in iniquity, __but rejoiceth in the truth; __Beareth all things, __believeth all things, __hopeth all things, __endureth all things. __Charity never faileth.

---

1. Jonathan Edwards, *Charity and Its Fruits*, (Edinburgh: The Banner of Truth Trust, 1998).

How do you measure up against these evidences of this biggest love of all through your life? If the Spirit has you, you measure up better than you have ever done before. No, you are not perfect yet. At the same time, you know you are improving. These signs of love are growing in your life.

How to Develop this Personality Trait Called Love

A peach tree grows not far from our back door. We enjoy picking the peaches when they are in season. Those peaches grow only when they are attached to the tree. The moment we pick them their growth stops. The same is true for us in the life of the Holy Spirit. We grow only so long as we are attached to Jesus, our "True Vine." He says, "I am the vine, ye are the branches: He that abideth in me, and I in him, the same bringeth forth much fruit: for without me ye can do nothing" (John 15:5).

The message is plain. If you want to experience this special Holy Spirit love in your life, stay close to Jesus. Read His word and spend time with Him in prayer. Put His instructions into action and watch his love grow.

The Fruit of the Spirit Is Joy

If the Spirit has me, I have joy. Joy, the opposite of misery, is the second fruit of the Spirit in Paul's list. No language has as many words for joy as does Hebrew. The idea of joy is transmitted by no less than thirteen Old Testament synonyms whose meanings convey the idea of possessing inward gladness, overwhelming mirth, or brightness of the heart that cannot be dimmed. "Thou wilt show me the path of life: in thy presence is fulness of joy; at thy right hand there are pleasures for evermore" (Ps. 16:11).

Joy Is Different from Happiness

Sometimes we confuse happiness for joy. The two may seem the same on the surface, but there are important differences between them. Happiness is a feeling. Joy is an attitude. Happiness is often temporary. Joy is permanent. Happiness depends on what is going on around me. Joy is the result of what goes on inside me: that is, in my heart.

Circumstances can steal happiness. Nothing can take away joy, for joy is an eternal fountain flowing from within me. Joy is God's gift to us.

GRIMALDI'S GRIEF

In 1835 a man visiting Florence, Italy, made an appointment to visit a physician. The doctor quickly discerned that the patient was filled with tension. He was uptight and complained of not having slept well in weeks. A thorough physical examination revealed that the patient was physically healthy. Experience told the medical man, however, that the patient's physical health would soon deteriorate if the emotional stress and tension in his life was not relieved. "Sir," said the physician, "you must learn to relax and enjoy life. Tell you what; there's a circus in town. Its star performer is a clown called Grimaldi. He is the funniest performer I have ever seen. Last night he had the people shaking with laughter. Go tonight and laugh with Grimaldi." The patient looked grimly into the face of his physician and said, "Doctor, I am Grimaldi!" He was able to put on a happy face and act like a clown, but he knew no joy.

There are a lot of people like Grimaldi in our world. Their external veneer hides their internal anguish and sense of purposelessness.

"How much money does a man need to be happy?" John D. Rockefeller had a ready answer for the people who asked him that question from time to time. "Always just a bit more than he has right now," Rockefeller replied. Ask people what would bring them joy. You will hear a lot of people say it would take winning the lotto or a new car or a bigger house or a face-lift or being famous or having power. History teaches us that these are not joy-bringers, although for a while they may bring happiness.

There is ample evidence that none of these things brings joy, however. Consider, for example, the famous, charming, handsome, and popular Lord Byron, who spent his life in pursuit of erotic sexual pleasure. His chase brought him the disease that finally took his life. Just before he died he wrote, "The worm, the canker and the grief are mine alone." Jay Gould was a multi-millionaire, yet as he was dying he said, "I suppose I must be the most miserable man on earth." Lord Beaconsfield was both powerful and famous yet concluded in a farewell letter to a friend, "Youth is a mistake; manhood, a struggle; old age, a regret." The obituaries almost daily carry the names of famous people, including some given star acclaim by the world, who take their own lives in abject misery.

How to Develop this Personality Trait Called Joy

How does true joy grow in our lives? By seeing all of life in the light of Jesus and His love. When we focus on the external circumstances around our lives, we soon lose our sense of Joy. This does not mean that we become otherworldly, like some kind of spiritual ostriches that bury their heads and pretend nothing around us matters. It does mean that we are not dependent upon appendages to our lives to bring us satisfaction. Joy is not in things but in us. It is in us because we are in Jesus.

The Fruit of the Spirit Is Peace

If the Spirit has me, I have peace for "the fruit of the Spirit is love, joy, peace," Paul writes. As a pastor I have observed people who look for peace in artificial anesthetics such as alcohol or other drugs.

Augustine of Hippo said it best, and we still quote him a millennium and a half after his death: "Our hearts are restless until they find their rest in Thee, O God." His words are as true and relevant today as they were the day he penned them. Jesus Christ says, "Peace I leave with you, my peace I give unto you: not as the world giveth, give I unto you. Let not your heart be troubled, neither let it be afraid" (John 14:27).

"Not as the world giveth," Jesus declared. There is no peace comparable to the peace Christ gives us.

Ask an unbeliever for a definition and chances are you will get a negative response: "Peace is the absence of war." That view betrays a defective understanding of human nature. I was born soon after World War II. Buildings in my hometown still bear the pockmarks of the air raids. I well remember the poverty and the rationing war can bring. War is an ugly thing. It is terrible. Yet there is something worse than war, and that is the man or woman or nation that believes that nothing is worth defending. Jesus still implores us to be peacemakers but not when the peace comes at any price.

Pure peace like pure joy is not external but internal. It can only come from God. Such a peace surpasses all human definitions of peace.

"The peace of God, which passeth all understanding, shall keep your hearts and minds through Christ Jesus" (Phil. 4:7). What makes that statement especially amazing is that a brutally whipped and dying inmate in a filthy, rat-infested Roman prison cell wrote it. After a lifetime of searching for peace, first by every external means imaginable and later as a missionary and church planter, Paul is able to say that peace, like joy, is not found in this world but in Jesus.

How to Develop this Personality Trait Called Peace

In a sentence, we grow peace through spiritual tenacity. Of this, the prophet Isaiah is very clear: "Thou wilt keep him in perfect peace, whose mind is stayed on thee: because he trusteth in thee" (Isa. 26:3). This is one of the clearest conditional promises in the Bible. Peace is assured to those who "stay" in God. The Hebrew verb means "to hold steadfast" or "to be resolute in our commitment." Let this thought control your mind and your life: You were made by God. You were redeemed by God. You belong to God. You owe your very being to God. "Let us hold fast our profession" (Heb. 4:14) and peace will grow in us.

The Fruit of the Spirit Is Patience

"The fruit of the Spirit is love, joy, peace, longsuffering" (Gal. 5:22). Patience, or longsuffering, is the Holy Spirit's fourth fruit according to Paul's list. If the Spirit has me, I have patience.

How Long Is Your Fuse?

I think I live in the city where all impatient drivers finally, somehow, end up. I love the story about the young woman whose car stalled in rush-hour traffic as the light turned green. All her efforts to start the engine met with no success. In only a few minutes she had a cacophony of honking horns filling her ears. The fellow in the car immediately behind her seemed to be the leader of the band. Gathering all the courage she could muster, she went to him with a proposal: "Since I can't get my car started, let's trade places. You go up and start my car and I stay here and honk your horn!"

Are you long-fused or short-fused? Is your temper fast or slow? Speaking personally, patience has been harder for me to learn than anything else on Paul's list. I am by nature a very impatient person. The story about the poor fellow who lay near the Bethesda pool for thirty-eight years before Jesus came has long convicted me. I would have never lasted that long. Either I would have pushed the people ahead of me out of the way, or I would have exploded like a total fool.

An anonymous (and obviously very patient) poet composed a wonderful little poem about an oyster:

There once was an oyster whose story I tell,
Who found that sand had got under his shell,
Just one little grain, but it gave him such pain,
For oysters have feelings although they're so plain.
Now, did he berate the working of fate,
Which had led him to such a deplorable state?
Did he curse out the government, call for an election?
No; as he lay on the shelf he said to himself
"If I can't remove it, I'll try to improve it."
So the years rolled by as the years always do,
And he came to his ultimate destiny: Stew!
And this small grain of sand which had bothered him so,
Was a beautiful pearl, all richly aglow.
Now this tale has a moral—for isn't it grand?
What an oyster can do with a morsel of sand!
What couldn't we do if we'd only begin
With all of those things that get under our skin!

How to Develop this Personality Trait Called Patience

The secret for growing patience is concealed in the wonderfully descriptive word for patience in the King James Version. That word is *longsuffering*. Patience, whether we like the idea or not, comes only through suffering. One of my minister friends claims to have never experienced any kind of suffering in his entire life. When he first told me this, it impressed me. Later, as I reflected on his testimony, I could understand why that man is very impatient. We cultivate patience not only through suffering but through suffering steadfastly. When trouble comes your way, as it surely will for all of us, respond to it by recognizing that God promises never to send suffering we cannot stand (see I Corinthians 10:13). When trouble comes your way, resolve to see it through. If you do, you will always be a better person on the other side. You will be better because you will be more patient.

The Fruit of the Spirit Is Gentleness

"The fruit of the Spirit is love, joy, peace, longsuffering, gentleness" (Gal. 5:22). When the Spirit has us, we are gentle natured.

The society I grew up in equated gentleness with weakness, femininity, and softheartedness. That, however, is not the picture the Bible conveys of gentleness. The Greek word is *praotes*. It means, among other things, "the ability to keep one's strength under control." As children, we sang a hymn about "Gentle Jesus, meek and mild." In my mind that created an image of Jesus as a pale-skinned, emotionally anemic wimp, which is, of course, anything but the truth.

Jesus was gentleness personified. With an infinitely soft touch, He cared for bruised reeds and broken hearts. He was never harried and never hurried with people in pain of any kind. His loving approach was, doubtless, part of their cure. He was gentle in saving an adulterous woman from death by stoning, yet bold enough to take a whip to those who abused His father's house. His was strength under control. He had the strength of character to be calm in the face of the Good Friday rabble. Yet He had compassion for a remorseful thief on a cross beside Him. Ultimately, because of His gentleness, Jesus won out. You see, the man who wins is not always the one with the Mr. Universe body. He is the one who can direct His passion the right way.

HOW TO DEVELOP THIS PERSONALITY TRAIT CALLED GENTLENESS

We cultivate gentleness by keeping in mind that God's image is present in every human being and that all creatures are His creatures. Thus, gentleness extends beyond human relationships and into the world of animals. Even a cockroach is God's creature!

146

The Fruit of the Spirit Is Goodness

"The fruit of the Spirit is love, joy, peace, longsuffering, gentleness, goodness" (Gal. 5:22). If the Spirit has us, we are good.

A happy Christmas ditty tells us to "be good for goodness sake!" Why? Because "Santa Claus is coming to town." Those words in context in that carol are not telling us to do good things for good reasons but because there is an implied expected reward. The Spirit's goodness is different. It is more about what we are than about what we do. Goodness is love, joy, peace, longsuffering, and gentleness in shoe leather. Dag Hammarskjold, the former secretary-general of the United Nations, once defined goodness as always living for others first. Charles Spurgeon instructed his students: "Do all the good you can, to all the people you can, in all the ways you can, as often as ever you can, as long as you can."

PEAS UP YOUR NOSE!

Prohibitions against bad behavior are not usually good motivators to good behavior. Good behavior based on a threat of punishment for bad behavior is built on a foundation that lacks integrity. Tell a child what not to do and expect that child to do it the first time he thinks you're not looking. That very thing will become the latest expression of forbidden fruit. A mother set out the ingredients to make vegetable soup, among them a packet of dried peas. Realizing that she was short one thing, the woman made a quick dash to the grocery store. Before she left home, she warned her children, "Don't put any peas up your nose." If we know anything about children, we can imagine what happened. The children were drawn to the peas by sin's powerful magnet. Mom came home to find each of her children with peas stuck in the very place they were forbidden.

We do good not because of negative motivation but because good is something we have become in the power of the Holy Spirit, the Breath of Abundant Life. The Spirit plants goodness inside us and watches it grow. We do good because He made us good.

How to Develop this Personality Trait Called Goodness

How is goodness grown? Only by the grace of God! Paul writes, "You, my brethren ... are full of goodness ... able also to admonish one another" (Rom. 15:14). In these words lies one of the keys to developing goodness. Because it is impossible for us to objectively grade ourselves on being good or evil, we can best grow this fruit by heeding the loving counsel of mature Christian friends. "Apply thine heart unto instruction, and thine ears to the words of knowledge" (Prov. 23:12).

The Fruit of the Spirit Is Faith

Faith is one of the first signs that the fruit of the Spirit is growing in a believer's life, for it is through faith that we are saved. If the Spirit has us, we have faith. "The fruit of the Spirit is love, joy, peace, longsuffering, gentleness, goodness, faith" (Gal. 5:22).

The Greek word translated "faith" is *pistis.* It is also translated "faithfulness." The fruit of faith is faithfulness, and that is the character trait that a life possessed by the Holy Spirit produces. What does faithfulness look like in human flesh? Faithfulness means doing what you said whether to a child or a king.

If you promised to be someone's friend, then don't be only a fair-weather friend. True friendships demand faithfulness.

If you told your children you would take them by McDonald's for ice cream after school, faithfulness to them and to Christ means you will take them there even if your day got complicated and off track because of other things.

If you promised your mother you would clean up your room, faithfulness to Jesus means you will do it even if your girlfriend calls on the phone to whisper sweet nothings you would really rather hear. Why? Because you said you made a commitment that preceded her call.

If you promised someone you would return a telephone call, faithfulness to that person as well as to Christ means you will return the call despite the fact that you don't especially like that person.

If you promised your marriage partner that you would always love, honor, and cherish him or her, faithfulness to Christ and your spouse means you will keep that promise always for better or worse, richer or poorer, in sickness and in health, until death doth you part.

If you told your boss you would accomplish some task, faithfulness to God and the boss means you will do it even if it means working unpaid overtime.

If you said your employees could have an extra day off over the Christmas holidays, faithfulness to God and to them means you do not renege on that promise even when it costs you more than you had calculated earlier.

Faithfulness means being dependable, and dependability means doing what I said I'd do even when it requires unexpected sacrifices on my part. That is what makes it such a vital evidence of the Holy Spirit in the believer's life.

Faithfulness, finally, is one of the few marks of the Spirit that brings its own direct reward. If you do all these things and others like them, one day you can expect to hear, "Well done, thou good and faithful servant" (Matt. 25:21).

HOW TO DEVELOP THIS PERSONALITY TRAIT CALLED FAITHFULNESS

Faithfulness comes from taking God's Word seriously in the sense of personal behavior patterns. We must learn to revere the Bible and its message and apply that message in practical ways in our lives. During the Exodus from Egypt, Moses chose men who were faithful, among other qualities, to be judges in the people's disputes. The key to all their qualities was that they revered God. We revere God when we constantly remember who He is and what He has done. If you want to cultivate the quality of faithfulness in your own life, this is what you must do.

The Fruit of the Spirit Is Meekness

What is meekness? Meekness is never weakness. Meekness is one of the most powerful demonstrations of the Spirit's strength we can ever show. It says we know we are not in charge of our lives and that someone infinitely wiser and all powerful leads us. The world outside Christ says, "Blessed are the strong, the canny, those who demand their own way and get it." Our generation puts a premium on self-assertion and self-promotion.

Jesus, on the other hand, teaches us, "Blessed are the meek: for they shall inherit the earth" (Matt. 5:5). The word for meekness comes directly out of the vocabulary of the animal trainers. A meek animal is disciplined to its master's commands. It has learned that what the master wants gets first priority in its life.

"He must increase, but I must decrease" (John 3:30). John the Baptist, who spoke those words, was one of the meekest men in all of human history. Yet he is one of the truly strong heroes in the Bible. He was no wimp. A rugged individualist, he ate locusts and wild honey for lunch. He even dressed in animal skins. That is a long stretch from quiche and Nino Ferragini! Rough and tumble John counted himself unworthy even of tying Jesus' sandal straps. Josephus, the noted first-century Jewish historian, writes about John's power and charisma years after John's enemies thought they were rid of him. According to Josephus, people still were emotionally moved when John's name was mentioned. Jesus' eulogy of John said, "Among them that are born of women there hath not risen a greater than John the Baptist" (Matt. 11:11). John was meek, but he was anything but weak. He challenged the moral standards of royalty. By his example, he teaches us that meekness is not frailty but potency. To be meek is to know that we operate on a limitless power that comes from above and to be humbled in that realization. Someone defined meekness by an acronym: *M* is for mighty. *E* is for Educable. *E* is for Emotionally stable. *K* is for Kind. If the Spirit has us, we are all these things.

How to Develop this Personality Trait Called Meekness

To develop this personality trait, first recognize what it is and what it is not. It is not, as has been said, weakness. To be meek is not to be a Casper Milquetoast. It is, rather, to be subordinate to our leader, whose name is Jesus.

The Fruit of the Spirit Is Temperance

"The fruit of the Spirit is love, joy, peace, longsuffering, gentleness, goodness, faith, meekness, temperance" (Gal. 5:22). When the Spirit has us, we are temperate, disciplined, or sound minded. "For God hath not given us the spirit of fear; but of power, and of love, and of a sound mind" (II Tim. 1:7).

150

Sober Reflection

Someone said, "When you wrestle with a pig, you both always get dirty—and only the pig enjoys it." Bad habits are pigs. To continue in them leaves us feeling dirty. We should not wrestle with them but declare them dead in Christ's strength. A great injustice has been wrought upon this word *temperance* by our current confinement of the word to the world of alcohol abuse. That limited notion of temperance comes out of the Temperance Movement that arose in response to widespread public drunkenness early in the twentieth century. The word t*emperance* is far bigger than that, however. We can be intemperate with many things. I have a friend who owns a red Ferrari (maybe I'm just jealous). That Ferrari is the pride of his life. He told his fiancée she could use anything he had except his Ferrari. We can be just as intemperate about cars or clothes or sports or sex as a drunk who falls down in the middle of the street. In God's view, intemperance extends far beyond alcohol. It is even possible to be intemperate about religion. I know a woman who is forever running to prayer meetings and Bible studies but whose children and husband are often neglected by her constant absence. She is intemperate, out of control.

Some newer Bible translations render the word for *temperance* as *self-control.* The whole idea of self-control, however, can be quite misleading, for it conveys the notion that we are capable of defeating our intemperance without any help. That is only true to some degree. It is possible for us to have a significant impact on the direction of our lives. However, reality is that there are many things that we cannot control. I could not, for example, control the color of my eyes—although I suppose I can do that better now than before with the new colored contact lenses some people wear. I certainly have no control over my height nor of the height of my two granddaughters, which their pediatrician has determined will eventually be four or five inches more than mine (is it cold up there Hannah and Cameron?). Those factors are all genetically predetermined (our five-foot-eight daughter Erin married six-foot-four Michael). Most of us also have no control over certain behavior patterns.

151

Self-control, if it is not properly understood in the biblical context, leads to an invictus attitude. *Invictus* is that poem by the humanist William Ernest Henley:

> Out of the night that covers me, black as a pit from pole to pole,
> I thank whatever gods may be for my unconquerable soul.
> In the fell clutch of circumstance, I have not winced nor cried
>   aloud.
> Under the bludgeonings of chance, my head is bloody but
>   unbowed.
> Beyond this place of wrath and tears looms but the horror of
>   the shade.
> And yet the menace of the years finds and shall find me
>   unafraid.
> It matters not how straight the gate, how charged with punish-
>   ments the scroll.
> I am the master of my fate. I am the captain of my soul!

Heady stuff that! And absolute rubbish! It breeds an attitude of self-sufficiency and pride that runs against the grain of what God's Word says. We are not, nor will we ever be, the captains of our souls nor masters of our fate. Perhaps the best proof of that is that Henley, the humanist who penned those words, finally committed suicide in utter despair. If that's the fate you want, his is the philosophy to live by.

Far better are the words of an unknown Christian who, in response to Henley's bragging self-sufficiency wrote *Christvictus!*

> Out of the light that dazzles me, bright as the sun from pole to pole,
> I thank the God I know to be, for Christ, the conqueror of my
>   soul.
> Since He's the sway of circumstance, I do not wince nor cry
>   aloud.
> Under that rule, which men call chance, my head with joy is
>   humbly bowed.
> Beyond this place of sin and tears, there is a life yet to be with
>   him; and he's the aid

That despite diminished strength and length of years keeps me
unafraid.

It matters not, though straight the gate, He cleared from punish-
ments my scroll.

Christ is the Master of my fate. Christ is the Captain of my soul!

We need Christ to accomplish temperance. Therefore, I go with the
King James translation that renders the word "temperance." Temperance
means "being moderate or restrained in thought and action." When Scripture speaks of the fruit of the Spirit as temperance, it means living our lives
by standards that honor Christ.

TWICE A CHAMPION!

Eric Liddell, the Olympic Champion runner who was the hero of the
movie *Chariots of Fire,* was a man of unusual temperance. After his
Olympic success, he gave his life to be a missionary to China. He was
imprisoned in North China during World War II. Yet even behind bars people around him witnessed his disciplined love for Jesus. Every morning
about six o'clock, with prison curtains tightly drawn to keep in the shining
of his peanut oil lamp lest the prowling prison guards would think someone was trying to escape, Liddell climbed out of his top bunk. He tiptoed
past the sleeping forms of his prison mates. Then at a small Chinese table,
he and another man sat together in the dawn's early light and studied their
Bibles. In whispered tones they discussed, prayed, and sought the Lord's
guidance together. They taught the other prisoners what they learned
from God's good Word during the long days behind bars. Eric Liddell's life
was disciplined by God's Word and by his trust that God's plan is always
the best for us.

SOMETIMES THE PIG WINS

Samson, on the other hand, lost his discipline to sexual lust. God has
endowed few people with greater potential than Samson. Yet he frittered it
away and failed miserably to reach the high prize for which God called
him. As a temperate, brave young man, he wrestled a lion and won. Yet he
could not wrestle and win against his own lusts. Samson wrestled with the

pig and lost the match. We live in a time of lust and loss of self-control. Principle figures in national scandals receive huge advances from publishers who want their books. Millions of people spend hard-earned money to read about other people's pig fights. We seem to quickly overlook the fact that these people have brought disgrace upon themselves and their nation. The message of those books holds nothing back when it comes to the lewd and lascivious. Counselors tell their clients to follow this pattern in their sessions.

When we turn to the Bible, however, a different kind of advice is advanced. Consider, for example, Paul the Apostle. Refusing to be a stained-glass saint, he acknowledges wrestling some pigs of his own. Although he never tells us precisely what his temptations were, we can imagine some of our own. In his list in his Galatian letter, Paul gives us a generalized list: "Now the works of the flesh are manifest, which are these; adultery, fornication, uncleanness, lasciviousness, idolatry, witchcraft, hatred, variance, emulations, wrath, strife, seditions, heresies, envyings, murders, drunkenness, revellings, and such like: of the which I tell you before, as I have also told you in time past, that they which do such things shall not inherit the kingdom of God" (Gal. 5:19-21).

THE PIGS ON PAUL'S LIST

Let us be honest about this subject. There is not a person on the face of the earth who can honestly deny that he or she has not been involved in some, if not all, of the sins in Paul's list. We should avoid at all cost the temptation to demonize others for their sins in hopes of elevating ourselves. That is a copout and a failure to be honest with God and with ourselves. "Why beholdest thou the mote that is in thy brother's eye, but considerest not the beam that is in thine own eye? Or how wilt thou say to thy brother, Let me pull out the mote out of thine eye; and, behold, a beam is in thine own eye? Thou hypocrite, first cast out the beam out of thine own eye; and then shalt thou see clearly to cast out the mote out of thy brother's eye" (Matt. 7:3-5).

Frank Harrington, who until his death was senior minister of the Peachtree Presbyterian Church in Atlanta, Georgia, the largest Presbyterian

154

Church in the Western world, often said, "I have never preached a sermon I did not need to hear myself." D. L Moody said, "I have more trouble with D. L. Moody than any other man to whom I preach." These men of God knew that the first job each of us has as Christians is to save us from ourselves. Paul knew it too: "Work out your own salvation with fear and trembling" (Phil. 2:12).

Cheese Up Your Nose

Some pranksters smeared Limburger cheese on the end of a sleeping hypocrite's nose. When he awoke, he immediately declared, "Somebody in here needs to take a bath." He moved among the people in the house with him, drawing near first to one person, then another. Each time after sniffing he would say, "Friend, you smell terrible. Take a bath!" Soon he had ordered everyone in the house with him to take a bath. He reckoned that if everyone bathed the wild odor he smelled would surely go away. Alas, it did not. Unable to stand it any more, he ventured outside for some fresh air. Once in the great outdoors, he breathed in deeply and declared, "I can't believe it; the whole world stinks!" It didn't, of course. Only he did. He alone needed to bathe. It is all too easy to blame the problem on everybody else. In fact, we need to clean up our own lives first.

Paul once assumed his biggest problem was with the followers of Christ and that his life's mission was to root them out for persecution. When he came to grips with his own sinful nature, he realized that his biggest problem was himself. How did Paul overcome his personal predicament? The same way we do today. He had to make a conscious choice to live a tempered life. Why does the Spirit call us to temperance? "He that ruleth his spirit [is stronger] than he that taketh a city" (Prov. 16:32).

How to Develop this Personality Trait Called Temperance

Remember the two things Samson forgot: First, who you are and, second, whose you are. Never forget you are a sinner. Soon after he was released from prison, Charles Colson declared that he had learned that there is "a little Watergate in all of us." He was right. The best of us is capable of doing the deeds of the worst of us, and we cannot afford to forget

155

that. Left to our own devices, there are no limits to how low human nature can sink.

Second, remember whose you are. You belong to Christ, who made you and bought you with His blood. When we remember our own potential for evil and combine that with an acknowledgment that we cannot make it to heaven alone, the Holy Spirit is better able to work the good God has in mind for us. The end result will be temperance.

It is very important as we conclude this chapter to understand the choices we must make. There is no such thing as a self-made man. We will finally succumb to a sin-controlled life or a Spirit-controlled life. Paul tells the Galatians that it must be one or the other. There is no middle ground, for the two are absolutely incompatible. In so doing, he makes a lie of the notion that there is such a thing as carnal Christianity. "This I say then, Walk in the Spirit, and ye shall not fulfil the lust of the flesh. For the flesh lusteth against the Spirit, and the Spirit against the flesh: and these are contrary the one to the other: so that ye cannot do the things that ye would" (Gal. 5:16).

Without a firm commitment to grow in Christ and to submit our lives to biblical authority, we will have no constant higher moral and ethical standards by which to guide and guard our lives. How can we achieve these high standards called "the fruit of the Spirit" in our lives? The answer is both short and long.

Let me illustrate the short answer with a story that is best told by my friend John Huffman. John speaks of a letter he received from his dying twenty-three-year-old daughter, Suzanne. Her doctors had just told her that she had between two and six weeks to live. Suzanne was so weak that she had to dictate these final words to her pastor and dad: "I want you to be more like Jesus Christ."[2]

Can you imagine receiving a letter from a sharp, beautiful, with-it daughter who is facing death with an attitude like that? As I reflected on Suzanne Huffman's letter later, I realized that the very act of writing, no dictating because writing is no longer possible, is a demonstration of Holy

---

2. John A. Huffman, Jr. *The Fruit of the Spirit Is Self-Control,* a sermon preached at St. Andrew's Presbyterian Church, Newport Beach, California on October 4, 1998. Used by permission.

Spirit discipline in her life. This is what she wants her dad to be more than anything else in the world. Her request has validity for her dad and for every dad in the universe. What she urges from John Huffman is what God has in mind for each of us, whether or not we are fathers.

"Be more like Jesus Christ!" That is the short answer. The longer answer tells us how to be more like Him.

First, live in the Holy Spirit. "If we live in the Spirit, let us also walk in the Spirit" (Gal. 5:25). This calls us to life on a scale that is not possible for us to achieve alone. We have already long ago learned that it is impossible to live the life of the Holy Spirit without help. We need Jesus.

Living in the Spirit requires that we be born again, for one birth alone is not sufficient. "Except a man be born of water and of the Spirit, he cannot enter into the kingdom of God. That which is born of the flesh is flesh; and that which is born of the Spirit is spirit" (John 3:5-6). Only in Jesus Christ can we be born a second time.

Second, Paul writes, "Let us also walk in the Spirit" (Gal. 5:25). I watched our granddaughter Cameron learn to walk not long ago. Her daddy, Michael, kept a close eye on her as she took a few tottering steps across the family room. After about three or four steps, Cameron would suddenly plop down on the floor. Her dad picked her up each time she fell, and off she went once more, paying no attention to his spoken directions, her chubby little arms flailing to keep balance. A few steps later she flopped down on the floor one more time. Picking Cameron up, Michael repeated his instruction each time. That routine was repeated so many times that I lost count of the number. Cameron took a few steps and flopped down on the floor. Michael picked her up and encouraged her to try once more. From the sidelines, I cheered Cameron on and marveled at our son-in-law's patience. I also wondered just how many more flops and how many more times the instruction and encouragement would need to be given before Cameron would make it all the way across the room unaided.

"The ways of the Lord are right, and the just shall walk in them" (Hosea 14:9). Through Hosea the prophet, God says we need to learn to walk again. With a bit of imagination, we can catch a mental image of God picking us up every time we fall. With a loving word of instruction and

157

encouragement, He sends us on our way each time we stumble. Our first steps of faith are just like Cameron's. We start out full of enthusiasm and confidence, but it's not long before we flop down. It is at those times that the Lord picks us up, dusts us off, and encourages us to go again until we make it all the way across this room called the Christian life. One day we shall walk through golden gates into the Father's house called heaven. One day His Spirit will finally have us completely.

10

The dynamite inside you

W e have the gift of the Spirit which, when we understand it properly, results in us experiencing the growing fruit of the Spirit. As we saw in chapter nine, the fruit of the Spirit takes a lifetime to grow in us. Now we come to yet another manifestation of the Breath of Abundant Life through us: the power of the Spirit.

The Christian gospel is nothing if not a message that God empowers ordinary men and women with confident hope to do great things that advance His kingdom on earth. A supernatural power is available to all Christians, and nothing in the world can equal it. At conversion the Holy Spirit takes up residence within us. After conversion the fruit of the Spirit grows in and through us. It is yet another thing, however, to be so filled with the power of this *Breath of Abundant Life* that He becomes the root of everything we think and do. Our Savior told His first disciples, "Behold, I send the promise of my Father upon you: but tarry ye in the city of Jerusalem, until ye be endued with power from on high" (Luke 24:49). Someone said that the pages of the New Testament are full of unexploded dynamite. That is true. Unfortunately, it appears to be not always true in the life of many Christians. There are Christian converts who live and die without experiencing the Spirit's power in their lives.

THE POWER IS NOT TURNED ON YET

Although I was but a child at the time, I well recall that day in 1950 when electricity was installed in my maternal grandmother's home. It was a big occasion for a little boy. Until that time her house was lighted by gas. I remember how the wires were laid neatly along the skirting boards, up the walls, and across the ceiling of each room. Switches were connected to the wires and fixed to the walls. Electric lights were hung from the ceilings. I recall my father coming in and flipping a wall switch the day the work was done, much as one might kick the tires of an automobile he was considering purchasing. When my dad turned the switch, nothing happened.

"It doesn't work, Robbie," my grandmother assured him, "because they haven't turned the power on yet. It will work after it's connected." She meant that the electrical power was not hooked up to the supply source because some houses on her block were not yet wired. So far as her home was concerned, however, all the proper fittings had been installed. Yet the power was absent because the vital connection was not made.

The same is true in the realm of the Spirit. While every Christian has the Holy Spirit since conversion, not every Christian has the power turned on yet. The right equipment is there, but the connection is not made. The result is anemic faith.

WHEN THE POWER GETS TURNED ON

"Ye shall receive power, after that the Holy Ghost is come upon you" (Acts 1:8). When the Sanhedrin took notice of the boldness of those two disciples they had previously considered unlettered and unlearned (Acts 4:13), it was because there was a power about their lives that made them different. It was not that Peter and John were suddenly more intellectually brilliant than before or that they had become men of culture, but it was that they could command the power of God.

The Greek word used for this power and for the power of all disciples of Jesus is *dunamis*. Its specific meaning is "miraculous power which results in ability, abundance, meaning, might, strength, and wonderful accomplishments that were previously unimaginable." That Greek word has made its way into our English language in such terms as *dynamic, dynamo, dynamite*. Yet nearly two thousand years past Pentecost, many Christians have so far only touched a minute portion of this divine energy. Far different the experience of the first generation of believers. They received Christ and accepted that power as a given. They subsequently became dynamic dynamos for Him. They knew not only that they had the power but also why they had it. Their witness has influenced world history as nothing before or since.

THE POWER OF JESUS

The power came to their attention first in Jesus. He went about doing things that no one had seen before. Through Him the blind were enabled to see, the lame to walk, lepers were cleansed, the deaf heard, the dead were raised, and the poor heard the gospel preached (see Luke 7:22). Tragically, many in the church today have tried to discount these He left us, said, "Verily, verily, I say unto you, He that believeth on me, the works that I do shall he do also; and greater works than these shall he do" (John 14:12). And "Heaven and earth shall pass away, but my words shall not pass away" (Matt. 24:35). Too often in our churches we have a great deal of activity but accomplish very little. Is there a corresponding parallel between experiencing this practical Holy Spirit power and belief in God's Word? I believe there is.

THE POWER OF THE DISCIPLES

For the disciples, the experience of this holy dynamite came first at Pentecost. What took place in the upper room in Jerusalem was a new experience of God that made itself real in and through those followers of Jesus from that day on. It changed life for them and changed them for life. It was not momentary but permanent. It was not strange but normal. They had seen it all before as they walked with Jesus. It was simply something He promised, and the promise was real because they believed it. They expected it. No promise is real until we expect it to happen and to happen to us. That is true of salvation—we must accept the offer of saving grace— and it is true of Holy Spirit power. There was for them and there is for us a new release of spiritual energy the like of which we cannot know otherwise.

This, of course, does not mean that the Holy Spirit was somehow dormant in the world before. We have seen that He was active all through the Old Testament as far back as Creation itself. The Holy Spirit has always been at work as the source of all the goodness, truth, and beauty in human history. What was different about Pentecost was that now the Spirit was the disciples. Just as the cross was a fresh symbol of the extent to which God's love for us would go, Pentecost in the upper room was the start of a new era in God's empowerment of His people. His energy through us was His chosen way of releasing His power upon ordinary people and sending it into the whole world. "Ye shall receive power, after that the Holy Ghost is come upon you: and ye shall be witnesses unto me both in Jerusalem, and in all Judaea, and in Samaria, and unto the uttermost part of the earth" (Acts 1:8).

THERE ALL THE TIME

A few days ago I attended the dedication of a church cornerstone. The building was erected five years ago, but the cornerstone was not dedicated until the mortgage was fully paid. It was interesting how many people attending that event admitted that even though they had passed the stone many times before, they had not noticed it. Yet now they were raving about its beauty and its message. It was there all the time, yet they missed it somehow. In somewhat similar fashion, Pentecost was a dedication of God's power through people on a scale and in a manner that, although it had never been absent from the world, was often not noticed.

Only occasionally do we read of the Spirit's activity in the Old Testament. Yet He was always there. He was always behind the scenes creating Bible heroes. He called Abram out of Ur of the Chaldees. He empowered Moses to face down the pharaoh and lead the Exodus out of Egypt. He raised up David and inspired his songs. He gave life to the preaching of the prophets. Yet His presence seemed mostly passive to God's people.

THE DAY THE FIRE FELL

That day in the upper room, however, the Spirit was anything but passive. "There appeared unto them cloven tongues like as of fire, and it sat upon each of them. And they were all filled with the Holy Ghost" (Acts 2:3-4). That small group of disciples became intensely aware of God's love, presence, and purpose. They saw and felt His presence in ways they had not experienced before. It was nothing new for the Spirit, but it was everything new for them. The Spirit who was always there now showed Himself real and alive and empowering.

THE LIGHT IN THE WINDOW

Thomas Kinkade is a committed Christian artist whose work catches attention because of his use of golden light. That light, which usually shines through a window, catches the eye of a passive observer. As he stops to study the picture, the light becomes the focal part of Kinkade's paintings. Study the light for a while, however, and soon other parts of the picture come into focus in a way that no other artist I know can imitate. There are times when the pattern seems to reverse itself. Some feature in one of Thomas Kinkade's pictures catches the attention of a bystander. Then as one studies that object, somehow the background light comes into focus in such a way that one realizes that it was, in fact, the light that really made the initial attraction stand out.

For the first disciples, the light was always there. It was just that now they suddenly were able to see it. Pentecost was like the cleaning of their spiritual windows to let the light shine through in an unprecedented way. And the light of the Spirit always led them to Jesus the Light of Life, for that is the Spirit's job. For all His power, the Spirit is modest. He never calls attention to Himself. His ministry is to call our minds and hearts to Jesus.

ECSTATIC SPEECH

"And they were all filled with the Holy Ghost, and began to speak with other tongues, as the Spirit gave them utterance" (Acts 2:4). The rapturous utterances of the disciples on Pentecost should not surprise us. Their ordinary vocabulary was far too limited for that moment. The only reasonable response to their experience was speechlessness, such as Zacharias, John the Baptist's father, had experienced when he heard that his wife whom he was convinced was barren would conceive in her old age, or utterance that could not be written with pen on paper.

Unusual phenomena like speaking in tongues have occurred in other times and in other places. Nor is it limited only to Christians. It occurs, I am told, in regions where Christ's name has not yet been preached and even in some of the cultic religions, including Mormonism. Ecstatic speech is not uniquely Christian.

Neither is it as unusual as we might think. Last week I ate lunch in a hospital cafeteria with a new dad. After a very difficult pregnancy, he and his wife had a beautiful, healthy baby girl. He was describing for me what it was like to be present at the moment his first-born came into the world when, suddenly, this normally articulate, in control of himself, young man stopped speaking. His lips were moving, but he could speak no more. Unlike Zacharias, it was not because his wife was pregnant. It was almost the exact opposite of that. The reason he could not speak was that words failed him. Nothing he could say at that moment could describe the experience they had just been through together. Tears of delight welled up in his eyes and ran down his cheeks. Those tears said what words could never tell. From my own experience, I knew what he meant. For the disciples on Pentecost, their unknown tongues expressed that now they knew for themselves that everything they had witnessed through Jesus was valid for them as well. The Greek text tells the story better than the English translations do. In the space of a few verses, three Greek words are translated into one English word. Those words are *glossa, laleo,* and *dialektos.* The one word is *tongue.* The three Greek words, however, help us see significant differences between these Pentecost utterances. There were different manifestations of tongues. One was a babbling sound. Another was a known language, which the speaker now spoke fluently even though he had never learned it. The third was more than a national language; it was a local dialect. One evidence of tongues spoke to the speaker himself about the power of the Spirit and the other two spoke to those who heard them, whether with articulation or with the local vernacular.

THE SECRET OF THE POWER

The book of Acts is the official history of the first-generation Christians. Luke the physician, who authored the book, set out under the Spirit's influence to put in writing how these changes influenced the everyday lives of the first Christians and their society. It is one of the most remarkable writings in all human history, and no person, Christian or otherwise, should be considered literate before reading it. The great theme of the book is the demonstration of Holy Spirit power through the dedicated lives of ordinary people.

From the pages of Acts, we can glean something more about the secret of this dynamic power in this first generation of believers. We have seen already that before He left them, Christ promised that the Holy Spirit would manifest His power among them. Like the first payment on a house mortgage, Pentecost was the first installment of that promise being fulfilled or to paraphrase Paul's words to the Ephesians, "the earnest of [their] inheritance" (Eph. 1:14).

How did they take possession of the Spirit's power and how did they demonstrate that they had it? In one sense, not only is Acts the historical record of that demonstration, but the rest of the New Testament is as well. We can examine only a limited number of instances where the power was seen.

POWER TO LIVE!

Ludwig Nommensen was a Danish missionary to the Batak people of Sumatra. When he first arrived among them, he sought out their tribal leader to make himself known and to present the chieftain with the claims of Christ. The headman listened carefully and asked how this religion Nommensen represented was different from the self-devised pagan creed they already followed. "From our fathers," the chieftain said, "we have inherited a religion that forbids stealing, telling lies, or lying with another man's wife. How is your religion better?" "The difference," Ludwig Nommensen replied, "is that we have a Master whose powerful Spirit enables us to keep His laws."

When the Spirit came upon the first Christians, it was not only what they had to forsake but also what they gained that made them powerful. They gave up old self-defeating moral attitudes and behavior patterns that promised momentary happiness for a wonderful dynamic ability to do things they once called impossible. The Breath of Abundant Life brought not just a set of rules but the power by which to keep them. They learned that life is better in Christ because it is built on a kinship with Him that works itself out in practical, helpful human relationships. Those relationships are based on forgiveness, trust, love, and fellowship that expands beyond a small local circle to brothers and sisters all across the world. Jesus had talked about this and demonstrated what it looked like. The disciples not only heard His message; they also saw it in action when he spoke to the woman at the well and Zacchaeus and the man who was blind from birth. They saw it in the way their Master ministered to the down and outs of His day. They heard it when He told the parable of a caring Samaritan that put to shame their old racist principles.

Pentecost power now fanned the flame in their hearts, and they set out to translate their newfound passion into reality. Wherever Christ's message was received, they were no longer strangers and aliens. They were brothers and sisters, once separated by accent, origin, tradition, and skin hue but now joined together as one family. The dynamite of the Spirit blasted away all the old barriers that had once separated people from one another. The experience was so unique and fresh in the Graeco-Roman world of their generation that it demanded the invention of a new word, *koinonia,* which means "fellowship." Their sense of kinship grew so strong that they finally combined their resources and formed a new economic system. Such a bond among the believers encouraged them to witness fearlessly. They told the story of Jesus in word and in deed to anyone who would listen.

THE POWER OF DETERMINATION

Another sign of Holy Spirit dynamism among the believers was confidence and determination. They knew that in Jesus they would always be more than conquerors and that nothing in this world could stop them. No matter what their background, when Jesus came in the power of the Spirit, there was a buoyancy and resilience that would not leave them no matter how difficult their mission or unwelcome their message.

"The disciples were filled with joy, and with the Holy Ghost" (Acts 13:52). What was the source of this joy? It was that they knew they were children of God and that He was their heavenly Father. They knew that this is His world and that He intentionally programmed it for their ultimate good. There was nothing for them to worry about. They were predisposed to a hallelujah mentality and no one could take it from them. Vance Havner once spoke at a chapel service at the University of Mobile where I was an undergraduate student. In typical Vance Havner style, he said many things, some witty, some profound, but none that has stayed with me like this: "A genuine glowing experience with God is worth a library full of doubts and arguments." Nothing is as contagious as genuine joy. It moves stone hearts and charms brutes. These disciples had learned, and were learning daily, exactly what Jesus meant when He said, "I am come that they might have life, and that they might have it more abundantly" (John 10:10). His Breath of Abundant Life had touched them.

They had learned their lesson well, for some had been with Jesus while others had witnessed His impact on the lives of their teachers. Even when Rome's authorities sanctioned their severe beatings before releasing them they went out "rejoicing that they were counted worthy to suffer shame for his name" (Acts 5:41). They remembered that no suffering they experienced would ever equal the suffering that their sinless Christ had taken in their place. They wore their suffering as a badge of honor. "I count all things but loss for the excellency of the knowledge of Christ Jesus my Lord: for whom I have suffered the loss of all things, and do count them but dung, that I may win Christ" (Phil. 3:8). Their joy was indestructible. Paul was in prison, his feet in leg irons, and his body bruised and lacerated with the merciless scourging of a Roman cat-o'-nine-tails and how does the Philippian jailer find him? Why, praying and singing praises to God (see Acts 16:25)! It is no wonder that the warder led his family to believe in Jesus that very night. Joy under pressure is always contagious. It will always achieve positive results.

Then there was Peter, living in constant danger, hunted and persecuted like a wild animal. Yet according to well-founded tradition, when he was finally captured and sentenced to die for Christ's sake, Peter deemed himself unworthy to die in the same way as his Master. He insisted that he be nailed upside down on a cross. There he hung for hours with his head directed at the ground giving testimony that One had gone this way before him of whom the world was unworthy. What does Peter write in his old age by way of instruction for the rest of us? "Rejoice with joy unspeakable and full of glory" (I Pet. 1:8).

The more you know of those early days of the faith and power of the Holy Spirit in the first believers, the more you are dazzled by their sheer

167

joy. In addition, the more you realize that we need the Lord to come on the church today with a new burst of Holy Spirit joy, power, and confident expectation. There is nothing ingrown about the fellowship, nothing small, nothing petty, nothing timid, nothing half-measured, and nothing self-focused. It was all for Jesus, and they counted every bit of it worthwhile.

LIFE WITH NO LIMITS!

When we turn to Paul's letters, we find that one of his favorite Greek words winds like a golden thread through them all. It describes the life philosophy that motivated the early Christians. That word is *abound*. The Greek is *pleonazo*. It means "to constantly increase, always be doing more, make no small plans, do no meager deeds, break all bounds and cross all the limits of your old belief system." In short, let nothing stop you from doing the right thing and the best thing and the biggest thing in the name of Jesus Christ.

Abound in hope, he tells the Romans. "Now the God of hope fill you with all joy and peace in believing, that ye may abound in hope, through the power of the Holy Ghost" (Rom. 15:13)

To the Corinthians he calls for abounding faith, speech, knowledge, diligence, love, and generosity: "Abound in every thing, in faith, and utterance, and knowledge, and in all diligence, and in your love to us, see that ye abound in this grace also" (II Cor. 8:7).

Abound more and more is his instruction to the Thessalonians: "We beseech you, brethren, and exhort you by the Lord Jesus, that as ye have received of us how ye ought to walk and to please God, so ye would abound more and more" (I Thess. 4:1).

To the Colossians it was that they must abound in the faith they found in Christ: "As ye have therefore received Christ Jesus the Lord, so walk ye in him: rooted and built up in him, and stablished in the faith, as ye have been taught, abounding therein with thanksgiving" (Col. 2:6-7).

EXUBERANT FAITH!

What does it mean to abound? It means to live out fully the abundant life Christ came to give us. It means we are to live fully supplied and filled with resources from a reservoir that will never run dry. It means to overflow, to have plenty, to teem with swelling abundance. It means that we enjoy life, not because of what happens in it, but rather often in spite of what life brings because to have Holy Spirit power is to know a life beyond this life.

For the first disciples, Christianity was above all else a large experience. It connected them to the God of heaven in a personal relationship through His Son. They believed His resources were at their disposal. It was bigger than anything else they knew or had ever experienced. No matter how great their sin, no matter how large their need, no matter how hurtful their suffering, they found in Christ One whose power would always be sufficient to forgive, supply, and heal. Theirs was above all else exuberant living. Life was on the move and would not be hindered by the mere resources of this world. It was surging. It was on the increase. It was rich beyond measure. It was stronger than anything it might come up against. It made them more than conquerors. This was life plus! Having been breathed upon by Jesus, now they possessed the Breath of Abundant Life.

Yet if we evaluate their possessions from this world's perspective, it is doubtful that any of them would have made the *Fortune 500*. They were unlikely candidates for the front of *Forbes* or those fancy airline magazines that promote headliners from the worlds of business and sports. They might have been, but that was not their motivation for living the high life. Their high life was founded not in earthly wealth and power but in the message and joy that was their endowment in Christ. "God hath chosen the foolish things of the world to confound the wise; and God hath chosen the weak things of the world to confound the things which are mighty; And base things of the world, and things which are despised, hath God chosen, yea, and things which are not, to bring to nought things that are: that no flesh should glory in his presence" (I Cor. 1:27-29).

Recognizing that we have no glory of our own was a great equalizer for them. With that sense of equality implanted in them by the Holy Spirit, they confronted the success standards of their day and declared them moot, just as Jesus had done. "For what shall it profit a man, if he shall gain the whole world, and lose his own soul?" (Mark 8:36). Having received a prize the world could never afford, they confronted this world's sin in all of its guileful forms. They spoke out against the same things Jesus did. They denounced moral corruption, devouring lust, indecency, injustice, immorality, unfairness, covetousness, and all the other forms of spiritual uncleanness around them. They called all that would listen not to a better way of life but to new life. "Ye have put off the old man with his deeds; and have put on the new man" (Col. 3:9-10). Their message said that however shameful the past, or however wasted, there is a fresh tide of exterminating forgiveness in the cross of Jesus Christ. "Put on Christ!" was their clarion cry, "Put on Christ and become new." "If any man be in Christ, he is a new creature: old things are passed away; behold, all things are become new" (II Cor. 5:17).

PENTECOST NOW?

"That ye might walk worthy of the Lord unto all pleasing, being fruitful in every good work, and increasing in the knowledge of God; strengthened with all might, according to his glorious power, unto all patience and long-suffering with joyfulness; giving thanks unto the Father, which hath made us meet to be partakers of the inheritance of the saints in light" (Col. 1:10-12).

What about today? Are there any indications that the same power of the Spirit that made the early church great is still available? Are the power, joy, enthusiasm, and ethereality available now? These are questions that every disciple of Jesus Christ needs to earnestly consider.

To be sure, the human needs are still present, for at its core human nature never changes. Only the environment in which it functions changes. Neither the mission of Christ nor its urgency has changed. Spiritual giants have pastored the congregation I serve now. Among the names of my predecessors on the bronze plaque in one of our hallways is Clarence Edward Macartney. Not long ago we came across some dusty 78rpm recordings of his sermons. Recorded in the 1930s and 1940s, the message Dr. Macartney preached still has relevance. Listening to the message on those discs was like a modern-day experience of "he being dead yet speaketh" (Heb. 11:4). I could not help but be impressed by the urgency of what he preached. Words like "Now! Today! This moment! While there is still time!" echo through his sermons.

Yet Clarence Macartney led the First Presbyterian Church of Pittsburgh in an era that was, in many ways, significantly different from today. He was called to Pittsburgh in 1927 and retired in 1953. He was here when the bubble burst on Wall Street and for that "day that will live in infamy" because of the bombing of Pearl Harbor. During the Second World War, when the steel mills dotting our city were white hot with munitions related orders, Dr. Macartney held forth about the relevance of this gospel to one nation under God. When the postwar affluence of the decade of the fifties started and the new more rounded shaped family automobiles made with Pittsburgh steel rolled off the production lines in Detroit, Dr. Macartney in his sermons spoke about the national need to see God's hand bringing America peacetime prosperity. He was a faithful herald of Christ, and I am honored to walk up the stone steps he climbed to preach each Sunday.

Nevertheless, I sometimes wonder if Dr. Macartney would recognize our city today. Steel is no longer king in Pittsburgh. Today our economy depends on medicine, education, and computers. The Three Rivers were here when he preached but not the stadium named for them. In those days the Pirates played at Forbes Field in another part of the city. The Steel City skyline is so different that even people who left Pittsburgh long after Dr. Macartney was here have trouble finding their way around when they come back home to Pittsburgh now. Dr. Macartney never rode the interstate I drive home on each night from downtown. It was not constructed until about thirty years after he died. The population of our city was twice as large in his day as it is today. America was different when Dr. Macartney's voice sounded from our pulpit and so was the church God called us both to serve. Clarence Macartney never sent a fax or typed on a computer keyboard. Dr. Macartney was brilliant, articulate, precise, a master of the English language, with a magnificent vocabulary, but the word *Internet* was not among his word stock. Satellites, if he even knew that word, were reserved for the realm of cutting-edge science fiction. Church records in his day were mostly handwritten. His sermon notes were pecked out on a manual typewriter. A lot of things are different now. Pittsburgh, still one of America's leading cities, will never be the same again. I like to think it will be better. The question we consider here, however, is has the message that inspired his sermons changed and do we still have the power that message promises?

The answer is that nothing about the gospel has changed. We still need the same Christ. The cross is the same. The urgency of preaching is the same. People without Christ are still lost. That is why it says, "Behold, now is the accepted time; behold, now is the day of salvation" (II Cor. 6:2). "To day if ye will hear his voice, harden not your hearts" (Heb. 4:7).

So where is the power? When the church stopped talking about the power, the business world stepped in and hijacked that word. It is in vogue in advertising. Washing powders have power and so do automobiles, according to the television commercials. We hear about power lunches, power words, power neckties, and power parties. The head coach of the Pittsburgh Steelers is Bill Cowher. When the Steelers are on a roll, our local sports pundits talk about "Cowher power." In the Christian world too, the word has sometimes been relegated to the realm of the Charismatics who have focused attention on the supernatural experiential manifestations of Holy Spirit power in tongues, healing, and exorcism. We have a great deal of talk about power but not much real power. Power is often talked about in shallow, meaningless, and godless ways.

A dear lady, the daughter-in-law of a once regionally well known pastor who was one of my long ago predecessors, corresponded with me often. On one occasion she graciously chastised me for what she termed "the revivalistic way you preach." Her admonition ended with this sentence, "It is as if you expect to see people converted in every service." She was right! Whether my preaching style was to her liking or not, she understood its goal. In my opinion, preaching that is not focused on calling people to conversion is not worthy of the name. Not only was she right about that, but, unwittingly perhaps, she was putting her finger on one reason that so much of preaching in our generation seems powerless. It lacks urgency. Any preacher who does not anticipate that souls will be saved through the message preached will almost certainly not see souls saved. Our expectations will largely determine our future experience.

BELIEVING IS SEEING!

"If ye have faith as a grain of mustard seed, ye shall say unto this mountain, Remove hence to yonder place; and it shall remove; and nothing shall be impossible unto you" (Matt. 17:20). Jesus was telling us that before we can see the supernatural happen we must first believe in the possibility of it. When the Holy Spirit came with power upon the first generation of Christians, it was, at least in part, because they expected to see God's power revealed. They had seen it before, and they would settle for nothing less. A mudpack in a blind man's eyes is not supposed to return his sight, but it did! Five loaves and two small fish are not enough to feed five thousand hungry people, but they were! Dead people do not come alive again, but they did! All these things and more they had seen at the hands of the One who told them, "He that believeth on me, the works that I do shall he do also; and greater works than these shall he do" (John 14:12). They expected Christ to keep His word and He did.

Do we really believe this today? Do you believe it? Have your expectations of Jesus and His power been dimmed somehow? Have you filed them away in the dark, dusty corner of what used to be? Will you be satisfied with less than those who passed the message of Christ along to you? What do you believe about God's ability to transform lives today? That is the final question each of us must answer. We experience no greater manifestations of His power than we are willing to believe, nay, expect. Whether we think Christ can and will, or cannot and will not, we will always be right. Our expectations become self-fulfilling prophecies.

SAVING POWER

There are those who say that today is different, that the Holy Spirit no longer works in power as He once did. To them I say, "Show me biblical proof for that assertion." Does He save? Ask the young man in our congregation who happened into church one Sunday morning. Having just gone through a breakup in his live-in relationship with a woman, he remembered the church and thought, in his own words, "It wouldn't hurt to go." Christ spoke to his heart that day with a warm invitation. "Come unto me, all ye that labour and are heavy laden, and I will give you rest" (Matt. 11:28). He was gloriously converted and today is preparing for the gospel ministry.

HEALING POWER

Does He heal? Ask Rachel Welty, the little girl in our congregation whose prenatal medical complications were so threatening that one doctor advised her parents, John and Rhonda, to consider abortion. At birth her prognosis was so somber that few people in medicine believed she had any long-term hope of living a normal life. However, of this her physicians were certain: The hole that modern technology had detected in her heart was healed. There was no medical explanation. That was not her only medical problem, however. For sixteen months, Rachel lay in a neonatal intensive care unit demonstrating more determination to hang onto life than anyone else I have seen in a quarter century of pastoral ministry. Last Sunday she was in church again, full of life. She is bright. She has personality plus. Her smile would melt the heart of a tyrant. As I write these words, she is registered for pre-school.

Or ask Marvin. Thirty-three years ago doctors opened him up to remove a cancerous tumor from his liver. What they found inside him they had seen before, and they knew his prognosis was hopeless. Marvin's internal organs were so horribly cancerous and metastasized that his surgeon closed him up without removing anything. Marvin went home with a thirty-day life expectancy and a prescription for pain medication. Neither chemotherapy not radiation treatments were prescribed because, in the estimation of his physicians, Marvin was too far gone for that. A year and a half later, a medical clerk called Marvin's wife and said, "We are closing out our records on your husband's illness and need to know the date of his death." Date of death! As the clerk spoke those words Marvin was replacing shingles on the roof of his house. All his bodily functions were normal. He had regained the weight he once lost to cancer and was back working at his old job every day. Today he shares his testimony of God's healing power with anyone who will listen. Radiology reports show that the organs that were largely gone earlier now are fully restored. There is, by the surgeon's own acknowledgment, no medical explanation for Marvin's recovery. It has to be the Spirit's healing power in response to the believing prayers of Christ's people. "The prayer of faith shall save the sick, and the Lord shall raise him up" (James 5:15).

If we were involved in a personal conversation right now, you might ask me why it is that some people, such as Rachel or Marvin, are healed while others are not when prayers of faith are offered. I would tell you that that is a good question for which I have no answer. What I do know is that God's Word says, "I will have mercy on whom I will have mercy, and I will have compassion on whom I will have compassion. So then it is not of him that willeth, nor of him that runneth, but of God that sheweth mercy" (Rom. 9:15-16). We should believe these words and have greater expectations about His ability to do great things in the Holy Spirit's power.

We should want this power to flow through us, not because of pride, self-importance, or any attention it might draw toward us, but because it will meet the needs of others and bring them to faith in the Savior. The number of spiritual gifts we possess or how stirringly we can call them up and display them does not make us more valuable as Christians. The only thing God values is our conformity to the character of Jesus. Whether He chooses to use us or not use us is for Him to decide.

No one can honestly read the Bible and conclude that God's power is not as real today as it was at Pentecost. It was, and is, God's intention for this Holy Spirit power to accompany the preaching of the gospel. It is a tragedy and a shame when that does not happen because we neither believe nor expect it. Paul writes, "Through mighty signs and wonders, by the power of the Spirit of God ... I have fully preached the gospel of Christ" (Rom. 15:19). For the apostle, for preaching to be complete it must be accompanied by the power of the Holy Spirit. Let us never be guilty of minimizing His mighty power. "God, who commanded the light to shine out of darkness, hath shined in our hearts, to give the light of the knowledge of the glory of God in the face of Jesus Christ. But we have this treasure in earthen vessels, that the excellency of the power may be of God, and not of us" (II Cor. 4:6-7).

Today we who are Christ's have a golden opportunity to proclaim Christ's excellent power. All across America and throughout the world, people yearn for more of what God has for them. A great spiritual vacuum exists in our generation. Even those who are not Christians are conscious of it. I have met them as God has allowed me to travel, from Belfast to Bangkok; London to Little Rock; Pittsburgh to Pascagoula; Hong Kong to Hattiesburg; Nairobi to Nashville; and places in-between. With communications satellites dotting the wild blue yonder, supersonic airplanes, and the World Wide Web, the world has shrunk into a single neighborhood. No previous generation ever had such an opportunity. Let us seize this moment and every available means it contains to tell the story of Jesus in Spirit-filled power as never before.

RECLAIMING PENTECOST

How do we tap into this supernatural power? The secret lies, I believe, in Paul's charge to young Timothy, "I put thee in remembrance that thou stir up the gift of God, which is in thee....For God hath not given us the spirit of fear; but of power, and of love, and of a sound mind" (II Tim. 1:6-7).

Timothy was overwhelmed by externals. Things around him seemed somehow to threaten what God had done within him. Paul tells him to remember what God gave him. Recall the gift that brings power. He had it. He must use it with love and strategic new boldness, power, love, and a sound mind. The message is plain for us. If we use some limitation or hardship as an excuse for falling short of God's best plans for us, it is time we changed our attitude. In the power of God we can be winners for Christ's sake.

God has endowed us with that same power. Let us come anew in humility and prayer with a repentant spirit and reclaim Pentecost. If we do, God will once again fulfill his promise. "If my people, which are called by my name, shall humble themselves, and pray, and seek my face, and turn from their wicked ways; then will I hear from heaven, and will forgive their sin, and will heal their land" (II Chron. 7:14).

Jesus says it plainly and Pentecost confirms it. If we will invite Him, the Holy Spirit will come right inside a human personality. That is not a special mystical experience reserved for a few special Christians. It is for ordinary people, people like you and me.

How will it happen? It will happen when we throw away that which does Christ no honor. It will happen when we expect it to happen and are prepared to pay the price, make the sacrifice, and surrender as much of ourselves as we know to Christ. It will happen when we take every thought captive and come with expectation, enthusiasm, vision, confidence, and determination like that of our first-generation brothers and sisters and walk in God's will.

In chapter eleven we will consider how we can know His will completely.

11

Gone for our good

"We think we have a great idea," they exclaimed, "but is it the will of God for us and how can we know for sure?"

Chapter ten concluded with a call to walk in God's will. That summons, which is after all basic to Christian discipleship, raises a question of its own: How can I know the will of God for my life? Put another way: How can we know the guidance of the Holy Spirit in everyday life so that we may follow in it? That, in turn, leads to an even more foundational question: Does God still guide today? Has He, as some might say, effectively gone out of the guidance business? What if I've already missed God's will? Is there a way back? Answering these and related important questions is the focal consideration of this chapter.

THE MOST IMPRESSIVE MOMENT IN HISTORY

Wouldn't you have loved to have seen it? For sheer drama, there is no more sensational sight in all human history than the grand finale of Christ's earthly ministry. The ascension of Jesus Christ from planet Earth stands alone as a unique event, even for Him.

There certainly were many other remarkable moments. The creation was phenomenal but the first five days of it happened without human witnesses. The advent of Christ into the world via a virgin's womb and Bethlehem stable was miraculous and phenomenal. Yet no one except Mary and Joseph really understood the full story of what God was doing at the time. Similarly, hundreds, perhaps thousands, witnessed Christ's crucifixion. Yet apart from a convicted thief, a solitary Roman centurion, and a few eyewitnesses, no one there was really impressed in any lasting fashion until after He died. Public executions were not rarities in that place and time. For the majority of spectators, this was just one more. The resurrection too was magnificent. Yet as many people as saw the risen Christ, there was no actual firsthand witness who could say they observed Him rising from the dead or walking away from the tomb. What we have is an empty tomb and a cocoon of undisturbed grave clothes where once the dead Christ lay. It was only later that the people with their own eyes beheld the risen Lord.

Christ's ascension was different, however. "He was taken up; and a cloud received him out of their sight. And while they looked stedfastly toward heaven as he went up, behold, two men stood by them in white apparel" (Acts 1:9-10). What a memorable spectacle! Jesus slowly rising into the air before being enveloped in a cloud created especially for that moment. Nothing like it had happened before or since. He had told His disciples, "It is expedient for you that I go away: for if I go not away, the Comforter will not come unto you; but if I depart, I will send him unto you" (John 16:7).

"It will be good for you," He said, "when I am gone. If I do not leave, the Comforter will not come." The message is plain: In Christ's estimation, His absence holds certain advantages for us. No wonder Dr. Luke makes note of their joy as they returned to Jerusalem. "He was parted from them, and carried up into heaven. And they worshipped him, and returned to Jerusalem with great joy" (Luke 24:51-52).

Jesus, the Son of God, "for the joy that was set before him endured the cross, despising the shame" (Heb. 12:2). Now He was vindicated from all His enemies said about Him and from every despicable accusation aimed at Him during His time on earth. Naturally, the disciples were filled with joy at this. Not only was He vindicated; they were vindicated too. His ascension, like the resurrection, was filled with both victory and promise for Him and for them as well. Never again would they doubt who He was or what He could do. Never again would they deny Him or walk away.

THE UNCERTAINTY OF ABSENCE

Only a few weeks before, doubt captured the disciples' hearts. The Hosanna chorus of Palm Sunday was by Friday an angry crucifixion cry. Just when it seemed that Jesus was finally coming into His own, every bright hope in their hearts was dashed by His death. The same multitude

Christ seemed to be winning over on Sunday became a bloodthirsty rabble in four short days. They cheered Him on, then turned on Him with all the fury hell could muster. We can easily understand the disappointment and frustration those who loved and walked with Him all along must have felt.

Then came the resurrection. It happened not only in the tomb. It happened inside them. There was a resurrected spirit inside each of them when they learned He had beaten cruel death. Life for each of them was jump-started. Even doubting Thomas came alive as never before at the recognition that Christ Jesus was indeed "the Christ, the Son of the living God." Who could deny that now? Thomas would never give in to doubt again. Like the rest of the disciples, he would go forward in new power. Tradition says that Thomas became the Lord's first missionary to India. Death was dead. It met its match in Christ. "O death, where is thy sting? O grave, where is thy victory?" (I Cor. 15:55).

All too soon Jesus announced that He must leave them again. Their resurrection joy was replaced by apprehension. He tried to explain in simple terms that He must go to prepare a place for them and that He would come back again one day. Still, with all of the emotional turmoil of a youngster being left with an unknown babysitter for an evening, His departure was unsettling for them. Christ said that they didn't need to fear. It was profitable for them that He should leave.

When We Lose the Ones We Love

In the last three years, I have stood at the graveside and watched the caskets of both my parents lowered into the ground. Today I know a bit more about death and grief than seminary could teach me. Yesterday I helped to conduct the funeral service for a very dear friend. A true Christian brother and confidant, Harry Coleman was wise, gracious, kind, gentle, and loving. He was a wonderful pastor to his congregation for over thirty years. He also was a quick-witted fun lover. Over the last few years, we have watched as Alzheimer's-like symptoms dragged away his once crisp mind. Yet when the end came, Harry succumbed to a heart attack.

How Harry died, however, or how my parents died, makes no difference for the long run. The loss of people we love for any reason is always sad. When we realize that we shall never see them again in this world, the loss hurts all the more. Their departure makes this world seem poorer. It leaves us feeling weakened and less well prepared for life's struggles.

Cogitating on these things, we can begin to sense the despair the disciples felt at Christ's announcement about leaving again. The only comfort came from His promise, "I'm going for your good, for if I don't go the Comforter will not come." We listen some more and He tells us why it is good for us that he is gone: "When he, the Spirit of truth, is come, he will guide you into all truth" (John 16:13). That was it! There was their hope. There would be new guidance for them by His Holy Spirit, the Breath of Abundant Life. Someone would come to lead them on toward heaven.

Does God still guide? The answer to that question is a resounding YES! According to the promise of Christ, God is still in the business of leading us through this present life. He directs our path by His Holy Spirit.

We should never doubt it. He was there for the children of Israel in the wilderness. "The Lord went before them by day in a pillar of a cloud, to lead them the way; and by night in a pillar of fire, to give them light; to go by day and night" (Exod. 13:21). He is, and will be, there to guide us.

HOKEY SPIRIT?

Well meaning but sometimes terribly misguided Christians have written and spoken a great deal of irrational nonsense about how God's guidance works for us. No wonder that some people outside Christ question whether or not there is valid guidance from heaven today. There is no grand mystery to the guidance of God. A seemingly deeply spiritual young woman attended a church where I was speaking. She caught my attention when she arrived late for every service. Instead of unobtrusively finding a quiet seat near the door she paraded down the center aisle, disturbing the concentration of others as she promenaded along. One evening, after the service was dismissed, she gushed, "I never do anything without a word from the Lord. Why, tonight I was almost here—I would have been on time too—when the Lord told me I had on the wrong dress. He wanted me to wear my green dress to encourage this Irish preacher. I noticed how green the trees are just now and I knew the Spirit was leading me. Those green leaves were my sign." I smiled politely and thought of how misguided she was. I replied, "Dear sister, when you came into the service late, you encouraged no one. Instead, you distracted some people from hearing God's Word." She was rather taken aback, but it was word in due season.

Does God care about the color of our clothes? Jesus said our heavenly Father clothes us better than the field lilies. We know from that and from other places in Scripture that God is interested in how we dress and in the other little issues of our lives. That lady in the church was wrong, however, in thinking that God was giving her a special sign about any relationship between the color of the tree leaves and the land of my birth. We do not always need a special sign. Her pastor later described this young woman as an unreasoning spiritual scatterbrain. She needed to recognize that finding and following God's will begins by living in obedience and response to present circumstances. His guidance is not mysterious. It is practical. If you are on your way somewhere dressed in blue or whatever color, stay with that color, especially when changing means arriving late and creating a disturbance.

A former employee of a church a friend of mine served had poor personal cleanliness habits. He seldom took a bath and left a foul smelling odor wherever he went. His teeth were dirty and decayed because he seldom, if ever, brushed them. His hair was matted and greasy from lack of grooming. On top of all this, the fellow had an obnoxious personality. Members of the congregation tried to reach out to him, but he rudely rebuffed them. Despite that, they kept trying to reach him. It was to no avail. My friend, in a last-ditch effort to help, tactfully raised the matter of personal cleanliness with the man. "Let me encourage you clean yourself up," he urged. The man's response told my friend the condition was intentional. "When it's time to clean up, God will tell me." Answers that invoke God can be made to sound pious. Most of us are reluctant to counter what God is reported to have said or, as in this case, not said. However, they are not always sound.

"Cleanliness is next to godliness!" That is what my mother told me. I was an adult before I realized those words were not a Scripture quote. It is true, of course, that Scripture does not tell us how often to bathe. The Bible does, however, provide life principles for our benefit. One is that we are to live in such a way as to avoid unnecessarily offending others (see I Corinthians 8:13).

In short, if you have body odor, take a bath. Take care of your teeth. (Or as a sign I saw once in a dental office said, "Ignore your teeth and they'll go away.") While you are at it, groom your hair. We may not keep any commandments by doing these things. However, if we wait for God to speak to us about them, we will wait throughout eternity, for God has already said all He is going to say and He will never change His mind.

HIS SIMPLE SUPERVISION

An old Bible professor of mine used to ask his students, "Do you want God's will? I'll give it to you: If your shoes are dirty, clean them. If you're sweaty, take a bath. If your hair is tossed about, comb it. But above all else, get your assignments to me on time or I'll dock your grade!" Then borrowing Paul's words, he added, "For this is the will of God in Christ Jesus concerning you!" (I Thess. 5:18). His hermeneutic might not have been on target, but his premise was sound. He was saying that there is order, balance, and reason to the guidance of God. He still leads us, but His manner, whilst occasionally mysterious and wonderful, is always practical. His plan for our lives is not otherworldly. His will is not disconnected from reality.

The children of Israel needed to find their way back home from Egypt. There was no local AAA office where they could pick up a map, so God, moving in a magnificent way, used one of His clouds along with some fire to get them where they needed to be. It was profitable for them to stay in step with God. They lost their way only after they stopped following His leadership.

IT'S A GOOD THING!

"It is expedient for you!" Another way to translate the Greek word *sumphero* is, "It is profitable for you," "It is in your best interests," or "It is to your advantage that I go away." There is no ambiguity about this. We find the same word, in both positive and negative contexts, elsewhere in the Gospels.

"If thy right hand offend thee, cut it off, and cast it from thee: for *it is profitable* for thee that one of thy members should perish, and not that thy whole body should be cast into hell" (Matt. 5:30).

"Whoso shall offend one of these little ones which believe in me, *it were better for him* that a millstone were hanged about his neck, and that he were drowned in the depth of the sea" (Matt. 18:6).

"If the case of the man be so with his wife, *it is not good* to marry" (Matt. 19:10).

"*It is expedient for us,* that one man should die for the people, and that the whole nation perish not" (John 11:50).

Every time *sumphero* is used, it is directed toward guiding people to a good path. Jesus was telling His disciples and through them us, "It is better if I go than if I stay so that the Comforter can come and guide you." We can hardly go wrong then if we recognize that God's guidance is not bizarre absurdity. It is not removed from the reality around us. God may not like some things about our present environment. Yet it is the one where He has come to us in Christ. It is, at least for now, the place where he has plans for us. He uses His disciples in practical ways and in real situations. His will is pragmatic and useful. It allows us to make some decisions (such as what color of dress to wear) for ourselves. Following the Spirit does not call us to be mechanical, unthinking marionettes. That is not the kind of mindless allegiance Jesus wants. "Thou shalt love the Lord thy God with all thy heart, and with all thy soul, and with all thy mind" (Matt. 22:37). God gave us minds because part of His intention for us is that we should learn to think His thoughts after Him.

FOUR KEYS TO UNLOCKING GOD'S WILL FOR YOUR LIFE

How can we learn God's will for us? The answer is simple rather than complex. There are four keys to discovering the leading of the Holy Spirit in your life.

THE FIRST KEY: WHAT DOES THE BIBLE TEACH

In a church our family attended when I was a child, the beadle placed the Bible on the pulpit lectern during each worship service. Having done that, he asked the preaching minister a splendid question taken directly from the book he had just carried, "Is there any word from the Lord?" (Jer. 37:17). The preacher responded, as does Jeremiah in that same place, "There is!"

Having thus answered, he directed the congregation's attention to the Scripture reading for the day. After reading the passage aloud, the minister proceeded to expose its truth in his sermon. I do not remember any particular sermon that man preached. I do not even recall his name. Yet that question and the response he made to it remains indelibly recorded in my memory bank. There is a word from the Lord for our generation.

PROFITABLE PROPHETS

"God hath spoken by the mouth of all his holy prophets since the world began" (Acts 3:21). "All scripture is ... profitable for doctrine, for reproof, for correction, for instruction in righteousness" (II Tim. 3:16). God, who gave us His Word, never directs us where the Bible does not go. The Holy Spirit in no way will ever guide us to do something that runs counter to God's revealed will in the Bible.

After over a quarter century in pastoral ministry, I assumed I had probably heard all a pastor was likely to hear by way of rationalization. I was proved wrong a few weeks ago when one couple told me that God told them they should cohabitate as husband and wife for a year before they made any wedding plans. They explained that as children, they had each endured the horrible emotional trauma of parents divorcing and they wanted to eliminate every possibility of failure. "How did God tell you it was okay to live together?" I asked them. "Well," the man said, "we talked about it and prayed about it and it just seemed like a good idea." I do not doubt that they sincerely believed they might test their suitability as marriage partners in this way. I quickly informed them that their lifestyle, all too common in today's culture, runs counter to God's Word.

"How could I be so sure?" they asked. "Because God absolutely never contradicts the Bible," I replied. His Word is His "lamp unto [our] feet, and light unto [our] path" (Ps. 119:105).

For Jesus' disciples, God's direct guidance has come through His Word for two millennia now. His Word, like His Spirit, is given for our profit. The promises of God are as sound today as they were the day they were issued. You can trust your life to them.

186

But what if someone may ask, God's Word is not true and reliable? If God's Word is not true, the Christian gospel, which has been the force behind major world movements in health, education, and Western civilization in general, is bankrupt. If the Bible is not true, we face a worldwide spiritual crisis greater than any other in history. But God's Word is true and it is reliable. He keeps all His promises to lead us to "Good works, which God hath before ordained that we should walk in" (Eph. 2:10). The Bible is filled from cover to cover with undying certainties that guide us all through life. Abraham Lincoln called it "the best book God has given to man. But for it we could not know right from wrong."

If you want to test whether a vision or idea is good, search the Scriptures. Never follow an idea, no matter how appealing it is, that does not have a biblical foundation. Every wise decision that has ever been made to benefit humanity, whether or not a Christian made it, is in line with what the Bible teaches us. The wisdom of God's Word is a sure guide to keep us in the right path.

THE SECOND KEY: PRAYER AND MEDITATION

After the Bible comes prayer and meditation. The couple who wanted to try their suitability for marriage never read the Bible. They relied only on prayer. And prayer that does not seek the Word of God through the Bible first can be misleading.

"Call unto me, and I will answer thee, and shew thee great and mighty things, which thou knowest not" (Jer. 33:3). If we sincerely want to know God's will for our lives, it stands to reason that we should talk to Him. That is what prayer allows us to do. The second key to unlocking God's will for us is prayer and meditation.

OUR DECLARATION OF DEPENDENCE

Prayer is more than a heaven directed 911 call for troubled people. Prayer is also more than asking God to do our will. At its heart, prayer is intended to be a daily declaration of our dependence on God. It implies that we know we need God to guide us. Prayer is one of God's ways of helping us to know and follow His will. Is it not interesting that even though the

Bible gives us several accounts of Jesus praying to His Father, it never once records a single word of what the Father might have said or done in response to Christ's prayers? Yet Jesus kept on praying. For us, prayer can bring patience. Sometimes we see the clear answer to our prayers immediately. We pray, for example, that someone might be healed and they recover quickly. Sometimes, however, the answer never seems to come. That may be God's way of telling us His answer is no and we are reluctant to accept it. Or it may be God's way of saying, "Wait a while. The timing is not right." Sometimes the answer is not what we want to hear. We think it is not to our benefit when that happens, but it is. In the shadow of the cross, Jesus prayed for the bitter cup to pass from Him. At first glance it looks as though God answers negatively. Yet wait a few days and the Father answers, "You can see now that I had something far more wonderful in mind."

Hank, a fellow from one of our congregations, prayed that God would help him secure a place on the basketball team at the university that he attended. When it did not happen as he had prayed, Hank was really disappointed. He wondered if prayer makes any difference or if God even cares. Suddenly, with no advance notice, Hank was selected for an opportunity to spend a study year abroad. He would have been unable to accept that opportunity had he been selected to play basketball.

How do I pray for guidance? There are three parts to a prayer for God to guide us. The first part is to admit that we are sinners. When you seek God's will in prayer, always begin by acknowledging your sins and asking his forgiveness. The second part is to remember who it is we are talking to. Praise God for who He is and for what He has done. Finally, in plain language tell God what you have in mind and ask Him to guide you to do the right things for the right reasons.

Meditation might be called the other side of prayer. If prayer is speaking, meditation is more concerned with trying to allow God to speak to us in silence. "They that wait upon the Lord shall renew their strength; they shall mount up with wings as eagles; they shall run, and not be weary; and they shall walk, and not faint" (Isa. 40:31).

When you meditate, go to a place where you can remain undisturbed for a while. Sit, lie, or stand quietly and comfortably there. It is important to be comfortable so that our posture does not disturb our time with God. Begin your time of meditation by asking for the illumination of the Holy Spirit. Specifically name the issues on which you want to know God's will and ask the Spirit to guide you to the right answers in the Bible. He will.

THE THIRD KEY: THE SPIRIT'S INWARD VOICE

Are you listening for God? Sometimes we become so preoccupied with the autocracy of the compelling forces around us that we fail to hear God's soul-stirring whispers.

"Behold, there came a voice unto him, and said, What doest thou here, Elijah?" (I Kings 19:13). Elijah knew that the still, small voice was God's. Not long before, he and the multitudes gathered on Mount Carmel along with the Baal prophets and witnessed fire fall out of heaven and consume a soaking sacrifice. For us, the message is plain: God does not always reveal His will in powerful, miraculous ways in the presence of large crowds. He speaks also in whispers that are audible to our hearts.

"The voice of the Lord is upon the waters: the God of glory thundereth: the Lord is upon many waters" (Ps. 29:3). Sometimes, says David the psalmist, God's voice thunders like a mighty ocean in a hurricane. At other times, He speaks with the whisper of a babbling brook. The third key to finding God's will is training the ears of our spirit to hear His voice however it comes to us. Listen carefully. God's opportunity could be knocking at your heart's door very softly.

THE FOURTH KEY: THE REALITIES AROUND US

The fourth key to finding God's will is to note the realities around you. "We are his workmanship, created in Christ Jesus unto good works, which God hath before ordained that we should walk in them" (Eph. 2:10). Nothing in our lives is accidental. Everything has its purpose. God has placed us where we are today as part of His greater plan for our tomorrow with Him. There are lessons to be learned where we are now that will make us more useful to Him in the future.

THE THINGS WE CANNOT CONTROL

God guides us through real life circumstances, even some we cannot control. As much as I like American politics, I am certain God does not want me to be president. How do I know that? Because the United States Constitution allows only natural born citizens to work in the Oval Office. I was disqualified from being president of the United States on the day I was born. That is an uncontrollable circumstance of my life and I must accept it. Barbara was born outside the United States also. Therefore, I have no expectations about becoming first husband either. My best hope for sleeping in the Lincoln Bedroom as a blood relative of the president comes through our American born daughter, Erin, or our American born grandchildren (any one of whom would make a magnificent president in my "totally unbiased" opinion).

The point is that there are factors beyond our control in all our lives that help us to discern God's desire for us. We should pay heed to them. They include genetic stipulations over which we have no power. Therefore, part of the fourth key to finding God's will is to recognize the circumstances about us we cannot change. He who hung the stars has also placed us, as we are, where we are.

AND THE THINGS WE CAN CONTROL

"But," I can almost hear someone protesting, "he is not where he was born. He moved to another city in another country an ocean away." You are right, of course! Yet as I reflect on my own life story, which was told briefly in an earlier chapter, it is all the more obvious that God's intention was to use me for whatever purposes He had in mind. We did not emigrate to America with the gospel ministry in mind. Our American dream was far removed from that. I am all too aware that even when neither Barbara nor I were Christians, God was working out His purpose for us. For example, the circumstances under which we gained legal residency in America happened in a way that God alone could have guided. Through a series of events over which we had no control, God opened doors that appeared to be closed and made possible some changed circumstances we could control.

Some things we can control and some things we can change. There are habits and self-defeating behavior patterns we can change through repentance. There are circumstances we can change by intention and, sometimes, personal sacrifice. When I sensed God's call to preach, I did not have a college degree. Yet the denomination to which I believed I was being called required not one, but two, degrees. I could not be president of the United States, but I could further my education in obedience to God's call. That call within my spirit was so strong that I resigned my financially stable and promising career with a major corporation and Barbara and I sold our home and invested the equity we received toward my education. After we made that first step in faith, we saw God faithfully provide for us in amazing ways through the years that followed. I can say out of personal experience that tomorrow God will open doors in your life that appear closed today.

BLOOMING (OR NOT BLOOMING) WHERE YOU ARE PLANTED!

Following Jesus meant abandoning similar environmental ties for His first disciples. Following God meant Abram had to make a choice between Ur and the inward voice that called him to step out to unexplored places. There is a certain undeniable parallel between "I am the Lord that brought thee out of Ur of the Chaldees, to give thee this land to inherit it" (Gen. 15:7) and "He ordained twelve, that they should be with him" (Mark 3:14).

In each case, a pre-condition of being in God's will was that they should abandon present security for an unsecured future in God's service. Catching fish and tanning hides were, and are, honorable occupations; but if they were really to be God's men, the disciples had to leave what was familiar "that they should be with him."

FORSAKING THE FAMILIAR

"Jesus himself testified, that a prophet hath no honour in his own country" (John 4:44). Their preparation for God's tomorrow was best accomplished away from the old familiar places and faces. Only in a new place could Christ have their essentially undivided attention. In the old places there were, perhaps, too many easily found distractions. Perhaps there were also familiar irresistible temptations. In a new environment and under a new power, they could experience an intimacy with Christ that would prepare them to change the whole direction of human history for generations yet unborn.

Having said this, Christ's call to "follow me" does not always involve an immediate nomadic relocation. Great works have been accomplished in Christ's name by people who heard His call to stay where they were. Some disciples are also called, it seems, to bloom near where they are planted in spite of any inherent distractions there. Certainly, where we are today is the place to begin our walk with Christ. If relocation is in His plans, we will know that at the right time.

LORD BUT!

The real issue is, are we willing to forsake the familiar? Our will is involved in finding the Spirit's guidance also. Before we can serve Christ with integrity, we must give up our will. "They straightway left their nets, and followed him" (Matt. 4:20). For those fishermen to surrender their nets to Christ was to give up every hope they held of future security. It was a demonstration of their obedience, their trust, and their willingness to go where Christ might lead.

That was not the case of the fellow who reasoned, when called to follow, "Lord, suffer me first to go and bury my father" (Luke 9:59). His problem was not a dead father. His problem was one of willingness. His word choice betrays his heart. That word *first* in "Suffer me first" was saying, "I am unwilling to surrender some of my personal plans to you, Jesus." His conflicted answer betrays an unsurrendered will. He calls Jesus "Lord," then immediately denies his Lordship. He was saying, "You are Lord, but ...!"

The Lord of eternity demands more than that from all of us. His Word says, "Thou shalt have no other gods before me" (Exod. 20:3). Jesus Himself said, "Whosoever he be of you that forsaketh not all that he hath, he cannot be my disciple" (Luke 14:33). "When Christ calls a man," wrote Dietrich Bonhoeffer as he reconciled his call to preach with a Nazi hangman's rope, "he bids him, 'Come and die!'"[1] Following Christ demands willingness to die to self and all our old appurtenances. "If any man will come after me, let him deny himself, and take up his cross daily, and follow me. For whosoever will save his life shall lose it: but whosoever will lose his life for my sake, the same shall save it" (Luke 9:23-24). To do less is to be trite about eternal things.

Following the Spirit's leading is no cheap, easy experience. For twenty centuries now thousands have suffered and are still suffering because of their commitment to follow Chris,t who offers no part-time openings for disciples. He wants all or nothing! A man told me not long ago that if he died his wife and children would be "fairly well taken care of." When asked what that meant, "I have a life insurance policy that will more or less take care of them."

There are no "more or less" disciples with Jesus. "Almost thou persuadest me to be a Christian," King Agrippa replied to Paul's invitation (Acts. 26:28). However powerful Agrippa seemed at that moment, he went down in history as a loser because of his unwillingness to surrender completely to Christ. Unlike Dietrich Bonhoeffer, Agrippa was not amenable to making the sacrifice that following Christ demands. Today, Bonhoeffer, who died with very little in the way of this world's goods, is remembered as a hero while Agrippa, who left enormous material wealth when he died, is remembered as one who finally failed at living.

The same is true in all of life. Anything worth having calls for a willingness to make a personal sacrifice. If we want to win, we must pay the price of surrendering our personal ambitions. "I have nothing to offer you but blood, sweat and tears," Winston Churchill told the British people as he laid his plan to hold back Hitler's oncoming forces and preserve democracy in Europe. Later Churchill said, "We need men who love their freedom wholeheartedly, not only with words, to join us in this fight."

Great business leaders know this too. Ask the men or women who built great corporations from scratch and you will hear a common thread of dedicated sacrifice running through their stories. They took risks and

---

1. Dietrich Bonhoeffer. *The Cost of Discipleship*, (New York: The MacMillan Company, 1957).

often paid dearly for success. It is said that the only place where success comes before work is in the dictionary.

Winning athletes, too, make sacrifices. They pommel their bodies and train their minds behind the scenes for years in hope of future glory. Great musicians do it also. I once asked James Galway how often he practiced playing the flute. He replied, "As often and as long as it takes to get it right." I learned later that after decades of playing in great concert halls across the world, the world's master flutist spends at least four to six hours in practice every day in preparation for bringing musical joy to the ears of millions. Success in any realm comes only through sacrifice, determination, and focusing on priorities.

Success with God comes the same way. "Seek ye first the kingdom of God, and his righteousness; and all these things shall be added unto you" (Matt. 6:33). "This one thing I do, forgetting those things which are behind, and reaching forth unto those things which are before, I press toward the mark for the prize of the high calling of God in Christ Jesus" (Phil. 3:13-14). In Vince Lombardi's words, "Winning is not the most important thing, it is the only thing!"

Finding the will of God for your life means putting the desire to serve Him first and everything else second.

What is your life's ambition? You say, "To follow Christ." Good! But are you willing to tear up all your other interests and go where He wants you? Until you are, you are not ready to be His disciple even at home. Following Jesus begins with an inward surrender to do His will right where we are today. Before you even turn to the next page, ask yourself, "Am I willing to follow Jesus anywhere, at any cost, whatever the pain, regardless of the sacrifice?" I must ask myself the same question before I write another page. If either of us answers with something other than a resolute "YES!" then this book ends here for us. We simply are not serious about being His disciples until we are absolutely resigned to follow wherever He leads. It is pointless to write (or to read) any more.

I just said, "YES! Lord!" Did you? If so, then we are ready to move on together and discover the next step in knowing the Holy Spirit's guidance for us. Only one thing is left before we do that. One more important question needs to be answered.

WHAT CAN I DO WHEN I MISS GOD'S WILL?

Is it possible for a Christian to take the wrong direction? Of course it is, for as we have seen, we are free moral agents. That freedom brings the risk that we might lose our way. We can miss God's direction intentionally or unintentionally. However, we cannot be happy for long walking the wrong way. Sooner or later, the Breath of Abundant Life will turn us back towards God's face. Abraham lied. Moses was a short-fused murderer. David fell repeatedly. The first disciples of Jesus betrayed Him, denied Him, and walked away when tough times came. We shall also fail Him. What is worse, we shall do it every day. "Let him that thinketh he standeth take heed lest he fall" (I Cor. 10:12). "If we say that we have no sin, we deceive ourselves, and the truth is not in us" (I John 1:8).

THE WAY BACK TO GOD

Yet even in our falling, God is present and He will work in the circumstances where we fall to teach us and redeem us. How can I come back to God? The answer has two steps to it. They are confession and repentance. Confession is our admission that we have not followed in His way. Repentance proves the sincerity of our confession. Repentance means to turn in the opposite direction. If we have been following our own will, we should turn back to God's will. When we confess our sins and repent from them, the Lord will always hear us, forgive us, and redeem us. Falling is a constant demonstration of how much we need Christ to redeem us.

If, on the other hand, what we really need is some kind of divine puppeteer, we will not find that in the God of the Bible. If what we are looking for is a Holy Spirit whose directions leave no room for misunderstanding, Christianity, as it is presented in the Bible, will frustrate us and drive us down. If it is fast-food answers about the complexities of life we want, we will always be disappointed by Jesus. That, however, is not what we need: "It is expedient for you that I go away: for if I go not away, the Comforter will not come unto you; but if I depart, I will send him unto you.... When he, the Spirit of truth, is come, he will guide you into all truth" (John 14: 16-17). Christ's ascension removed from our presence the Light of the World, the Way, the Truth, the Life. "Into all truth" implies that we are predisposed to drift away. "Prone to wander Lord, I feel it. Prone to leave the God I love."[2] Visible guidance was withdrawn so that invisible grace could be given to us. The good news is that when we take the wrong path, God through Christ provides a way back to the right one, just as He did for Abraham, Moses, and David. The first disciples (with the exception of Judas) were given a second chance.

Freedom allows us to make bad decisions and sin. Freedom also allows us to surrender to Christ's voice within us and make informed, good choices. Life is far more exciting, more livable, more real when I don't know all the answers and don't have easy access to a push-button deity who will tell me what color of dress to wear tonight. It is always more exciting to be a partner than a puppet.

In our resolve to make good choices, we find the guidance of the Holy Spirit, the Breath of Abundant Life. Through Him we live the life as God intends it. This is the beginning of true success. In chapter twelve we will consider how God's success moves our lives long term as we walk in fellowship with the Breath of Abundant Life.

---

2. From the hymn "Come, Thou Fount of Every Blessing," by Robert Robinson, 1758

12

Successful living in fellowship with the Spirit

Edward Vernon Rickenbacker first saw the daylight in a modest Columbus, Ohio, neighborhood. Even as a child, Eddie was impressed by mechanical things and by speed. Automobiles fascinated him, especially fast ones. Nobody was surprised when he found his way to the racing circuit, where he quickly became a champion. Then the accomplishments of two other Buckeye State citizens, Wilbur and Orville Wright, caught his fancy. It seemed to him that a whole new frontier was opened by their successful flight on North Carolina's outer banks. Given his love of powerful engines and fast cars, flying seemed to be a natural transition for Eddie.

When the United States Army organized its first aero unit, Eddie was more than ready to allow Uncle Sam to bankroll his air exploits. It was a "win-win" relationship. His flying expertise already well established, Eddie would serve his country doing something he loved. Promptly promoted to unit commander, he quickly established himself as America's leading flying ace. Now he was a hero on the road and in the sky.

When peacetime came, Eddie was recruited by the business world. Commercial flying was a new frontier, and the leadership experience he had gained in the U.S. Army Air-Corp served him well. Combined with his personality, hard work, and quick, visionary thinking, it moved him rapidly up the corporate ladder. A few years later, Eddie found himself in the corporate pilot's seat as chairman and president of one of the country's great airlines.

Then along came another war. When America entered World War II after Pearl Harbor, Eddie volunteered once more for service with the Air Corps. He served with such distinction and courage that he was awarded the Congressional Medal of Honor, the highest honor his country could bestow on him.

Eddie Rickenbacker was a bigger-than-life legend in his own time. Despite that, people who knew him remember him as a modest man. He was not one to brag constantly on his own achievements.

One of my favorite Eddie Rickenbacker stories dates back to 1942, one year after the United States entered the Second World War. Eddie was on an overseas trip, inspecting island military bases in Asia. He and his crew were forced to ditch their plane somewhere in the Pacific. So far over the ocean were they that no land base could hear their mayday signals. After watching their plane sink to its watery grave, they bobbed helplessly on a nine-foot raft for three weeks. It was widely assumed that the sea had consumed them. Each day Captain Rickenbacker and one of his men led the little band in morning prayer and Bible study. Their food rations quickly dwindled until there was nothing left. One morning, weakened by malnutrition and facing the prospect of starving to death at sea, they prayed for God to save them from a watery grave. A few minutes later, God came in the form of a stray seagull that landed on Eddie Rickenbacker's hat. At whiplash speed, Eddie reached up and trapped the bird in his bare hands. He quickly killed, cleaned, and dressed that raven of the ocean and divided its meat among his men. Each one received only a morsel, which he ate raw. It wasn't much, but it was enough to keep them alive and renew their hope. What was more, the bird's entrails provided them with fish-bait and the intestines of the fish they caught became the bait for catching more fish. Thus, one wayward seagull and a fast thinking, fast acting leader established a food cycle. A diet of fish and occasionally dried seaweed was not exactly what these military top-brass were used to as they traveled from base to base, eating in the officers' quarters and nice hotels. For Eddie Rickenbacker, however, it was evidence of the Lord's practical grace. He and his crew survived to talk about God's amazing provision. Spotted by a ship after nearly a month on the ocean, they were rescued. When the war was over, Eddie Rickenbacker was every man's hero. He sought no accolades for himself however. "Whatever success I am credited with is not mine but Jesus Christ's," he declared. "Whatever I was doing, I tried to keep Him as my homing beacon."

In chapter eleven, we heard Jesus say that He must leave for our benefit. How that initial work of the Holy Spirit begins to show itself in our daily lives was the focus of what was said there. In this chapter, we will see how His Holy Spirit works out His benefit in us today and leads us to success.

Success! What is it and how will we measure it? How do we know when we have it? Or if we do not?

"The one who dies with the most toys wins!" Those words blaring from a bumper sticker on the back of a screaming red Ferrari that passed me on Sixth Avenue yesterday seem to define success for many people in our generation. The problem with those words is that they fail to tell the truth, the whole truth, and nothing but the truth. What they don't say is that whoever dies with the most toys is just as dead as whoever dies with no toys. When the owner of that Ferrari breathes his last, he will be buried in the same size cemetery plot as the penniless pauper who spends his nights sleeping between the portals of our church building. After a quarter century of standing at gravesides with my people, I can testify that it doesn't matter if the body in the casket rubbed shoulders with the rich and powerful or slept in a night shelter. Grave holes are one-size-fits-all. Jesus Christ has a better idea that flips our commonly held notions of success over on their ear. His beliefs about success permeate the whole New Testament understanding of true prosperity and have stood the test of two thousand years.

THE GIFT THAT KEEPS ON GIVING

What is real success as taught by Jesus? Let me suggest a summary definition straight from the inspired pen of the most read writer in human history: "The grace of the Lord Jesus Christ, and the love of God, and the communion of the Holy Ghost, be with you all. Amen" (II Cor. 13:14). Real success, according to this definition is to experience for ourselves Christ's grace, God's love, and the constant companionship of the Breath of Abundant Life. What a gift that is for all who receive it! The two things that never die and that we can take with us into eternity are Christ's grace and God's love. In the meantime, there is fellowship with God and His Son Jesus through the Holy Spirit. This really is the gift that keeps on giving, for it promises success for this world and the next. Now, that's real success!

This picture of success that meets us on the pages of the New Testament is remarkably different from what we read in *People* magazine or *Investor's Business Daily,* or see on *Lifestyles of the Rich and Famous.* It is not that there is anything inherently wrong with success as defined in these other places, provided that it is properly understood. Such success not properly understood can be very temporary and short-lived and a source of unimaginable misery. If you ever doubt that, think about some of the people the world has termed successful and how they ended their lives.

Curt Cobain was one of his generation's most popular rock stars. He lived life, as he knew it, to the hilt. Pleasure was his password, sex his byword, and drug abuse his favorite recreation. He pursued all three with reckless abandon only to find that pleasure plus sex plus drugs bring neither success nor happiness. He died of an intentional drug overdose.

Nor is success found in wealth. Christina Onassis, heiress of her father, Aristotle's, shipping fortune, told a reporter only a few weeks before she died, "Anyone who believes money can buy happiness has not looked at my family."

Success is not synonymous with fame and following. Jerry Garcia was trailed by the masses. People, even well-regarded professional people, put their careers and businesses on a back burner to pursue the life of a "Deadhead." Few entertainers reach the long-term popularity status of Jerry Garcia and the Grateful Dead. Yet Garcia died as a repeat patient in a drug detoxification center. Fame does not equal success.

Success should never be equated with power, control, or family connection either. Saddam Hussein's sons-in-law, the fathers of his grandchildren, died by the bullet by which they had lived. Each of these people the world regarded as "successful" met an end that none of us would work to achieve. Their experience of success was short-lived and came at a price too high for anyone to pay.

If only they had taken to heart the gripping story Jesus told about a man who invested well, worked hard, and reaped bountifully: "He thought within himself, saying, What shall I do, because I have no room where to bestow my fruits? And he said, This will I do: I will pull down my barns, and build greater; and there will I bestow all my fruits and my goods. And I will say to my soul, Soul, thou hast much goods laid up for many years; take thine ease, eat, drink, and be merry. But God said unto him, Thou fool, this night thy soul shall be required of thee: then whose shall those things be?" (Luke 12:17-20).

From Christ's words we can compose a personality profile of this man the Master had in mind. This is how we might describe him if he lived in our neighborhood: "He is a nice fellow, really, and obviously, a great success. His business is good. He is on an expansion program. There is no hint of immorality about his life. He is not a crook. Perhaps he is generous. He certainly provides for his family's long-term well-being."

Yet Jesus saves the strongest word He ever used for this man the world would call successful: "Fool!" Fool? What did he do that was so stupid? Only that he failed to make adequate preparation for eternity. In all of his getting, he forgot he had a soul to save. Charles Wesley wrote, "A charge to keep I have, A God to glorify, A never dying soul to save, And fit it for the sky."[1]

The television newsmagazine *Dateline NBC* reported a story about an adventuresome young man from an affluent family, who full of dreams for a great future, chartered a plane and pilot to fly him to a remote area of the desolate North Country of Alaska. His expressed goal was that he might find himself among the natural beauty and mysteries in that largely unexplored part of our planet. He cashed in part of his inheritance and for months went through the process of gathering up everything he thought he might need. He bought plenty of clothes and supplies to keep warm. He stockpiled over five hundred rolls of film, several cameras, and fourteen hundred pounds of food and provisions. He purchased two or three guns and ammunition to ward off any unpleasantness he might encounter on his great adventure. He bought several spiral notebooks, which he planned to use as diaries. Use them, he did. He vividly recorded the Far North's splendor. His excitement with his discoveries is not hard to detect, especially among the words of his first diary entries. "Awesome!" "Stupendous!" "Majestic!" All these and other words describe the sights he

---

1. Charles Wesley, (1762). Taken from *Hymns for the Living Church.* (Grand Rapids: Hope Publishing).

captured there. Slowly, however, the tone of his writings begins to change. Excitement gradually is replaced by the hard cold fact that he realizes he has forgotten one thing. His final words are the unheard siren call of a horrifying nightmare. He died in a nameless valley by a nameless lake about 225 miles northeast of Fairbanks. He left his abundant collection of things and friendships back in the "lower 48." His final diary entry says, "I should have used more foresight in arranging my departure."

Carefully laying up everything he imagined he might ever need for his time in the wilderness, he forgot to plan his exit. His badges of success were neatly stacked nearby. Wonderful family photographs! Extraordinary life! Hundreds of beautiful pictures and striking descriptions of the wild frontier! All these things were near his emaciated, frozen body when a search team found it. Have you planned your way out? "It is appointed unto men once to die, but after this the judgment" (Heb. 9:27). If you achieve all the things this world counts wonderful but fail to make plans for your way out, you will die a failure, even if you leave a fortune. To be truly successful is to know beyond a shadow of doubt that you will spend eternity with God in His heaven. Like the man who envisioned bigger barns, that young man's success was great but short-lived.

Long-Lived Success

Success as defined by the apostle Paul, however, is always long-lived. Sometimes it calls for jettisoning elements that others call necessary parts of success.

Success Symbols

Eddie Rickenbacker wanted everyone to know that front-page photo-ops, powerful positions, popularity polls, a household name, and a high figure net worth statement did not define his measure of success. True success means achieving God's plan for your life. For Eddie Rickenbacker that was a living relationship in fellowship with God's Son, Jesus Christ. Possessing a lot of "toys" did not make Eddie a winner. Honing in on the will of Christ and walking in fellowship with Him was Eddie's measure of real success.

WINNING THROUGH LOSING

If the most toys makes a victor, Paul the Apostle was born a winner and died a loser. "Though I might also have confidence in the flesh. If any other man thinketh that he hath whereof he might trust in the flesh, I more; circumcised the eighth day, of the stock of Israel, of the tribe of Benjamin, an Hebrew of the Hebrews; as touching the law, a Pharisee; Concerning zeal, persecuting the church; touching the righteousness which is in the law, blameless. But what things were gain to me, those I counted loss for Christ. Yea doubtless, and I count all things but loss for the excellency of the knowledge of Christ Jesus my Lord: for whom I have suffered the loss of all things, and do count them but dung, that I may win Christ" (Phil. 3:4-8).

Paul's was the red Ferrari success story of his time. He had "all the toys" a Jewish lad could gather. Yet he writes, "My success began when I gave up everything I once counted worth having. The things that were gain to me, those I counted loss for Christ." The Greek might be just as literally translated, "My success began the day I lost the symbols I once called valuable." Paul, the born winner, was born again a loser. He started out with a silver spoon in his mouth and ended up with nothing except a few books and a coat. Yet he dares to call himself a success! How can that be? It can only be because Paul traded all he owned for the greatest treasure there is: Fellowship with Christ in the power of the Holy Spirit, the Breath of Abundant Life.

Saul of Tarsus was a product of the finest breeding, a winner from the start as far as his peers were concerned. Birth! Breeding! Secure upbringing! Education! He had it all. His was the then first-century equivalent of an Ivy League education, for he studied under the finest teacher of his day, Gamaliel. His life was a predictable pattern. His success was a given, or so it seemed!

We've all known people like Paul. Where I grew up such folks were sometimes known as "the landed gentry." Born into a good home, often with a noble title attached to their name, frequently they start out near the top of the corporate ladder. As a friend told me one time, "Their biggest problem is how long their father might live and keep them from moving into the corner office!"

TOP TO BOTTOM!

Paul was among the most elite on the social register of his time and place. Then, he says, something unexpected and uncharacteristic happened to him. It changed the whole direction of his life. When it did, Paul once a winner became Paul a loser. Could it be that God has plans to bring you to the same place?

The answer is yes! For with Christ the way up is always down. It always begins with a diminishing sense of self and an increasing sense of Christ. "He must increase, but I must decrease" (John 3:30).

During the early days of His earthly ministry, Jesus outlined this abundant life success in ways that both Paul and Eddie Rickenbacker learned to understand. His message has been passed on to us as the Sermon on the Mount. "Blessed are the poor in spirit: for theirs is the kingdom of heaven. Blessed are they that mourn: for they shall be comforted. Blessed are the meek: for they shall inherit the earth. Blessed are they which do hunger and thirst after righteousness: for they shall be filled. Blessed are the merciful: for they shall obtain mercy. Blessed are the pure in heart: for they shall see God. Blessed are the peacemakers: for they shall be called the children of God. Blessed are they which are persecuted for righteousness' sake: for theirs is the kingdom of heaven. Blessed are ye, when men shall revile you, and persecute you, and shall say all manner of evil against you falsely, for my sake. Rejoice, and be exceeding glad: for great is your reward in heaven: for so persecuted they the prophets which were before you" (Matt. 5:3-12).

This is the course outline for successful living as taught by the most dynamic teacher in all history. With poetic rhythm, he reinforces each lesson with one word: "Blessed!" That word goes to the heart of everything He taught us to be and do while He walked among us. If you want to be successful and know the power of the Spirit's constant companionship throughout this life, make this word your clarion call: "Blessed!"

A EULOGY FOR GOD?

The Greek is makarios. It might also be translated "supremely successful, flawlessly fortunate, infinitely well-off." The precise Greeks used two words for blessed, and makarios is one of them. The other word is eulogia, also found in the New Testament. The second word is the foundation for our word eulogy. We usually associate the word *eulogy* with a funeral service, although the American Heritage Dictionary does not limit its use exclusively to that setting. Nor does the New Testament, where we read of Zecharias, father of John the Baptist and the one whom God dumbfounded by the news that he and his barren wife, Elisabeth, would bare a child, that "His mouth was opened immediately, and his tongue loosed, and he spake, and praised God" (Luke 1:64).

The Greek text could be interpreted as saying that Zecharias *eulogized* God. He did not, of course, belong to the "God is dead" school. Indeed, his experience was to the contrary. Instead, his dead religion took on life in a personal relationship with the God of heaven. As a result, he was unable to speak throughout Elisabeth's pregnancy. However, when the baby boy he was promised arrived, suddenly Zecharias found his voice again. This verse and others in the New Testament help us understand the difference between the Greek words *eulogia* and *makarios*. One is praise as directed from human beings to God (*eulogia*). The other (*makarios*) is blessing that comes the opposite way, or from God to humanity. Thus, it can only come through the Holy Spirit. This success as defined by Jesus in His Sermon on the Mount and delivered in the power of the Holy Spirit will be the focus of the remainder of this chapter.

CHRIST'S FIRST SUCCESS SYMBOL:
SUCCESS MEANS POVERTY

"Blessed are the poor in spirit: for theirs is the kingdom of heaven."

This poverty of spirit that Christ encourages has nothing to do with material indigence. Nor does it mean being spiritually poor. To be "poor in spirit" is to realize we need a power beyond ourselves if we are to live life to the full. It is humility. It isn't easy to humble oneself, and it runs against the grain of everything that we are inclined to be and do. Yet the Lord is looking for teachable, trusting hearts. He will honor those who humble themselves.

Max Cleland first impressed me when one of our former churches hosted a group of international business leaders that we took to the Georgia State capitol. Max Cleland was Georgia's secretary of state at the time and, though in a wheelchair, one of the most vibrant and fulfilled personalities I have met. Since then, he has been one of my heroes. Before that I had no idea how well Max Cleland's life models what Jesus had in mind when He laid out this first success principle.

Early one morning in 1968, Captain Max Cleland awoke an energetic young U.S. Army captain. When the sun set that evening, Captain Cleland was fighting for his life in a M-A-S-H hospital, his body torn into rough edged pieces like an ugly homemade jigsaw puzzle. A Vietcong grenade took away both his legs and one arm. Months of excruciating mental and physical torment lay before him. Against the odds, he survived by sheer will power. Back in Georgia, Max Cleland was elected to two terms in the state legislature. After that, he ran for the state's number two office and was soundly defeated. He said later that the idea of his own people rejecting him at the ballot box was more agonizing than all the pain that grenade in a far-off country brought him. Eventually he was hired as a staff assistant in Washington, D.C. In that capacity he was driving through the nation's capital in a blinding rain one evening when he began to experience flashbacks. His life with all its broken parts and defeats bore in on him in a way he had not experienced before. He said later, "I was in a mess. Three of my four limbs were gone. I felt like less than half a man. I thought again about being rejected by my own people and concluded no one cared what I had gone through for the country. I was overwhelmed by a sense of being a burden to the people around me. For the first time, I felt as though I simply couldn't take any more. I pulled over to the side of the freeway and wept like a baby. 'Oh, God help me. Nobody cares,' I cried. Tears rolled down my cheeks, off my chin, and onto my shirt. As I wept, I sensed new power rise up inside me. It was like nothing I had experienced before. I knew that God cared and that I was all the man God needed. He made me strong at my broken places." Today, United States Senator Max Cleland represents the State of Georgia in our nation's capital. That night on a rain-soaked freeway near Washington, D.C., Max Cleland met someone else who was rejected by His own people, Jesus Christ, of whom it is written, "He came unto his own, and his own received him not. But as many as received him, to them gave he power to become the sons of God, even to them that believe on his name" (John 1:11-12). Max Cleland discovered for himself that a God-given power comes upon us as we surrender our own strength and lean fully on God's Son, Jesus. It is the power of the Breath of Abundant Life. When He comes, we have taken the initial step up the stairway of His kind of success, true success.

THE SECOND SYMBOL:
SUCCESS MEANS TEARS

"Blessed are they that mourn: for they shall be comforted."

For over thirty years, Clyde (not his real name) had connections to the organized crime network that ruled the Gulf Coast underworld. Clyde ran an illegal back room "gambling and girls" operation in the area. Rumor had it that every local law enforcement officer of significant rank was unofficially on Clyde's payroll. Clyde started to attend church soon after his granddaughter was severely injured in an automobile accident. For a long time, her survival was in question. Tears flowed down Clyde's cheeks each Sunday as I presented the message of God's amazing grace and forgiveness through Calvary's cross. Every attempt I made to minister to Clyde was thwarted. "One day we'll talk," he told me repeatedly, "but not yet."

After several weeks, Clyde's "one day" came! Arriving at our back door unannounced late that afternoon, he said, "I can talk now." We sat down together at the kitchen table. He started talking by acknowledging the nature of his business and said he knew he had to close, which he had done six weeks earlier. Since shutting his shop, Clyde had been busy. His days and evenings were spent seeking the forgiveness of everyone he believed his business had harmed. He apologized not just to his old clients but to his former employees and all their family members as well. He traveled from house to house and from business to business, wherever he had to go, asking for the pardon of everyone that he thought he might have harmed. It was a thorough demonstration that Clyde meant to do business with Christ from now on. He said, "I want to be baptized and join the church. "Sure," I responded. Then I added, "I have only one question, "Why do you weep when I preach?" "For the wasted years of my life," Clyde replied.

"Blessed are they that mourn: for they shall be comforted." Jesus says that tears are necessary to success. In Clyde's case, the mourning of conviction had to precede the morning of conversion. The deep sense of individual sin must be felt before we can rejoice in the success of salvation's full victory.

THE THIRD SUCCESS SYMBOL:
SUCCESS MEANS BEING SADDLE-BROKEN

"Blessed are the meek: for they shall inherit the earth."

Editorializing a few days after Lincoln's Gettysburg address, the *Chicago Times* called it a "silly, flat, dish-watery utterance." Lincoln's speech is, of course, recognized as one of the greatest examples of oratory in the history of the English-speaking world. Someone asked President Lincoln what he thought of the editorial. He replied, "It's an editor's right to say what he thinks. However, I still like my speech." Of all the symbols of success Jesus taught in His Sermon on the Mount, none is more misunderstood than meekness.

What does it mean to be meek? First, it certainly does not mean to be weak. Weakness and meekness are not synonyms. In fact, they are nearer antonyms. The Greek word for "meek" gives us the first clue. It seems at times to be a favorite of Aristotle in his ethics. For him, life's virtues are almost always defined as the midpoint between excess and deficiency. Courage, for example, is a virtue according to Aristotle because it is the midpoint between cowardice (a deficiency in courage) and foolhardiness (the outcome of two much courage). By that logic, meekness is a virtue because it is the midpoint between exorbitant anger and that Casper Milquetoast personality that never expresses anger for any reason. Meekness is not weakness but knowing when and how to express anger or differences of opinion positively. It is, finally, having control of oneself at all times.

THE MEEKEST MAN IN THE WORLD!

"Now the man Moses was very meek, above all the men which were upon the face of the earth" (Num. 12:3). These words about one of the Bible's strongest leaders are written about a time when he was undergoing personal turmoil. Moses responded meekly to a rebellion led by his sister, Miriam, and his brother, Aaron. Miriam and Aaron were jealous of Moses' success. Since they could find no fault with his leadership skills, they chose another area of his life to criticize. They faulted Moses for marrying a Cushite woman after Zipporah, his first wife died. Specifically, their complaint was that Moses' new marriage was interracial. As a result of Miriam's negative reaction, God says, in effect, "If you think your light skin tone is superior to her dark skin let me make you lighter still!" (see Numbers 12:4-10). God struck Miriam with leprosy, which, among its other symptoms, turns all skin snow white. Miriam was marked for life in a way her culture regarded as a curse. What was Moses' respose to Miriam's predicament? Did this man with an infamous temper lash out, "Gotcha!"? Did he scream, "Serves you right!"? No. Once upon a time he might have responded like that. Now, however, his comeback is bathed in grace born of God's Spirit. Moses prays for God to heal his sister. Meekness is learning to balance our responses in moments that are loaded with potential for destructiveness without compromising our convictions. That is the third success symbol on Jesus' famous list.

THE FOURTH SYMBOL:
SUCCESS MEANS PURSUING GOOD FOR GOOD REASONS

"Blessed are they which do hunger and thirst after righteousness:
for they shall be filled."

How can I achieve God's finest plan for my life? Surely that would be the pinnacle of success! A car wash sign I saw some time ago declared, "Your clean car will run better!" It certainly seems that way, doesn't it? It's the winter months and your car gets all dirtied up in slush and muck. It looks ugly! You step in and out carefully, trying not to wipe your best clothes against it. You drive it to the car wash for a shampoo and blow dry. Before you know it, you feel as though you are driving a different automobile.

The same principle holds true for our minds. Hungering and thirsting for righteousness is all about directed mental activity. Ralph Waldo Emerson said, "A man is what he thinks about all day long." Fill your mind with slush and dirt and gunk and that is what your life becomes. Someone even wiser than Ralph Waldo Emerson said, "As he thinketh in his heart, so is he" (Prov. 23:7).

A man went to his psychiatrist's office and said, "Doc., sometimes I feel like a dog." The psychiatrist replied, "Relax on my couch and tell me more." "Oh no, " said the patient, "I'm not allowed on the couch. That's part of the problem!"

That story contains a certain undeniable life truth kernel that each of us needs to remember every day. It is that what we pursue determines what we become.

Our student days were spent in a wonderful rural Mississippi community called Helena. We lived in a house that had its own water supply. One of our farmers there loved to tell about his neighbor who bragged that his well provided better water than the rest. It was cool, sweet, and pure. It bubbled up on demand through a pipe that ran deep into the ground and fed a barrel just above ground level. One morning the neighbor went to fetch some water and found four sleepy eyes looking back at him. Somehow, two great bullfrogs got into the tank. There they sat on the bottom looking up through the sparkling clear water. How they got in there, no one knows. What everyone does know is that no one in that family wanted any of that water until the frogs were removed and the barrel was flushed out.

Over the years I've remembered those bullfrogs many times, for they have a message for us. Those bullfrogs represent the filthy thoughts that come into our minds when we drop our mental guard. The barrel is our heart. When our thought life is debased, the words and actions that flow out of our lives will be corrupt. Jesus said, "Out of the heart proceed evil thoughts, murders, adulteries, fornications, thefts, false witness, blasphemies: these are the things which defile a man" (Matt. 15:19-20). In short, evil is not at the X-rated movie show but in us. We act the way we do because we are the way we are. Conversely, when we intentionally pursue pure thoughts, our lives and lips will produce good fruit. One naturally follows the other. Let us then work on "bringing into captivity every thought to the obedience of Christ" (II Cor. 10:5).

THE FIFTH SYMBOL:
SUCCESS MEANS DEMONSTRATING MERCY

"Blessed are the merciful: for they shall obtain mercy."

Shakespeare's *Merchant of Venice* has a splendid line that goes to the heart of this success symbol: "The quality of mercy is not strained. It droppeth as the gentle rain from heaven. Upon the place beneath. It is twice blessed: It blesses him that gives and him that takes." In that one phrase, the Bard of Avon recognizes mercy's double blessing. It blesses the giver and the recipient. If you want to be successful, demonstrate mercy.

Here's how it works: If you want to be successful, work at helping other people succeed. It begins by treating others as we like to be treated. I heard about a deer hunter who spotted a fine looking buck struggling in a mudbog. It was hopelessly bogged down. It was such an easy target that the hunter's first impulse was to shoot it right there. As he aimed his rifle, he had a vision of himself plodding into the bog then out again with a hundred pounds of muddy dead deer meat across his shoulders. What seemed like a better idea came to him. He called for his partner to bring a rope and fashioned a lasso with which he roped the terrified animal. Slowly but surely he and his partner dragged the uncooperative deer through the mud to solid ground. Now with the lasso still around the big buck's antlers, his friend said, "I'll hold the rope. You shoot him." The once ambitious hunter's response startled his friend, "No. Let him go." "Are you crazy?" the friend asked. "No," he replied, "it's just that as he came out of the mudbog, I caught him looking me straight in the eye. I even saw my own reflection there. With his eyes he asked me, 'What would you have me do to you if the tables were turned?'"

Are you having difficulty extending mercy? May I be so bold as to suggest that in the eye of your imagination, you turn the tables? What would you want the other person to do if your roles were reversed? Do it and your one step closer to success.

THE SIXTH SUCCESS SYMBOL:
HEART EYES

"Blessed are the pure in heart: for they shall see God."

Sir Isaac Newton, the brilliant scientist and committed disciple, said he could take his telescope and look into the face of millions of stars. He quickly added, "Yet when I enter my room, shut the door behind me, and fall on my knees to pray, I see more of heaven and its Lord than if I was looking through all the telescopes in the universe."

Left to its own devices the human heart can be a terribly destructive instrument. "The heart is deceitful above all things, and desperately wicked: who can know it?" (Jer. 17:9). The New Testament Greek word for heart is *kardia,* which is the root for our word *cardiac.* The Greeks, however, understood the heart to be far more than just the internal organ that beats in the chest. For them, the heart was the hub of human personality development. It involved the mind, the will, and the emotions. If you want to be successful by the standards that Jesus Christ taught, it is necessary that you learn to subject all these things to His Lordship.

How do I become "pure in heart"? There are three steps involved in this success symbol. Each one is founded on that Greek idea.

THINK UP

The first is that we learn to think up. Thinking up is about the mind but not necessarily about IQ. It has more to do with SQ, the spiritual quotient. It acknowledges that faith is no more related to intellect than it is to ignorance. SQ is recognizing the difference between knowledge and wisdom. Across the years of my ministry, I have encountered saints who did not have much opportunity for formal education, yet they are wise people. Some of them developed successful businesses. One man I know did not finish high school, but he has Ph.Ds and law school graduates on his payroll. Another man has two earned doctorates, but he cannot hold a steady job. His relationship skills are practically non-existent. The first has wisdom. The second possesses only knowledge. "Incline thine ear unto wisdom, and apply thine heart to understanding" (Prov. 2:2).

WILL UP

If thinking up impacts the mind, will up has to do with the human spirit, the attitude. "After thy hardness and impenitent heart treasurest up unto thyself wrath" (Rom. 2:5). A paraphrase of this passage is, "Because of your unwillingness to change, you are making trouble for yourself."

GROWING OLD WITHOUT GROWING UP!

Do you know any stubborn old people? Not many, I'll bet. Why? Because most of them are dead already! Ask any cardiologist and you will hear confirmation about the absolute relationship between stubbornness and coronary artery disease. To will up is to graduate from old self-defeating negative attitudes into positive ones. It is to allow God's Spirit to transform your unhappiness into joy, which always wells from inside us (see John 15:11). It is to cooperate with the Spirit in turning your discontentment into contentment. Paul writes, "I have learned, in whatsoever state I am, therewith to be content" (Phil. 4:11). That, too, wells up from inside us. It is to collaborate with the Spirit in searching out the good and the redeemable in all situations. "Whatsoever things are true, whatsoever things are honest, whatsoever things are just, whatsoever things are pure, whatsoever things are lovely, whatsoever things are of good report; if there be any virtue, and if there be any praise, think on these things" (Phil. 4:8). Christians whose conversation always focuses on what is wrong give the Devil free publicity. He doesn't deserve it!

LIVE UP!

To be "pure in heart" is to find the highest causes in which to invest your life in order that you may accomplish as many positive things as possible for God's glory. Eddie Rickenbacker called Christ his homing beacon. He followed Paul's example: "I follow after, if that I may apprehend that for which also I am apprehended of Christ Jesus" (Phil. 3:12). Paul is telling his favorite church that his homing beacon is to accomplish everything he can for Christ his Savior. As part of our seminary training, we went through an exercise of writing our own obituary. It was a way of accomplishing three goals. First, it brought us face-to-face with our own mortality in order that we might better minister in the context of death. Second, it impressed upon us the urgency of the gospel we were called to carry. Third, it forced us to center on what we really wanted to accomplish with our lives. It set the important over the urgent in order that our lives would be better focused.

One family gathered to hear the reading of their wealthy father's last will and testament. One sentence said everything: "Being of sound mind, I spent it all!" How will your obituary read? How would you like to be remembered when you die? Start out in that direction today. Do not let your life come to an end so that it will be said of you:

Mr. Meant-To has a comrade,
And his name is Didn't Do;
Have you ever chanced to meet them?
Did they ever call on you?
These two fellows live together
In the house of never-Win,
And I'm told that it is haunted
By the ghost of Might-Have-Been![2]

To be pure in heart is to see the unavoidable connection between eternity and today. It is to avoid the one-day-hope-for way of living some dreamers follow. To rephrase John Wesley's words, it is to do all the good you can for all the people you can for Christ's sake today. Tonight your soul may be required of you! Start making your best dreams come true today in the Holy Spirit's power and you will find success.

THE SEVENTH SYMBOL:
SUCCESS MEANS MAKING PEACE WITH GOD, YOURSELF, AND OTHERS

"Blessed are the peacemakers: for they shall be called the children of God."

Toward the end of his life, John Newton, who wrote what is probably the best-known hymn in Christendom, often told those who gathered to

---

2. William J. Bennett, *The Book of Virtues for Young People.* (New York: Simon and Schuster, 1997), p. 150.

hear him preach, "I was once an infidel and libertine but now I am a child of God." John Newton, involved in the lucrative slave trade, sailed from Africa to England and back repeatedly with shiploads of captives who were sold into bondage. John Newton himself was a slave to sin. Caught off Ireland's beautiful wild western coast in a ferocious gale, John Newton and his crew were certain their ship would be lost and they would all drown. Someone called out for prayer that God would show mercy on their slave-trade souls. John Newton knew he had no right to ask God for mercy. Yet certain he would die at any minute, he gave his life to God and promised that if perchance he survived, he would turn his life in a different direction. Amazingly, against all odds, the crew and their human cargo survived. John Newton walked away from slavery in all its vicious forms as a redeemed servant of the King of kings. "Now being made free from sin, and become servants to God, ye have your fruit unto holiness, and the end everlasting life" (Rom. 6:22). John Newton was freed from sin and enslaved to God. He spent the rest of his life speaking out against slavery and sin. Later he wrote the words that Christians around the world sing, "Amazing Grace, how sweet the sound that saved a wretch like me." "For he is our peace, who hath made both one, and hath broken down the middle wall of partition between us" (Eph. 2:14).

THE EIGHTH SUCCESS SYMBOL:
SINGING IN THE RAIN!

"Blessed are they which are persecuted for righteousness' sake:
for theirs is the kingdom of heaven."

A newly ordained minister took up his first assignment with a wise old pastor who had served Christ faithfully for many years. Six months later, the depressed, brokenhearted young man tendered his resignation. "Why are you quitting?" the older man asked him. "I can't take it any more," the young fellow said. "Since the first month I've been here, I've been insulted almost every week." He added, "How on earth can you keep on going with all these ungrateful insulting people?" The old man's eyes twinkled. He smiled in response, "I don't know what you mean about insults. The worst I've experienced is having a few doors slammed in my face, an occasional hate letter, some slander or being cursed out, and called dirty names. And, of course, one fellow hit me with a baseball bat a long time ago, but I've never been insulted!"

"Blessed are ye, when men shall revile you, and persecute you, and shall say all manner of evil against you falsely, for my sake. Rejoice, and be exceeding glad: for great is your reward in heaven: for so persecuted they the prophets which were before you." The gospel that saves us was born on a rough Roman cross and nourished on suffering, sacrifice, and rejection. Following Jesus Christ is not an invitation to a popularity contest. We will not need to seek out persecution in any of its forms. It will find us itself, for the one who hates the cross is still alive and well on planet Earth. Indeed, if there is not evidence of persecution for righteousness sake in our history, we might even now be missing our calling.

The question is, how will we resolve to respond to it? A wonderful parable tells about three birds that were chatting with one another when an unexpected thunderstorm passed overhead. The duck was indifferent. The rain ran right off its back. The chicken became unbearable. Helpless in the downpour, it squawked off in misery. The robin, however, kept right on singing. For robins always sing in the rain. Ornithologists will tell you that this little bird—often called the bird of the cross—saves his sweetest song for when it is raining. Perhaps the robins remember that bad news never lasts. And so must we, for after the cross comes the resurrection.

When persecution comes, as it will for you if you belong to Christ, avoid the temptation to retaliate. Instead, with head held high, move forward in God's strength knowing that Christ loves you. You are walking in good company "for so persecuted they the prophets which were before you." Persecution is the best evidence we have that we are on the track to real success with Jesus. His Spirit shall lead you home. Make Him your homing beacon. Fix your focus on Him and walk forward boldly; you are a child of the king and don't ever forget it.

Go forward also aware of this: The road to victory has potholes, hurdles, and a few unexpected curves. How to overcome them in the power of the Holy Spirit, the Breath of Abundant Life, is the central theme of the final chapter.

13

Let nothing stop you now!

It was 1951. The place was Madison Square Garden, New York City. Preacher's son, Gil Dodds, had broken the world's record for the fastest mile ever run on an indoor track. After accomplishing his feat, Gil Dodds came forward to the accolades of the roaring thousands that witnessed his achievement from their seats in the stands. The crowd thundered its approval. They had never seen anything like this before. After the medal was hung around Gil Dodds's neck, the master of ceremonies asked him if he had anything to say. The people in the stands shouted for his voice to be heard. Silence fell across the arena as Gil took the microphone. He started by saying that he was not an accomplished speaker and that his dad was the preacher in the family. Gil's talent was running. Nervously he paused and looked out across the sea of smiling faces. As he raised the microphone toward his mouth again, the multitude waited. Gil spoke. "Whatever talent I have came from God. I didn't win this race tonight," he told them, "He did! I couldn't do the one thing coaches say a long-distant runner must do. I couldn't sprint at the end of the race. But the Lord took care of that. In place of the sprint, He gave me stamina."

Gil Dodds's victory that night at Madison Square Garden and throughout his career came from his capacity to run consistently from the beginning to the end of a race. Other runners could run faster. There were moments when some of them could leave Gil in the dust, but nobody could match Gil's stick-to-it-iveness. They could run faster, but only for a while. Winded, they soon petered out and lost their advantage, at which point Gil took the lead again. Did Gil sometimes look slower than the other runners did? Maybe, but he was more likely to finish. Therein lay the secret of his success. His enduring strength made him a winner, and he knew the source of his strength was beyond himself. It was from God's Breath of

Abundant Life. His victories came not from his ability to sprint—there were many better sprinters—but from his robust ability to not slow down until the race was over. That was Gil Dodds's special gift from God's Spirit.

SPIRITUAL STAMINA!

"Ye did run well; who did hinder you?" (Gal. 5:7).The thought Paul conveys to the Galatians, like many of his other figures of speech, is borrowed from the world of competitive sports. The journey to success in the style and manner of Jesus Christ, as outlined in chapter twelve, is a race.

Paul recalls for the Galatians the enthusiasm with which they first received his message. They listened attentively to the word of his lips. They regarded him as the Lord's messenger and would have even traded their healthy eyes for his apparently weak, possibly injured, eyes. Since his departure, however, things have changed. Something negative has dimmed their spiritual zeal. False teachers have come in like a computer virus and corrupted their walk with Christ. They are confused between the true gospel they heard from Paul and the false teaching they have received from others. Now, trying to blend certain parts of the old Jewish practices that were part of their former religious system with faith in Jesus Christ had watered down their eagerness for the gospel of grace. Their gospel was compromised by their actions. For that reason, Paul writes his letter to them.

What a miracle of grace it is when the Holy Spirit, the Breath of Abundant Life, calls a sinner to conversion! It is the work of the Spirit from start to finish. "Salvation is of the Lord." "By grace are ye saved through faith; and that not of yourselves: it is the gift of God" (Jonah 2:9; Eph. 2:8). If someone is saved, it is not because of what he or she has done but because of what Jesus did on the cross.

A newly converted person has already passed some hurdles, but there are others. Getting over them takes a lifetime. This gospel we are called to has a long history of trouble. Since before the cross, people have been persecuted for preaching it or following it. That has not changed. In chapter twelve we saw that a rough Roman cross was the birthplace of our message. Suffering, sacrifice, and rejection have been its trademarks since its earliest days. Following Jesus Christ is not an invitation to a life of luxury on easy street. It is, in fact, an ongoing reveille that reminds us that we are called to war. As I outlined this book, I questioned whether this chapter or the preceding one should go last. I decided that this one should be the final one because the war still goes on. The conflict is described throughout Scripture. What is worth noting is that it is always depicted with present tense verbs: "Put on (present tense) the whole armour of God, that ye may be able to stand (present tense) against the wiles of the devil. For we wrestle (present tense) not against flesh and blood, but against principalities, against powers, against the rulers of the darkness of this world, against spiritual wickedness in high places. Wherefore take unto you (present tense) the whole armour of God, that ye may be able to withstand (present tense) in the evil day, and having done all, to stand. Stand therefore, (present tense) having your loins girt about with truth, and having on (present tense) the breastplate of righteousness; and your feet shod (present tense) with the preparation of the gospel of peace; above all, taking the shield of faith, (present tense) wherewith ye shall be able to quench (present tense) all the fiery darts of the wicked. And take (present tense) the helmet of salvation, and the sword of the Spirit, which is the word of God: praying always (present tense) with all prayer and supplication in the Spirit, and watching thereunto (present tense) with all perseverance and supplication for all saints" (Eph. 6:11-18).

If the war Paul writes about was history, his verbs would have been written in the past tense. The verbs are all present because the conflict is not over. I am told that the First Presbyterian Church of Pittsburgh has the largest collection of Tiffany stained glass in any church building in the world. It would be impossible to replace them today. What is most intriguing about those windows is that they tell the story of Jesus on two levels. On the lower level, the windows represent Bible scenes from His earthly life. The upper level represents Bible scenes from His heavenly life. In a similar way, we also live on two levels. There is an earthly dimension to our lives and there is a heavenly dimension. We live between the two. We are in the world but not like it. Therein lies the hindrance of which Paul speaks to the Galatians, "Ye did run well; who did hinder you?" We might also translate it, "Who stunted your growth in Christ? Who kept you back from being all Christ meant for you to be?" This chapter looks at hindrances to running the race and suggests some ways to overcome them.

DON'T BE HINDERED IF THE TALK ISN'T WALKED!

"Example is not the main thing in influencing others," Albert Schweitzer often said. "It is the only thing." A few years ago a newly elected president of the United States was selecting the members for his cabinet. He had enormous difficulty in finding someone to take on the position of chief law enforcement officer of the country as attorney general. One nominee, after first denying it, admitted when confronted with the evidence to knowingly hiring an illegal alien to care for her children. A second admitted to illegal drug use. Another had written law articles that advocated the overthrow of parts of the United States Constitution. Each of them was a lawyer and each had taken an oath to uphold and defend the laws of the country. Yet each had violated that oath. The talk was not walked!

Not long ago the City of Pittsburgh decided to clamp down on unpaid parking tickets. High priority was given to repeat parking offenders who did not pay their tickets. A computer search was conducted of the outstanding ticket files. Guess what! The biggest violators of Pittsburgh's parking laws included some local law enforcement officers who parked in no parking zones around the courthouse building. Someone suggested that maybe they were inside taking care of business, perhaps including giving evidence against other people who were in court for parking violations. Their walk did not match their talk!

It was people in the church who caused Mark Twain to repudiate the Bible and the Christian faith. In his adolescence he heard elders and ministers use the Bible to justify slavery and witnessed them abuse the slaves they owned. He heard men using filthy language and watched them give short measure in their businesses during the week after having been in leadership in the service the previous Sunday. His wife and mother loved Christ genuinely, but Twain was hindered by the fact that many others were not sincere. They were, to his way of thinking, saints on Sunday and devils through the week. Their walk was different from their talk!

The same is true where you live. Feelings of disappointment with inconsistent behavior by Christians are among the reasons given by many people who have forsaken the Christian faith or the church. "I used to be a Christian but I dropped out because there are so many hypocrites in the church," one young man, once a ministerial student, told me not long ago when I invited him to attend our services. "I know," I replied. Then I added, "Do you have a better plan for where they might be on Sundays?" He had no answer. The truth is that neither one of us like the fact that there are hypocrites in the church. Yet the fact remains that church is the best place a hypocrite can be. Maybe he or she will hear the gospel there and get converted. Then walk and talk will be consistent!

That fellow's charge against us is a siren call reminding us that we are being noticed, even when we don't realize it. A lad and his dad were driving along a country road when they passed a watermelon patch. Dad said, "Son, watch out for me while I climb through that hole in the hedge and get us a couple of those good looking watermelons." Sneaking through the hedge, the dad called back, "Now be sure to look both ways and holler if you see anybody coming." He grabbed a couple of choice melons and cut them from the vine. "Is anybody coming?" he asked. "Look both ways, now." The lad asked, "But Daddy, don't I really need to be looking up?" Someone "up there" who knows our every move is always watching. We need to remember the responsibility for our influence over others as well. At the same time, we must acknowledge that none of us lives now in sinless perfection. That does not excuse us when there is an ongoing inconsistency between walk and talk.

"What is that to thee? Follow thou me" (John 21:22). It was after the resurrection, and Peter wanted to know about John's future. Jesus replied that Peter should not concern himself with that. We have a tendency to measure our lives by the actions of others, whether to rationalize or justify our own behavior, but Jesus tells us not to do that. Your place with Christ is to follow him. "The arm of flesh will fail you."[1] We will always end up disappointed if our model is another person. The nearer we keep to Christ's cross and to a sense of our own need to grow in him, the less influence

---

1. From the hymn "Stand Up, Stand Up for Jesus," by George Duffield, 1858.

others will hold over us. Christianity is not faith in other disciples. It is faith in Jesus only. If the Christian faith depended on those who name Christ as Lord to live consistent lives, it would have died before the end of its first century when there was Judas who betrayed Jesus and Peter who denied Him and a host of others who abandoned Him when times got tough. Yet the gospel goes on, despite the poor examples of its devotees. It continues because of the beauty and glory of its Lord whose life was marked by absolute consistency. In the meantime, before we go to be with Jesus, rise above the hypocrisy of other believers and focus your eyes on Jesus alone. You will never be disappointed.

DON'T LET OPPOSITION STOP YOU NOW!

"He came unto his own, and his own received him not" (John 1:11). When the very people God had chosen to prepare the rest of the world for His Messiah opposed and rejected Him, drove Him out of their synagogues, and eventually nailed Him to a cross, Jesus didn't flinch. He didn't give up and return to heaven with His mission unaccomplished. Nor did His disciples surrender to the voices of the opposition after the Holy Spirit came upon them with power at Pentecost. Nothing could stop them! They knew they were involved in a mission that had sent its leader to a cross and sent them into the world in supernatural power. They also knew that opposition and persecution are parts of the package when we receive Jesus Christ as Lord and Savior and the Holy Spirit comes into our lives. Along with many blessings, they are also givens of discipleship.

At the height of his popularity with the British people, Winston Churchill was invited back to Harrow, his old school. The prime minister remembered all too well the price he had paid to get where he was. He recalled the nights spent underground at Whitehall, consulting his cabinet officers and military advisors while bombs were exploding all around. He remembered the pain of rejection a few months after victory. He recalled the time he spent in exile when he might have expected to live with the status of a hero and the opposition he had faced with political opponents from all parties, even his own. When he rose to speak to these students who were seated now where once, decades before, he sat listening, he asked himself what might be the best advice he could give them. Laying aside his prepared manuscript, the wise old man stepped before them and said, "Never, ever quit." He paused, then repeated, "Never, ever quit!" He paused a second time before saying, "Never quit!" With that, Sir Winston Churchill returned quietly to his seat. It was the best advice he could give them and, as far as he was concerned, that was all they needed to hear.

HAMMERED BUT NOT BEATEN!

The Waldensian church has a marvelous symbol. It pictures an anvil with several worn out hammers lying beside it. Underneath is this inscription, "One Anvil but Many Hammers." We will be beaten upon as Christians and we should prepare ourselves as best we can for it, but the hammers will wear out before we do. The anvil stands long after all the hammers fail. When the Holy Spirit comes upon us, we are built of stronger stuff.

Before we belonged to Christ, we did not face the same opposition we face since we received Him. Before we came to Him, we belonged to the one Scripture calls the prince of this world (see John 14:30). As disciples of the world's prince, we were no threat to him. Now, however, we belong to another. We are aliens in our former homeland. In truth, we don't fit in here. Satan knows that and his hammers are aimed at us. They will come in the form of opposition and persecution that is verbal, emotional, physical, and spiritual. We should expect that and prepare ourselves for it. When it comes, it always brings thoughts of throwing in the towel. There are times when the old life appears, for the moment, more attractive. Yet it is not and never will be. Remember always, that that is the life you walked away from. It is the life that forced your Savior to die for you. Never, ever quit.

DON'T QUIT!

An unknown poet left us this gem:

> When things go wrong as they sometimes will,
> When the road you trudge seems all uphill,
> When funds are low and debts are high,
> And you want to smile but you have to sigh,

When care is pressing you down a bit,

Rest if you must, but don't you quit!

Life is strange with its twists and turns,

As everyone of us sometimes learns,

And many a failure turns about,

When he might have won had he stuck it out.

Don't give up though the pace seems slow

For you may succeed with another blow.

Success is failure turned inside out,

The silver tint of the clouds of doubt

And you never can tell how close you are,

It may be near when it seems so far.

So stick to the fight when you're hardest hit,

It's when things seem worst

that you dare not quit.

As a young minister, I felt burned out, beaten up, unappreciated, and bent out of shape. I decided to resign and felt an obligation to break the news to my uncle Sam, my chief mentor, under whose ministry I had come to Christ and sensed the call to preach. "I'm going to resign," I told him. "I've had enough. It's too hard and too many people are criticizing me." He realized right away that I was in the throws of a pity party and responded appropriately. His answer plays back in my memory bank even today. Without a moment's hesitation he asked, "Why are you telling me? I didn't call you. When you started toward the ministry you told me the Lord called you. Don't you think you'd better present your resignation to Him first?" "But," I protested, "what if its not His will?" "If its not His will," he said, "I think you'd do well to stick it out." Then he added, "Just remember this, 'No man, having put his hand to the plow, and looking back, is fit for the kingdom of God.'" His quote from Luke's Gospel was what I needed to hear. Christ never said following Him would be easy. Quite the contrary, He warns us, "If any man will come after me, let him deny himself, and take up his cross daily, and follow me" (cf. Luke 9:23,62).

Expect opposition, even from unexpected places and people. Turn it around and use it to cultivate the Christian virtue of endurance. Let nothing stop you now. Never, ever quit!

DON'T LET TRIALS STOP YOU NOW!

I was speaking in Enterprise, Alabama, on one occasion when someone there pointed out a monument to a bug near the center of the town. That's right, a monument to a creepy crawler! Carved out of a fine piece of stone is the likeness of a boll weevil. That pest became a local hero. Here is what happened: In early plantation days cotton was king for the community around Enterprise. The economy of that region rose and fell according to the cotton market. If the price of cotton was up, everybody in Enterprise profited because of it. If the market for cotton was down, everybody tightened their belt and tried to make it through. Then came pestilence in the form of the boll weevil, a small beetle that thrived by puncturing the boll in the developing cotton crop, preventing it from coming to maturity. Farmers facing hardship and bankruptcy met to pray together about their predicament. Out of those meetings came a determination to face the problem head on.

A number of scientists, led by George Washington Carver, a dedicated Christian, were enlisted, and they applied their knowledge to the situation. They conducted tests to find a new crop that would resist the tiny nuisance. Raising peanuts was their recommendation. Boll weevils don't like peanuts and either move on or die once peanuts are planted. Besides, peanuts grow with less effort and are harvested more often than cotton. In time, peanut warehouses replaced cotton gins. Enterprise quickly gained a worldwide reputation for the fine quality of its new crop. Local farmers quickly recouped their losses and learned they could earn more from peanuts than cotton. Later they realized that had it not been for the infestation of the boll weevils they might never have realized that they were living in the future peanut capital of the world. They were convinced that God sent the boll weevil as a blessing in disguise. Good news came out of their trial. Today that monument stands in the heart of Enterprise as a reminder that somewhere in the midst of every trial stands the providence of a loving heavenly Father. If you've eaten a lot of candy bars, it is likely that you have eaten some Enterprise, Alabama, peanuts. Give thanks for the boll weevil and remember the God of the boll weevil has wonderful plans for your life too.

225

JOY IN TRIALS!

"Count it all joy when ye fall into divers temptations; Knowing this, that the trying of your faith worketh patience. But let patience have her perfect work, that ye may be perfect and entire, wanting nothing. If any of you lack wisdom, let him ask of God, that giveth to all men liberally, and upbraideth not; and it shall be given him" (James 1:2-5). Notice that James does not say "if" we face diverse temptations (the Greek is *peirasmos* and is often also translated "trials"). The issue is not if we will face trials, but when we face them. They, too, are part and parcel of life in this world.

GOD'S CHILD-TRAINING PLAN

Trials produce faith. Faith, in turn, produces patience and patience produces growth toward perfection of character. The boll weevil sent the cotton crop to ruination but it sent the people of Enterprise to their knees in prayer. That prayer, in turn, developed perseverance and perseverance, peanuts! The peanut capitol of the universe!

THE WORLD'S BEST CHILD TRAINING PROGRAM

When we become God's children, we are automatically enrolled in the best child-training program in the world. The Lord allows trials to come as a way of allowing us to learn if we really meant it when we said yes to His Holy Spirit, the Breath of Abundant Life. Through trials we are turned towards God. "Cast thy burden upon the Lord, and he shall sustain thee: he shall never suffer the righteous to be moved" (Ps. 55:22). When we turn toward God, we are strengthened inwardly and refined: "He shall sit as a refiner and purifier of silver" (Mal. 3:3). In addition, trials deepen our faith: "The trial of your faith, being much more precious than of gold that perisheth, though it be tried with fire, might be found unto praise and honour and glory at the appearing of Jesus Christ" (I Pet. 1:7).

Are you caught up in a trial? Just before my dad went to heaven, my ministry was facing strong opposition that seemed to have no limits in the depths to which its advocates would sink. I saw the church at its shameless worst. Allegations and charges were leveled against me that thinking people knew were without foundation. They were built on false and

226

twisted hypotheses. Nevertheless, I also believed then, and still believe, that Christians often are convicted in the courts of public opinion on trumped up allegations, and I feared that would be my end also. Why shouldn't it be? Our Leader was convicted like that! I stood at my dad's graveside a few days after he was buried knowing that people I once trusted were leveling false allegations against me. My spirits were already low, for I had watched my father suffer terribly during his final months and wished every day that somehow I could have been present to support him and minister to him. As I stood there, the convicting voice of the enemy of my soul came upon me with unusual boldness. He taunted me, saying, "Your dad died and found out when he got to heaven that his son, of whom he thought so much, was facing the possibility of being disciplined, perhaps even defrocked! How does that make you feel, preacher boy?" A tear rolled down my cheeks and on to my tie. My heart was broken. I walked slowly away from his grave with my aged mother. We arrived back at the car and began to drive away. I could think of nothing to say that would break the silence of that wretched moment and comfort her. Then, like the sun bursting through a thundercloud, the Word of the Son of God, who gave Himself up for my soul, came charging through the spiritual blackness with words I had studied often. They came so alive in the depths of my being that they might have been written just for me: "Who shall lay any thing to the charge of God's elect? It is God that justifieth. Who is he that condemneth? It is Christ that died, yea rather, that is risen again, who is even at the right hand of God, who also maketh intercession for us. Who shall separate us from the love of Christ? shall tribulation, or distress, or persecution, or famine, or nakedness, or peril, or sword? As it is written, For thy sake we are killed all the day long; we are accounted as sheep for the slaughter. Nay, in all these things we are more than conquerors through him that loved us. For I am persuaded, that neither death, nor life, nor angels, nor principalities, nor powers, nor things present, nor things to come, nor height, nor depth, nor any other creature, shall be able to separate us from the love of God, which is in Christ Jesus our Lord" (Rom. 8:33-39).

In the sunlight of God's inspired Word I found brightness and courage to trust my trials to Christ. God vindicated my heart that day in an

Irish graveyard as surely as He vindicated my soul on Calvary. I knew that eventually truth would rise to the surface and all would be okay. In time it was. What a wonderful Savior we serve!

I was not the first nor shall I be the last to face false accusations. We all face misunderstanding and indictments as disciples of Jesus. Joseph, too, faced false allegations and a mockery of a trial. Genesis 41 records his amazing vindication. All the sufferings and pain he endured prepared him for the higher calling of his hour of triumph. Joseph would never have been a blessing to his own people and accorded hero status in the history of Israel were it not for his determination in the face of family trials and the false accusations of some people in Egypt.

As disciples of Jesus, we are called frequently to pass through the dark clouds of trial before we can experience the sunshine of the Savior's love in a new and more wonderful measure.

Legend tells about a farmer who was sowing seeds when one of them cried out, "Sir, please don't bury me in the dirt. Allow me to remain a while longer in the warm sunshine." The farmer, ignoring that plea, dropped the seed into the hole he had just made in the ground and covered it over. As he did, another seed, unnoticed, fell on a smooth stone nearby. "Ah," said the second seed, "I have achieved the dream of the first seed. I shall lie here basking in the sunshine. What a lucky fellow I am." Alas, the second seed lay there in the sunshine, but it never germinated. Nothing ever developed from its life. The buried seed, however, sprouted a small delicate stem, which, with time, developed a bud, then a flower, followed by delicious fruit. Growth only happens through dirt! Don't let trials stop you from becoming all Christ in the Spirit's power dreams for you to be. Wouldn't you choose to be a fruit-bearing disciple over a dead one rotting in the sunshine anytime? Of course, you would!

DON'T LET THE WORLD'S SIREN SONG HOLD YOU BACK!

The apostle Paul was more than an evangelist. He was also a pastor who poured his heart into his converts for Christ. Some of them became his close personal friends and ministry partners. One like that was called Demas. "My fellow laborer," Paul calls him writing, to Philemon. In his letter to the Colossians, Paul sends greetings on behalf of Demas (see Colossians 4:14). Yet the apostle's anointed pen writes no sadder sentence anywhere than this: "Demas hath forsaken me, having loved this present world" (II Tim. 4:10). The allure of the world's bright lights was more than Demas could resist. He gave up a promising future at the side of the greatest missionary in all Christian history because of something Christ, out of love, could not permit in Demas's life.

THE PRESENT WORLD FOR THE WORLD TO COME!

Don't allow anything in this world to hold you back from serving Christ fully. We live, as has already been noted, between two worlds. Therein is an inherent tension that shall never go away so long as we are alive on earth. It is the struggle between this world and the world to come where we shall sing in the presence of Him who loved us all the way to Calvary and loves us still, the temporary straining against the eternal, the brief today against the endless tomorrow, the froth and foam of this world for the security of eternity with Christ, the temporary hollowness of the now against the eternal weight of glory. The pull, the suck, the drag of this world's trinkets sometimes is chosen over streets of gold and precious stones for all of forever. The result is always the same. To slide back into the world is to be a loser in the only race worth winning. There is no more common epitaph in the spiritual cemetery of potentially great Christians than this: "They gave up on Jesus!" Do not allow it to be yours. Cling fiercely and determinedly to Christ every single day. Stay in prayer, in God's Word, and in fellowship with His people. Demas gave up Paul. More important, Demas gave up Jesus. When you give up Jesus, you give up everything worth having.

"The backslider in heart shall be filled with his own ways" (Prov. 14:14). You will notice that it does not speak of the back jumper or the back runner nor even about a back walker. I suspect it is because intention and effort are needed to jump, to run, or even to walk. Sliding, on the other hand, requires no effort and often happens unintentionally. Our granddaughters, Cameron and Hannah, chuckle with delight when they play on their backyard swing set. They like to swing and they like to slide even more. Sliding takes less energy than swinging. In swinging they must muster the momentum to keep the swing moving back and forth. For sliding, however, they only have to be raised up to a higher level and simply sit down. There is no effort to sliding.

Backsliding is like that too. You go walking in the hills and mountainsides of County Antrim or coastal California. From high above, the coastline below looks seductively beautiful. You stop to admire it. In an absent-minded moment you cease concentrating on holding your grip and focus on what is below you. Before you know it, you are sliding away from where you wanted to be, moving in the wrong direction with no real effort. So it is in the spiritual life. We loosen our grip on Christ and begin to slide away, easily, comfortably, and effortlessly. Whatever reason or excuse we may give for backsliding, the fact is it only happens when we no longer exert effort to follow the Savior. When we backslide, we are "give-up" Christians, people who simply stopped trying to follow the Master. We may not lose our salvation, for He keeps His promises even when we do not keep ours, but we certainly lose the joy of it. It was the joy of it that David yearned for most of all. "Restore unto me the joy of thy salvation; and uphold me with thy free Spirit" (Ps. 51:12). Sometimes the first evidence that we see of backsliding is that our old joy has gone. To backslide is to stop running the race of faith and risk losing true joy. Do not allow the siren song of this temporary world to hinder your eternal life with Christ! "Seeing we also are compassed about with so great a cloud of witnesses, let us lay aside every weight, and the sin which doth so easily beset us, and let us run with patience the race that is set before us, looking unto Jesus the author and finisher of our faith; who for the joy that was set before him endured the cross, despising the shame, and is set down at the right hand of the throne of God" (Heb. 12:1-2).

DO NOT ALLOW STUBBORN DISOBEDIENCE TO STOP YOU

"Then spake Jeremiah unto all the princes and to all the people, saying, The Lord sent me to prophesy against this house and against this city all the words that ye have heard. Therefore now amend your ways and your doings, and obey the voice of the Lord your God" (Jer. 26:12-13).

Jeremiah was God's anointed messenger, sent to proclaim to his generation that they must repent and turn anew to God. The people who heard his message branded him a traitor when he told them that God would destroy both their city and the temple because of their sinful habits. They intentionally chose another path and reaped the consequences of their hardheadedness. We have lived long enough to know from what happened following Jeremiah's warning that God lets no sin go unpunished. There are only two ways for sin's punishment to be borne. Either we will bear it ourselves for all eternity or we will accept the pain Christ bore on the cross as sufficient penalty and out of gratitude repent and turn back to Him.

Despite the consistent and plain message of the Scriptures, there are still Christians who have slowed up in the race for Christ. Their testimony for Him is not as strong as it once was. They have willfully chosen to disobey His commandments. These folks have considered Christ's cross and rejected it as being of no account for them. Unlike the hapless backslider, they willfully choose to walk a path they know Christ would never approve. They started well in the race for Christ then purposely stopped running and walked away from Him, breaking His laws and disobeying the voice of the Spirit within. The net result is always a great dissatisfaction with life.

During World War II some British soldiers found a wounded, bleeding German officer lying in a filthy ditch. They rushed him to a field hospital where army surgeons quickly placed him on a gurney, cleaned his wounds, and rushed him to surgery hoping to save his life. The man saw that a blood transfusion was being set up for him in the operating theater. In heavily accented English he adamantly refused to accept a transfusion. Doctors explained that without a blood transfusion, surgery was impossible. If they operated now, they could save his life. If they did not operate, death was certain and very painful. He responded abruptly, "I will die before enemy blood goes into my veins!" He was right. He did die! Doctors stood by helplessly and watched him breathe his final breath. It was one of the great public acts of personal foolishness in that war. That man had much to gain and nothing to lose. His stubbornness cost him his life.

Courage is often better demonstrated by changing a long-held opinion rather than sticking to it. What long-held determination might keep you from running the race and achieving the prize Christ has for you?

Could it be an unforgiving spirit? Think about this: "Then came Peter to him, and said, Lord, how oft shall my brother sin against me, and I forgive him? till seven times? Jesus saith unto him, I say not unto thee, Until seven times: but, until seventy times seven" (Matt. 18:21-22).

Some years ago in a small Irish village, a man and his teenage son argued violently. They fell out, and each said he would never speak to the other again. Bitterness and a lack of forgiveness mastered them both. The son soon left for the city and vowed never to set foot in the home again. The mother cried and begged her boy not to leave under those circumstances. Her son ignored her pleas. The wiser father soon regretted the way he had treated his son. With a heavy heart, he packed a few things and left for the city to find him. Day after day, he tramped the streets searching for his boy. When, after several weeks, he was still unable to find him, he decided he would place an advertisement in the local newspaper. It said, "Seamus, all is forgiven. Your mother and I are heartbroken. We want you to come home. Meet me at the statue in front of the city hall next Friday at noon. Let's talk about it. I love you. Your dear Father."

When twelve o'clock came on Friday, that boy walked up to his father and the two embraced. That was not all. They found themselves surrounded by over twenty young men called Seamus, every one of whom hoped it was his father who placed that advertisement in the newspaper. Each one wanted to be reconciled with his father!

Stingy Forgiveness!

Life is too short to allow an unforgiving spirit to hold you back from being all God has created you to be in Jesus Christ. At the heart of the prayer Jesus teaches all His disciples is this petition, "Forgive us our debts, as we forgive our debtors" (Matt. 6:12). It is the only conditional sentence in the entire prayer. It forces us to petition the Father for the same forgiveness that we are willing to give. Is your forgiveness stingy? Is that what you want? Or do you need more? Do not allow an unforgiving spirit to hinder your race for Christ.

Let nothing stop you now! "If we live in the Spirit, let us also walk in the Spirit" (Gal. 5:25). When the USS *Missouri*, a famous World War II battleship, came to Pascagoula, Mississippi, for refitting and re-commissioning, I was privileged to be given a captain's tour. It was an unforgettable experience to stand on the strong planks of her wooden deck where history was made when General Douglas MacArthur, the official representative of the United States of America, met the appointed representative of the Japanese emperor, a Japanese admiral. I recall a story told me by Admiral Floyd Schultz, a member of our Pascagoula congregation. He said that when that Japanese admiral stepped up on deck and walked across those planks on the *Missouri's* deck toward General MacArthur, he extended his hand as a gesture of friendship. The American general had another interest, however. He wanted to see proof that the handshake was genuine. Through his interpreter he told that admiral, "Sir, first your sword please!" General MacArthur would take no chances with his former enemy. Once that Japanese officer's sword was surrendered, General MacArthur shook the man's hand. Now the peace process could really begin. Until the weapons of war are surrendered, genuine peace cannot start.

DROP YOUR WEAPONS!

This principle holds true for Christian warfare as well. Total surrender of all the weapons and warring ways of our old life is crucial to spiritual advance. Every part of our lives belongs to God. We can pray the sinner's prayer for mercy all day long, every day. If, however, we truly want to move forward in the power of the Spirit, our challenge is to surrender all our lives to Him. High aspirations, enthusiastic feelings, careful planning, and being able to express yourself well are all great gifts. We should use them to the best of our ability in Christ's service. However, when it comes to living for God in the life that is abundant, we find that these things are not what the Christian life is all about. Living our lives as Christ intended in the Spirit of God is about total surrender and living to the hilt. Whatever your weapons are, drop them now and come completely. Let nothing stop you from living the abundant life God has in mind for you through His Son, Jesus, in the power of His Holy Spirit, the Breath of Abundant Life.